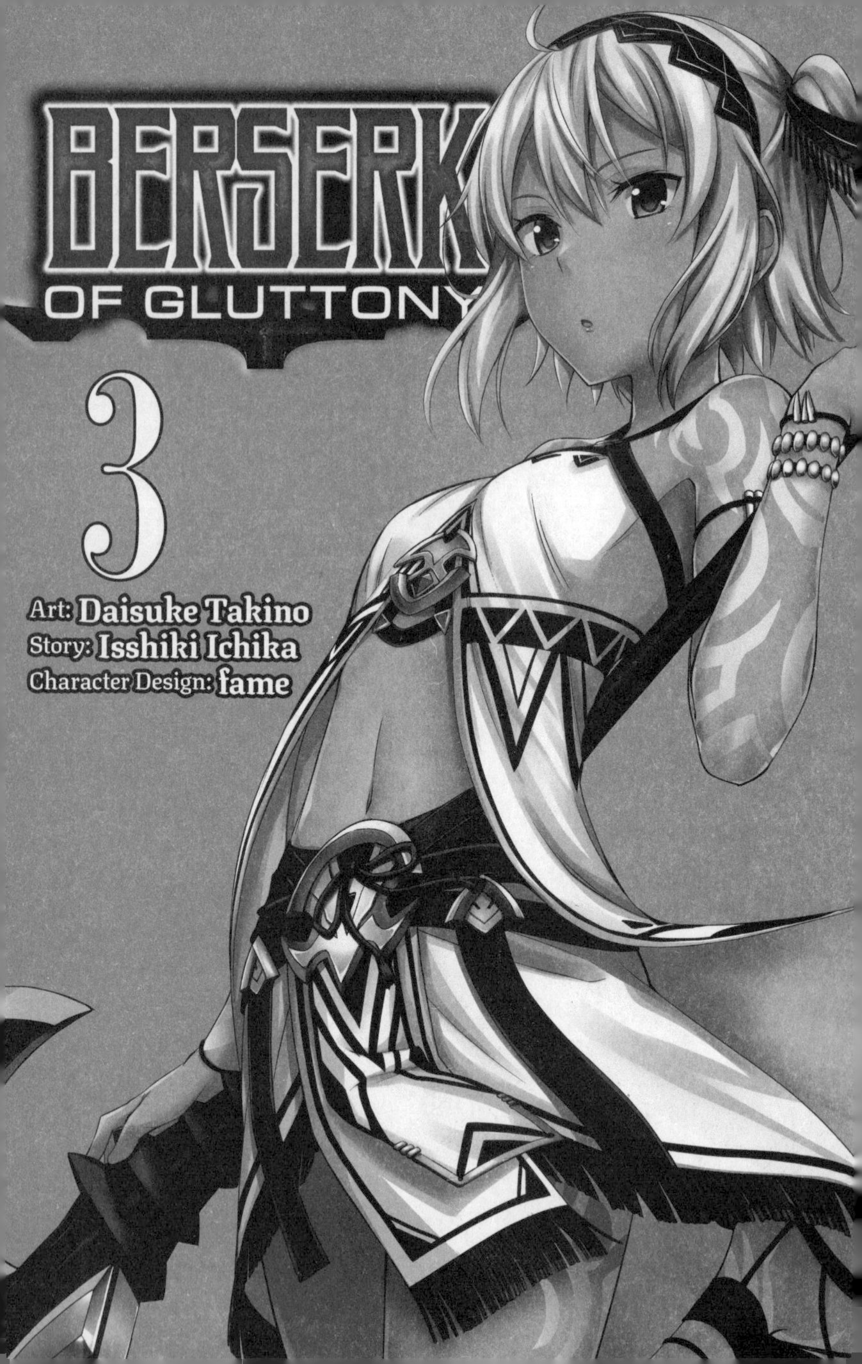
BERSERK
OF GLUTTONY
3
Art: Daisuke Takino
Story: Isshiki Ichika
Character Design: fame

CONTENTS

Chapter 11	The Second Level	003
Chapter 12	A Village Suspended in Time	033
Chapter 13	The Weight of a Fist	059
Chapter 14	The Desert of Extinction	091
Chapter 15	The Fearsome Beast of the Sandstorm	121

Chapter 11 ⸭— The Second Level

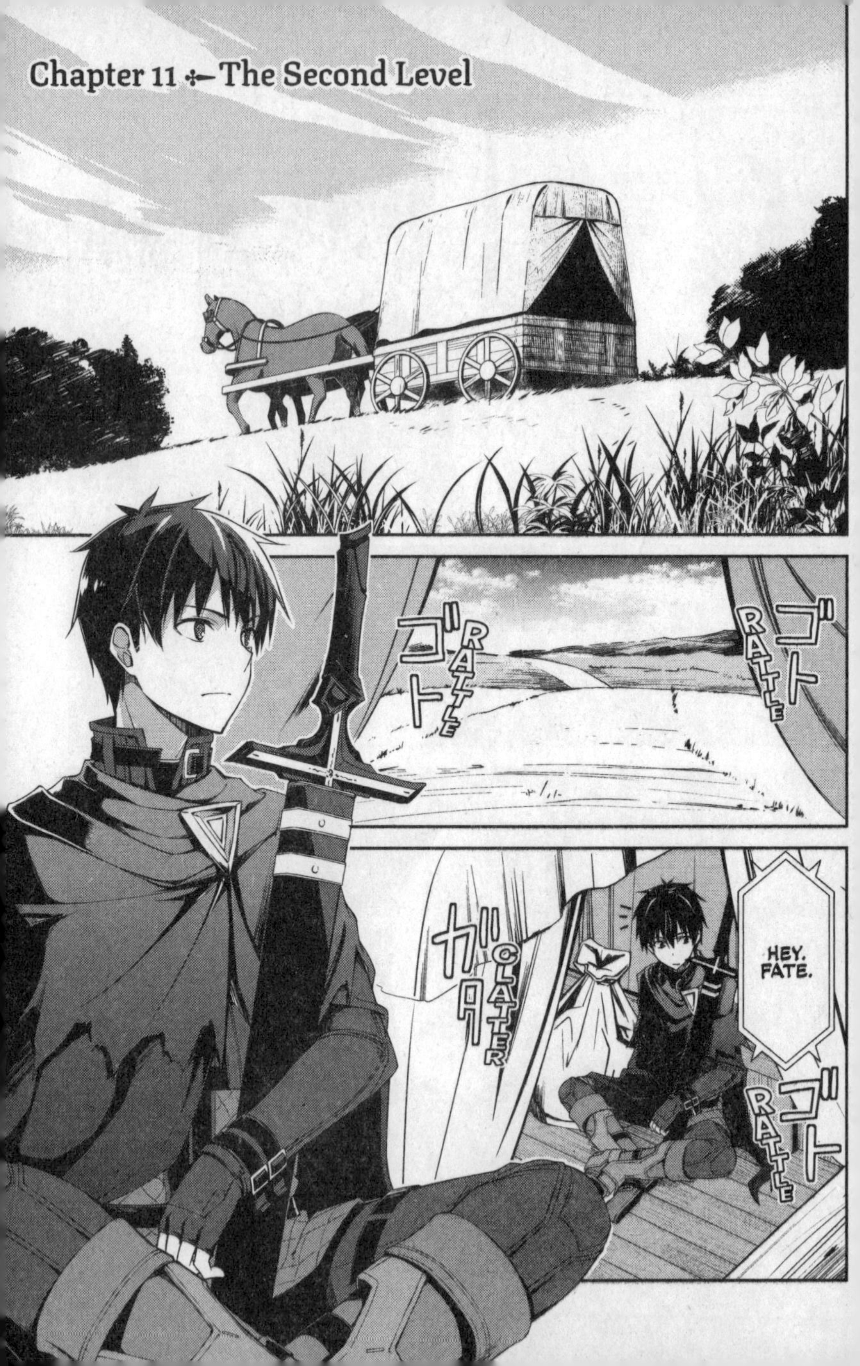
ゴト
RATTLE
ゴト
RATTLE
HEY. FATE.
ガタ
CLATTER
ゴト
RATTLE

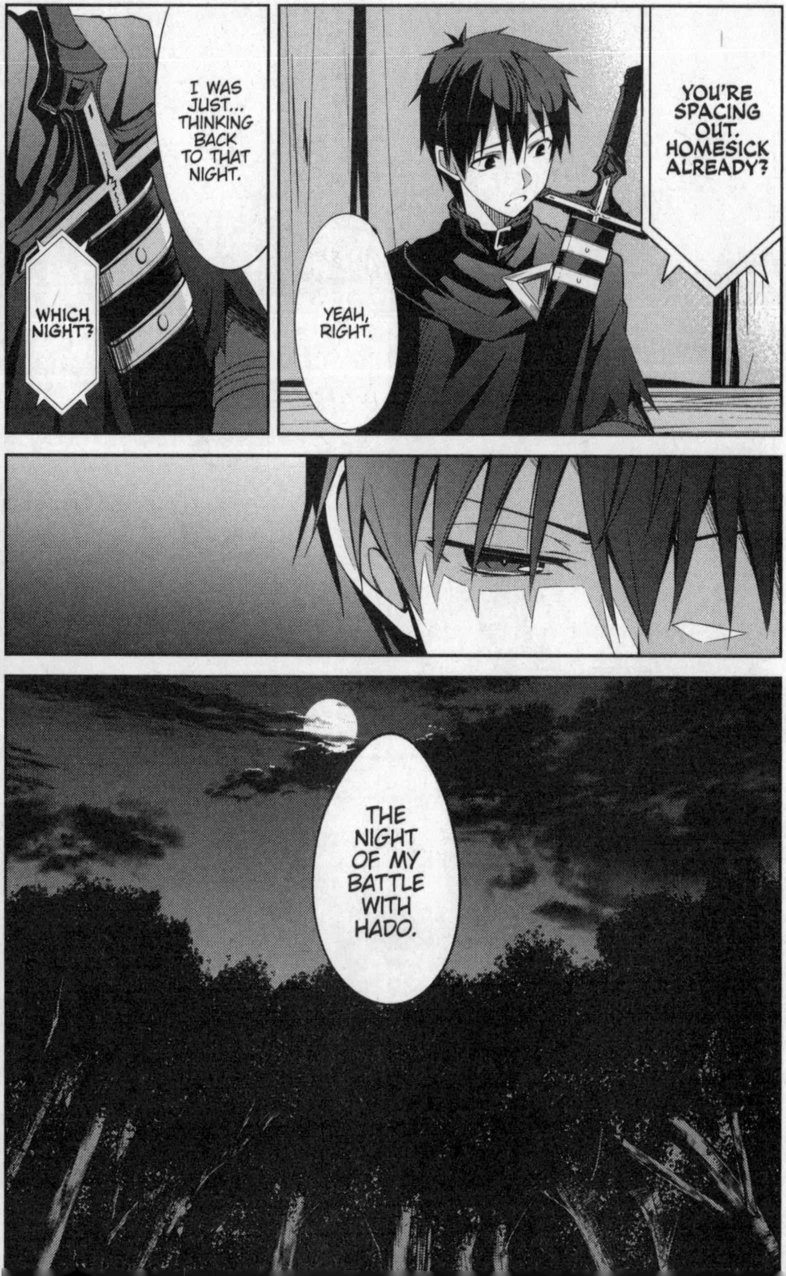
YOU'RE SPACING OUT. HOMESICK ALREADY?
YEAH, RIGHT.
I WAS JUST... THINKING BACK TO THAT NIGHT.
WHICH NIGHT?
THE NIGHT OF MY BATTLE WITH HADO.

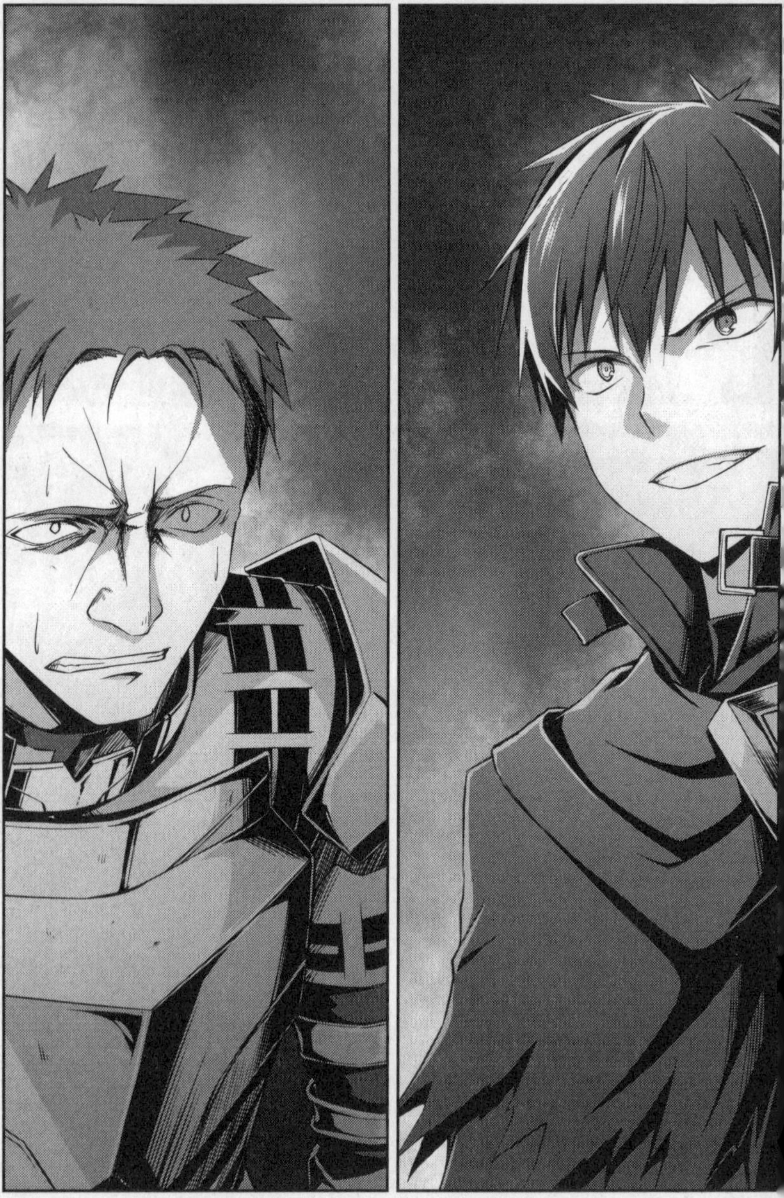

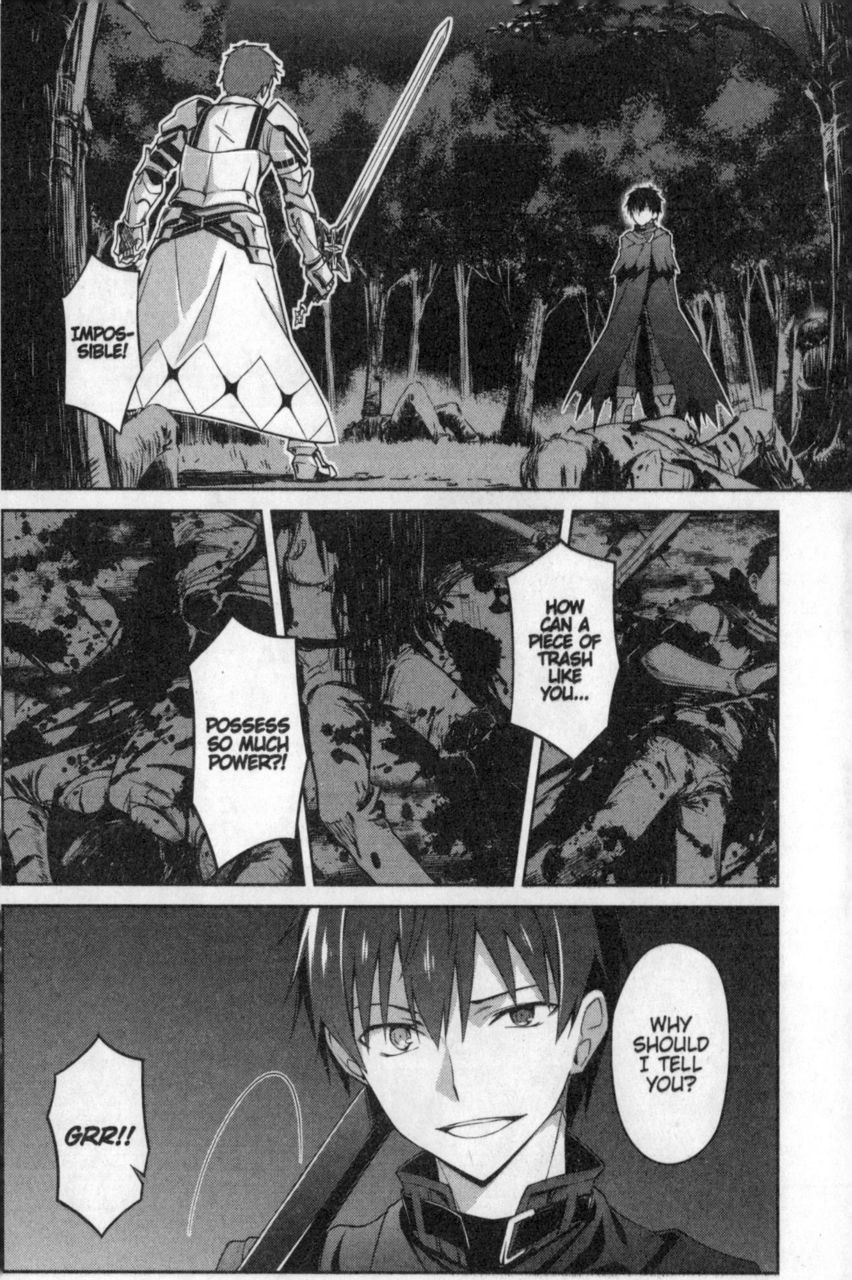
IMPOS-SIBLE!
HOW CAN A PIECE OF TRASH LIKE YOU...
POSSESS SO MUCH POWER?!
WHY SHOULD I TELL YOU?
GRR!!

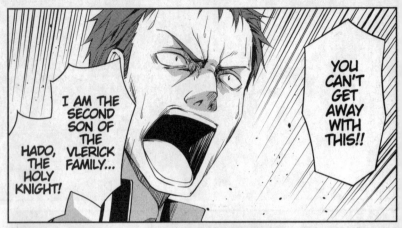

I AM THE SECOND SON OF THE VLERICK FAMILY... HADO, THE HOLY KNIGHT!

YOU CAN'T GET AWAY WITH THIS!!

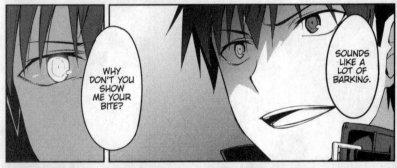

WHY DON'T YOU SHOW ME YOUR BITE?

SOUNDS LIKE A LOT OF BARKING.

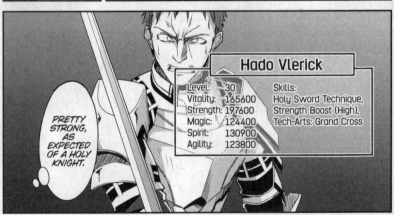

PRETTY STRONG, AS EXPECTED OF A HOLY KNIGHT.

Hado Vlerick

Level:	30	Skills:
Vitality:	165600	Holy Sword Technique,
Strength:	197600	Strength Boost (High),
Magic:	124400	Tech-Arts: Grand Cross
Spirit:	130900	
Agility:	123800	

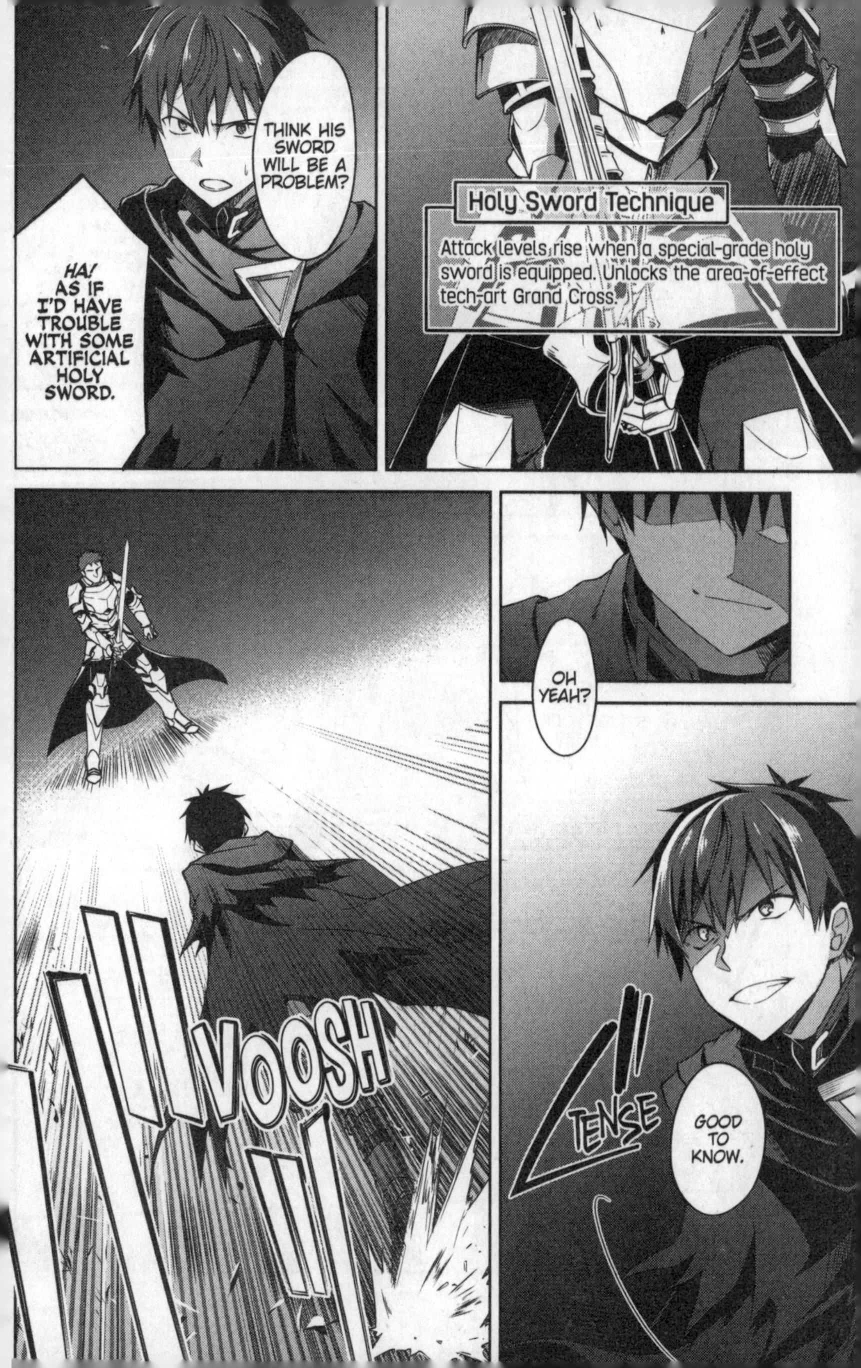
Holy Sword Technique
Attack levels rise when a special-grade holy sword is equipped. Unlocks the area-of-effect tech-art Grand Cross.
THINK HIS SWORD WILL BE A PROBLEM?
HA! AS IF I'D HAVE TROUBLE WITH SOME ARTIFICIAL HOLY SWORD.
OH YEAH?
TENSE
GOOD TO KNOW.
VOOSH

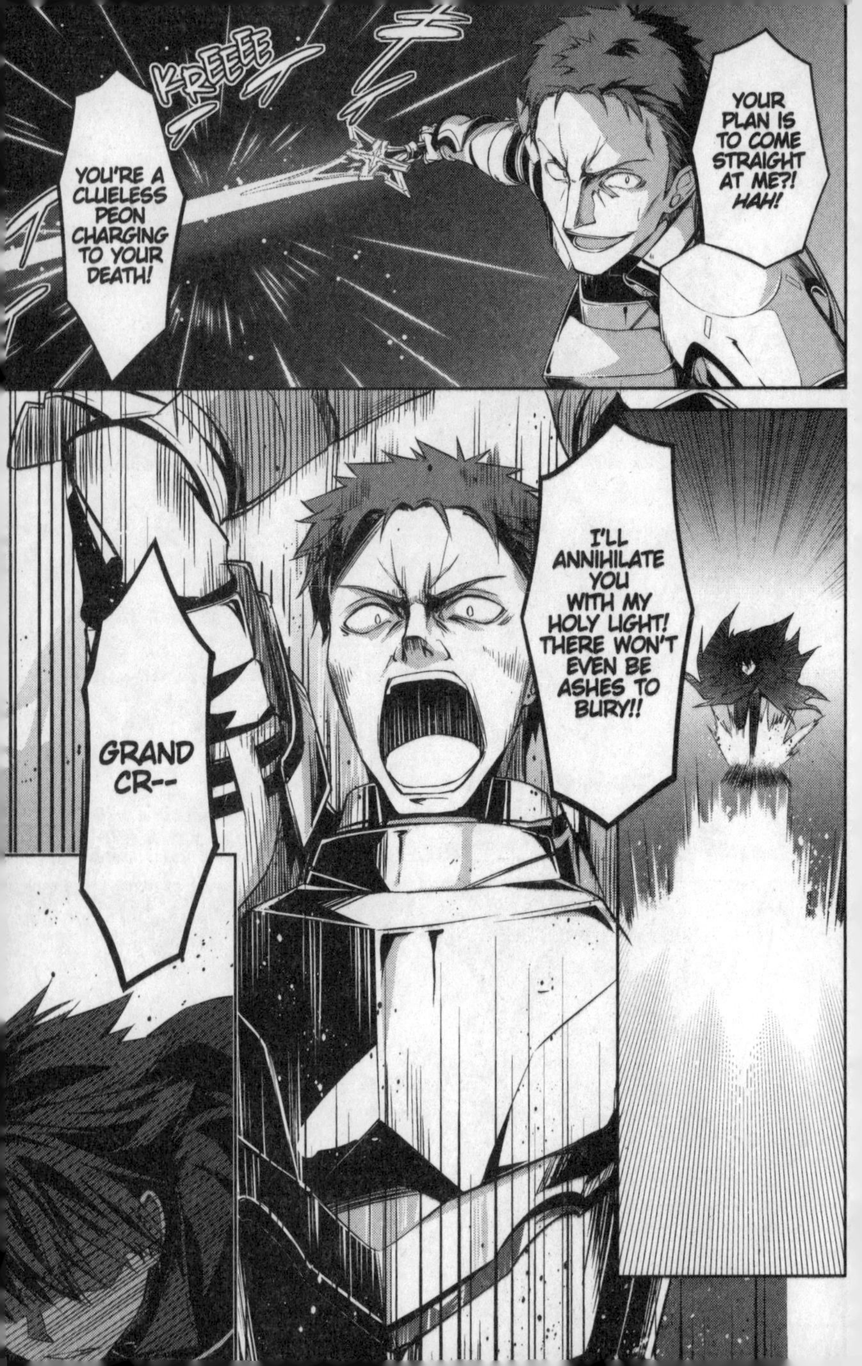
YOUR PLAN IS TO COME STRAIGHT AT ME?! HAH!
KREEEE
YOU'RE A CLUELESS PEON CHARGING TO YOUR DEATH!
I'LL ANNIHILATE YOU WITH MY HOLY LIGHT! THERE WON'T EVEN BE ASHES TO BURY!!
GRAND CR--

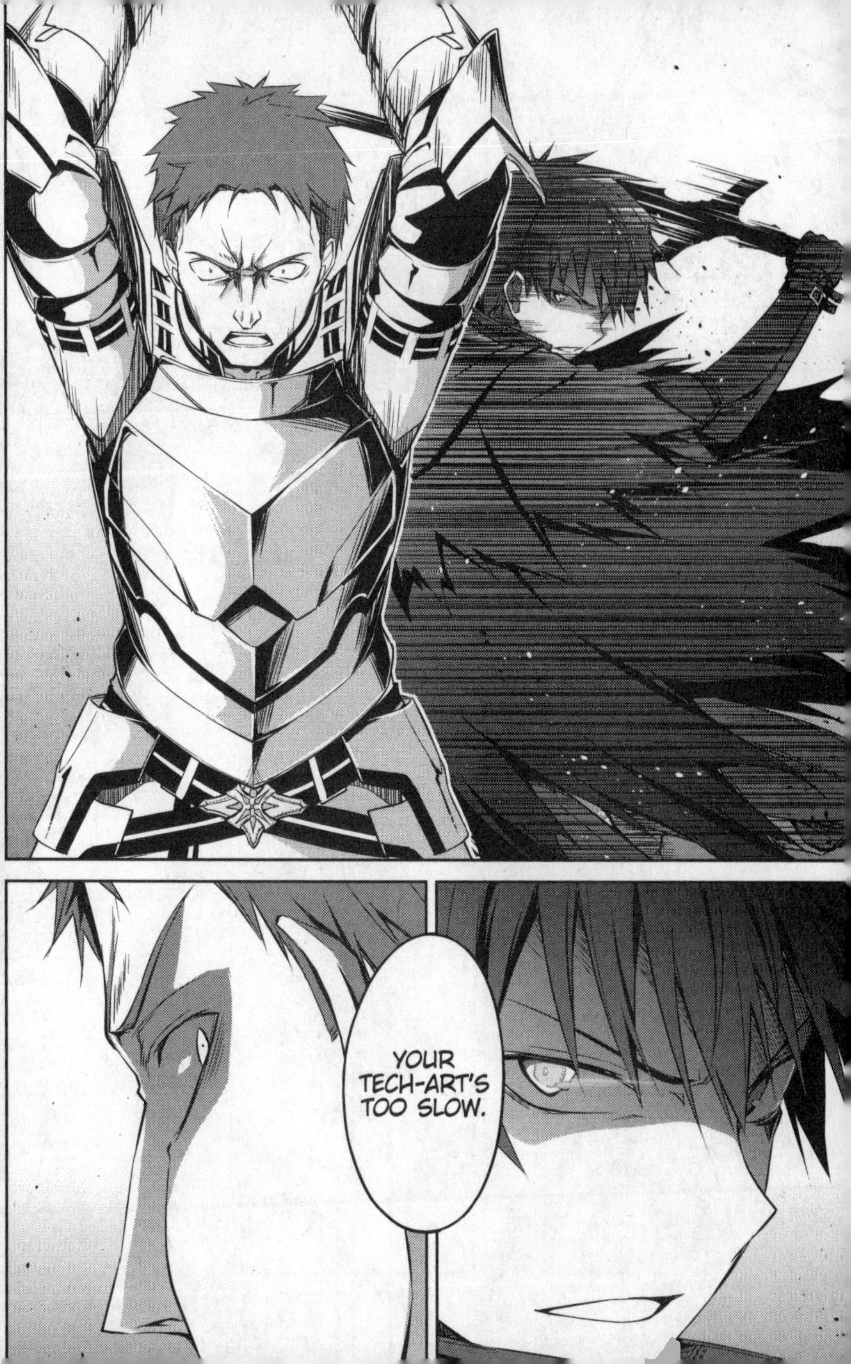
YOUR TECH-ART'S TOO SLOW.

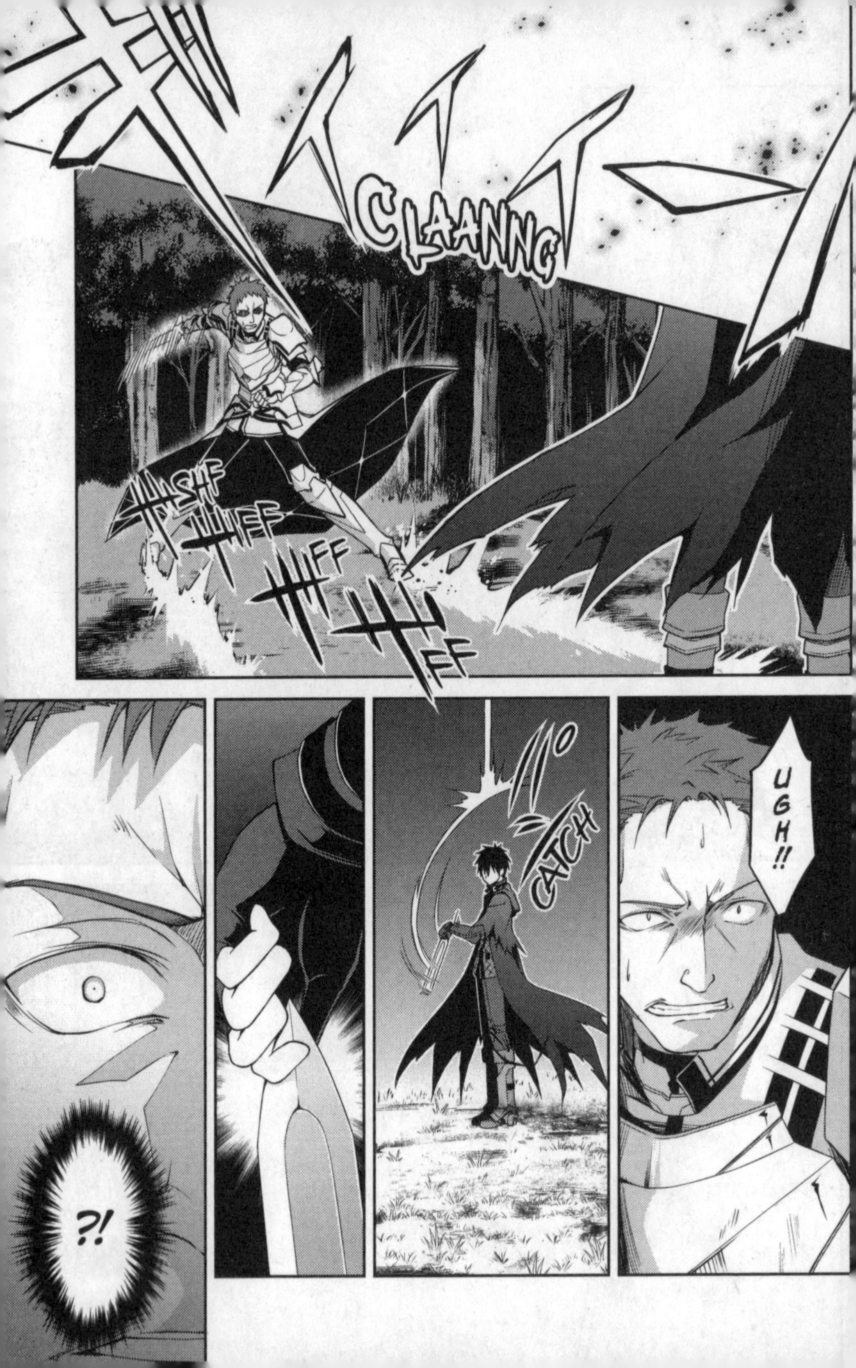
CLAANNG
SHF
HUFF
HUFF
HUFF
UGH!!
CATCH
?!

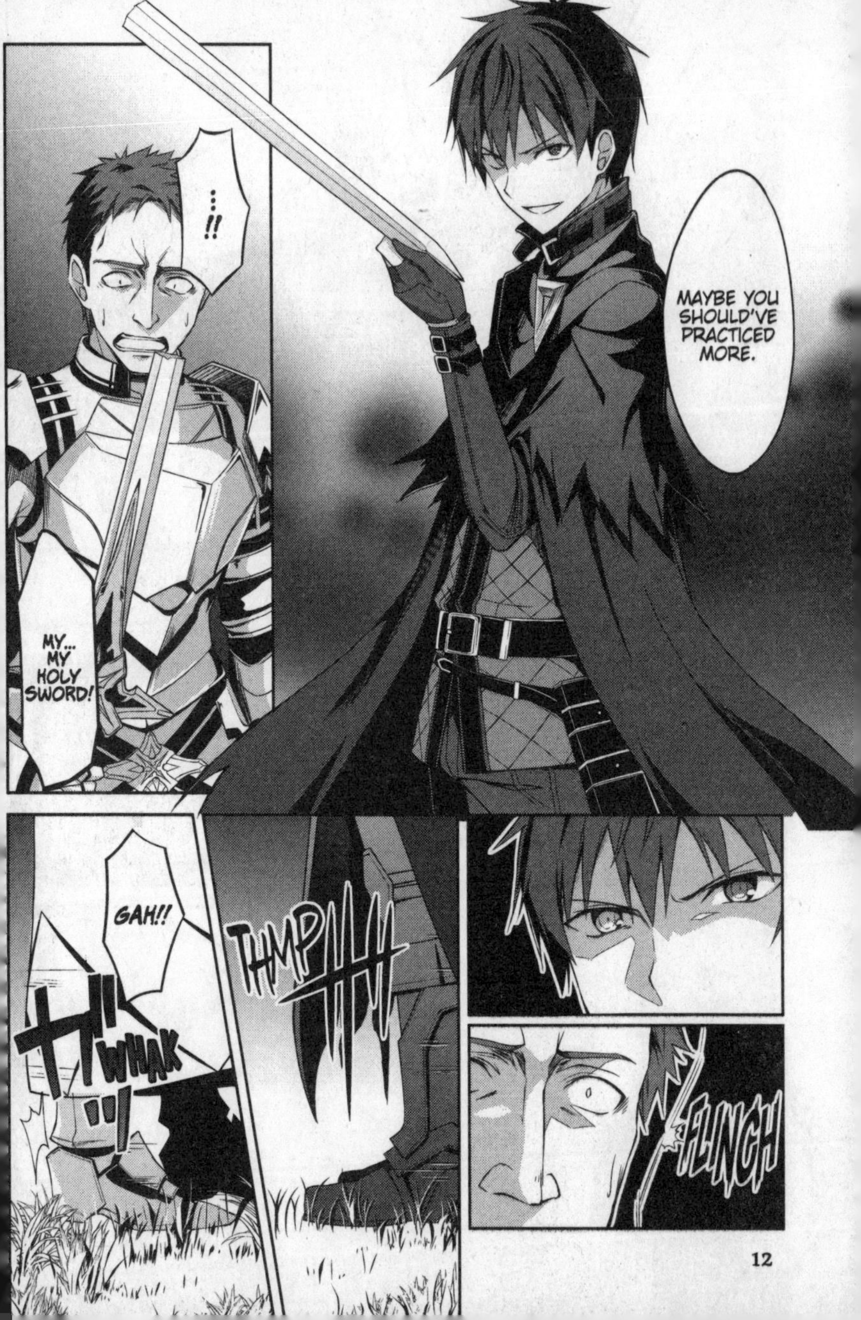
MAYBE YOU SHOULD'VE PRACTICED MORE.
...!!
MY... MY HOLY SWORD!
FLINCH
THMP
GAH!!
WHAK

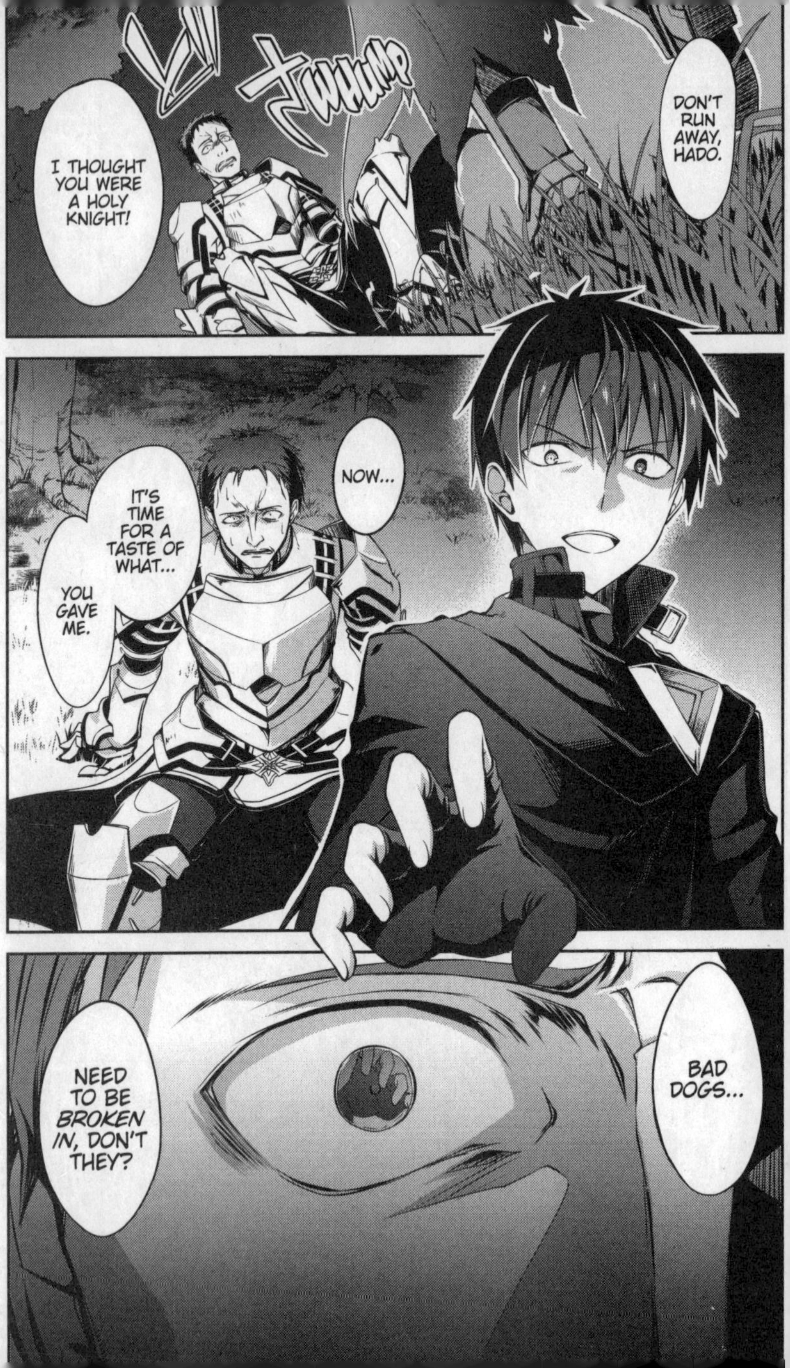
DON'T RUN AWAY, HADO.
I THOUGHT YOU WERE A HOLY KNIGHT!
NOW...
IT'S TIME FOR A TASTE OF WHAT...
YOU GAVE ME.
BAD DOGS...
NEED TO BE *BROKEN IN*, DON'T THEY?

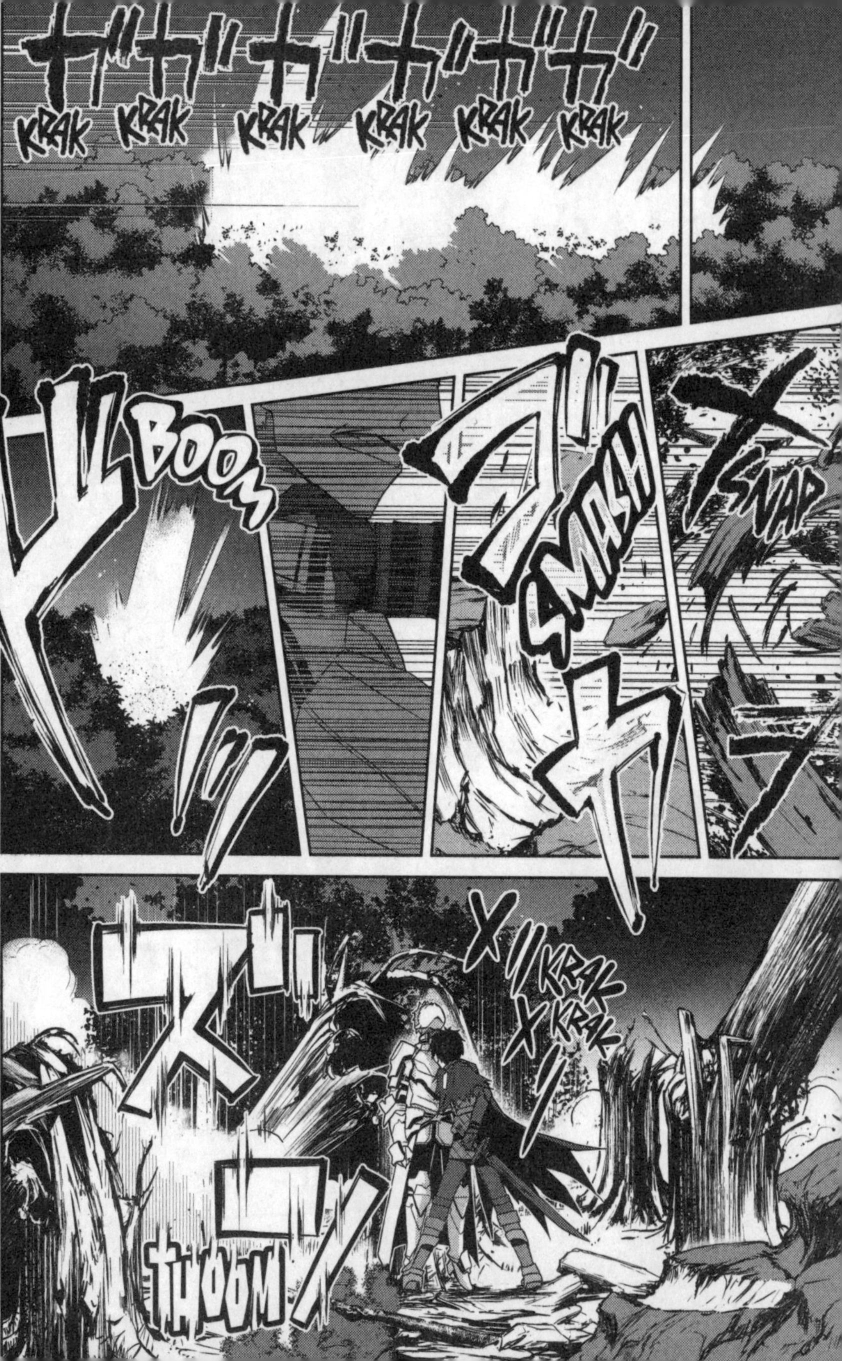
KRAK KRAK KRAK KRAK KRAK KRAK
SNAP
SMASH
BOOM
KRAK KRAK
THOOM

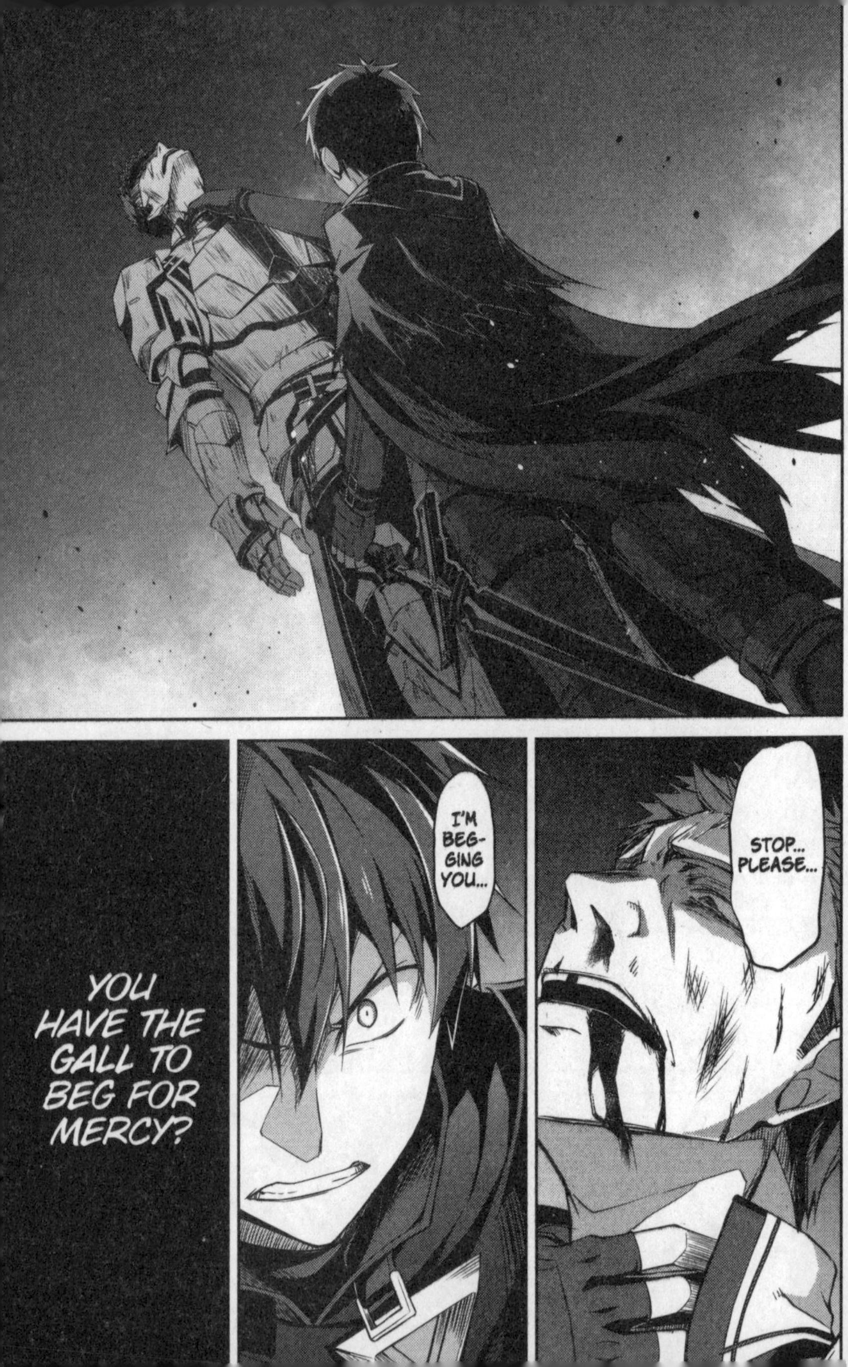
STOP... PLEASE...
I'M BEG-GING YOU...
YOU HAVE THE GALL TO BEG FOR MERCY?

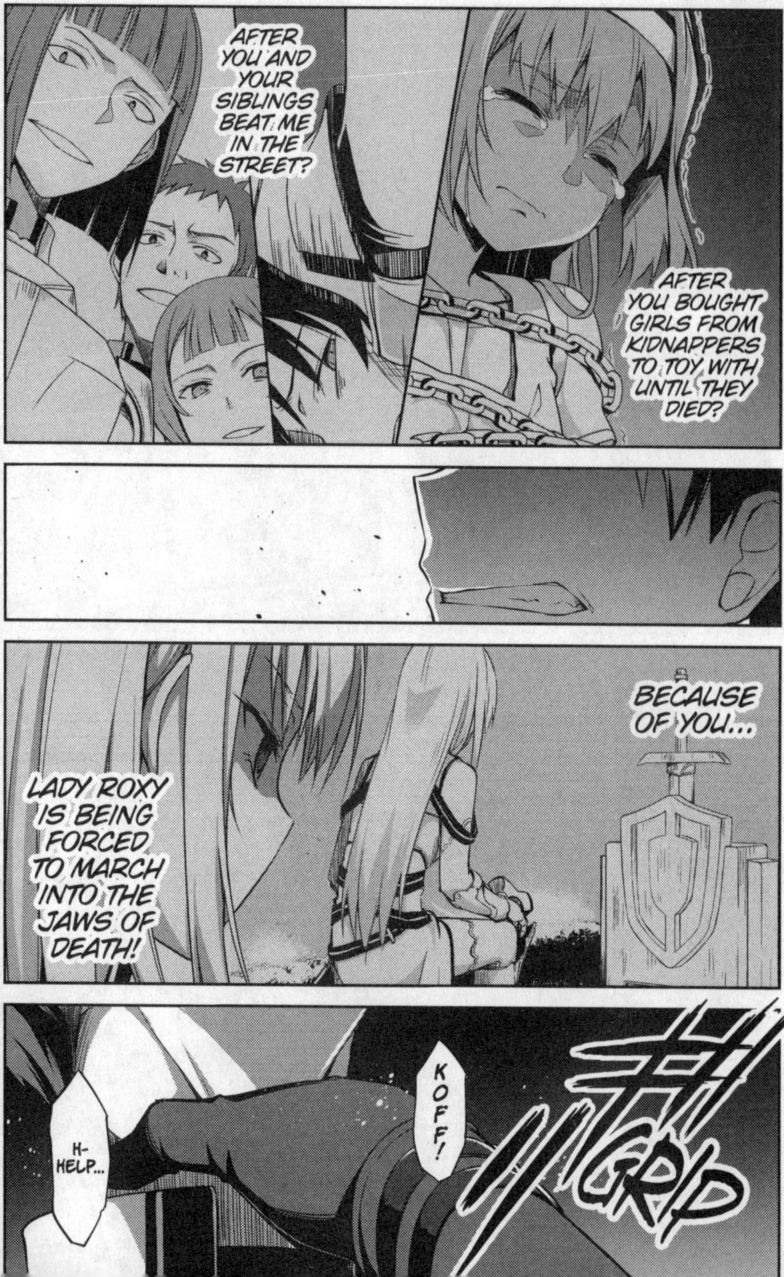
AFTER YOU BOUGHT GIRLS FROM KIDNAPPERS TO TOY WITH UNTIL THEY DIED?
AFTER YOU AND YOUR SIBLINGS BEAT ME IN THE STREET?
BECAUSE OF YOU...
LADY ROXY IS BEING FORCED TO MARCH INTO THE JAWS OF DEATH!
GRIP
KOFF!
H-HELP...

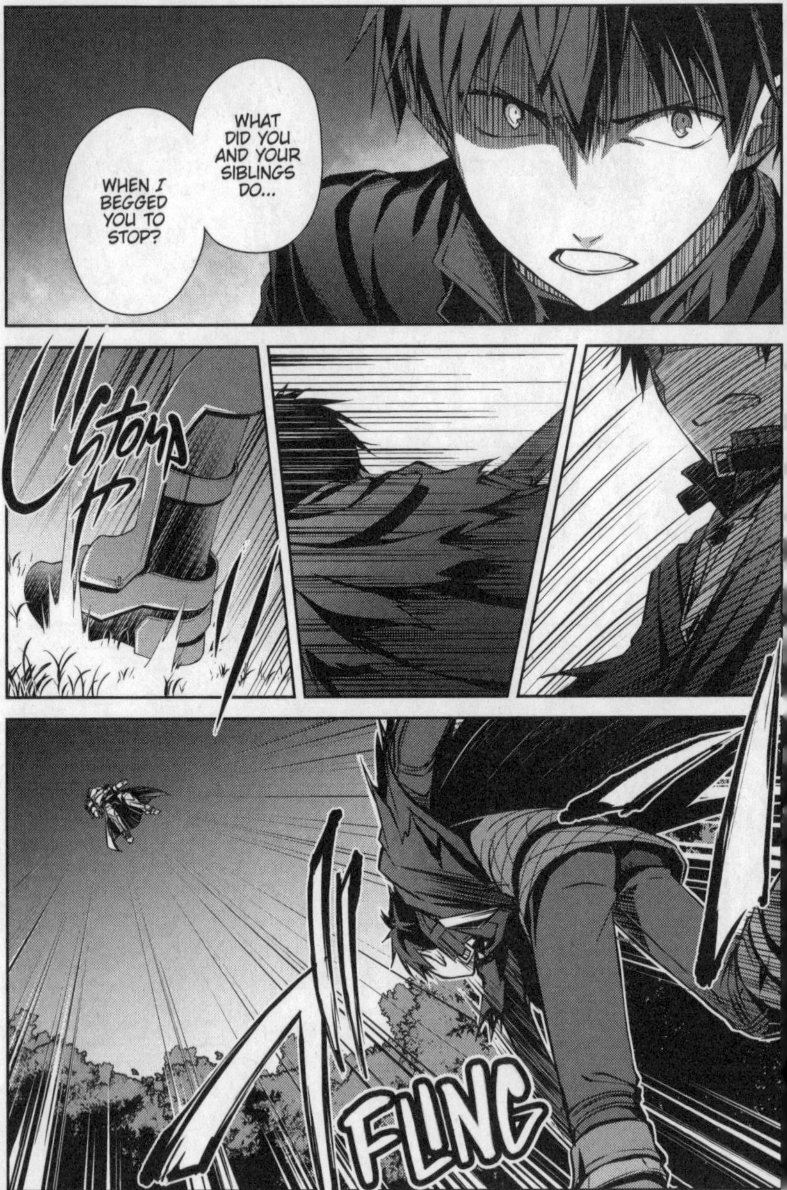
WHAT DID YOU AND YOUR SIBLINGS DO...
WHEN I BEGGED YOU TO STOP?
STOMP
FLING

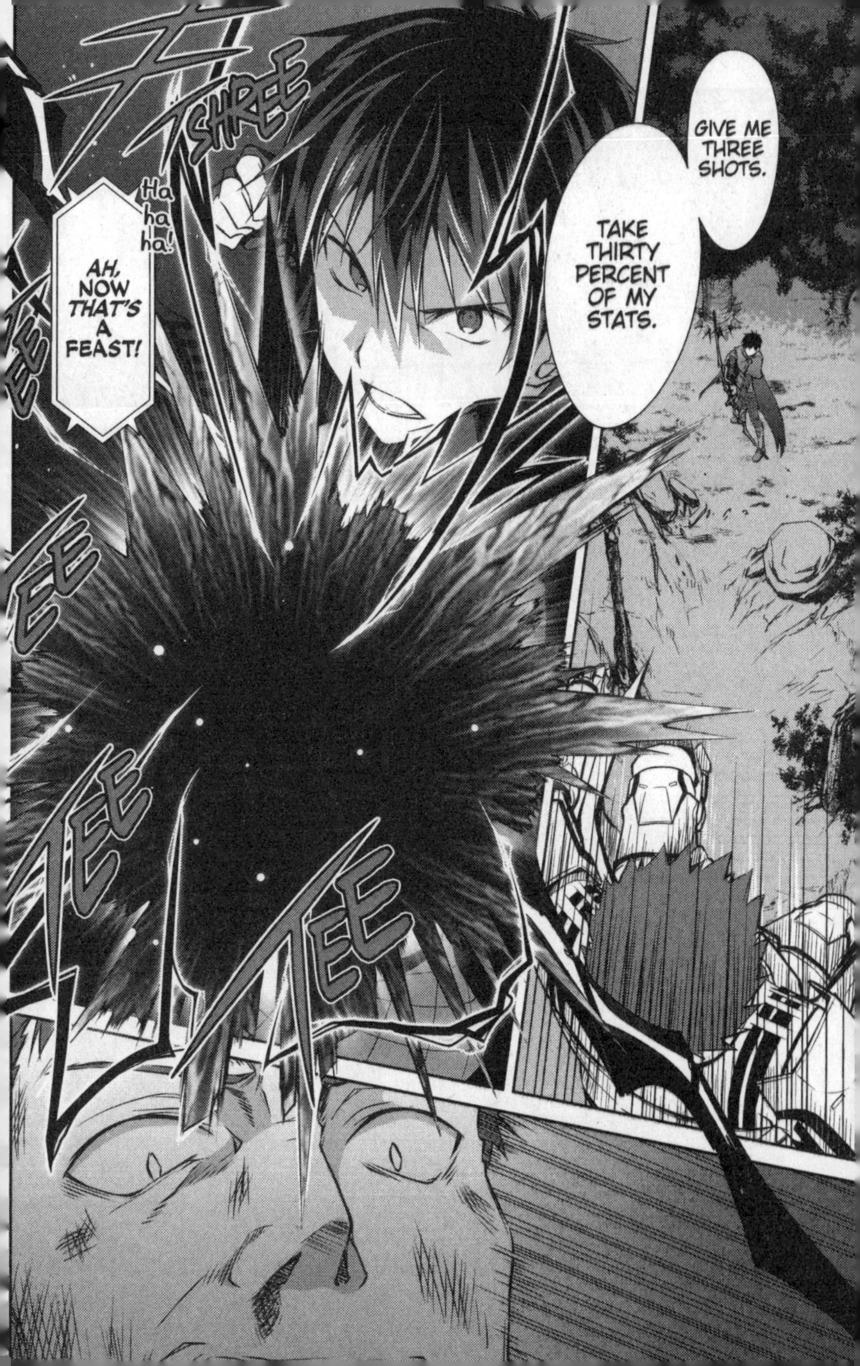
GIVE ME THREE SHOTS.
TAKE THIRTY PERCENT OF MY STATS.
SHREE
Ha ha ha!
AH, NOW THAT'S A FEAST!
EE
TEE
TEE
TEE

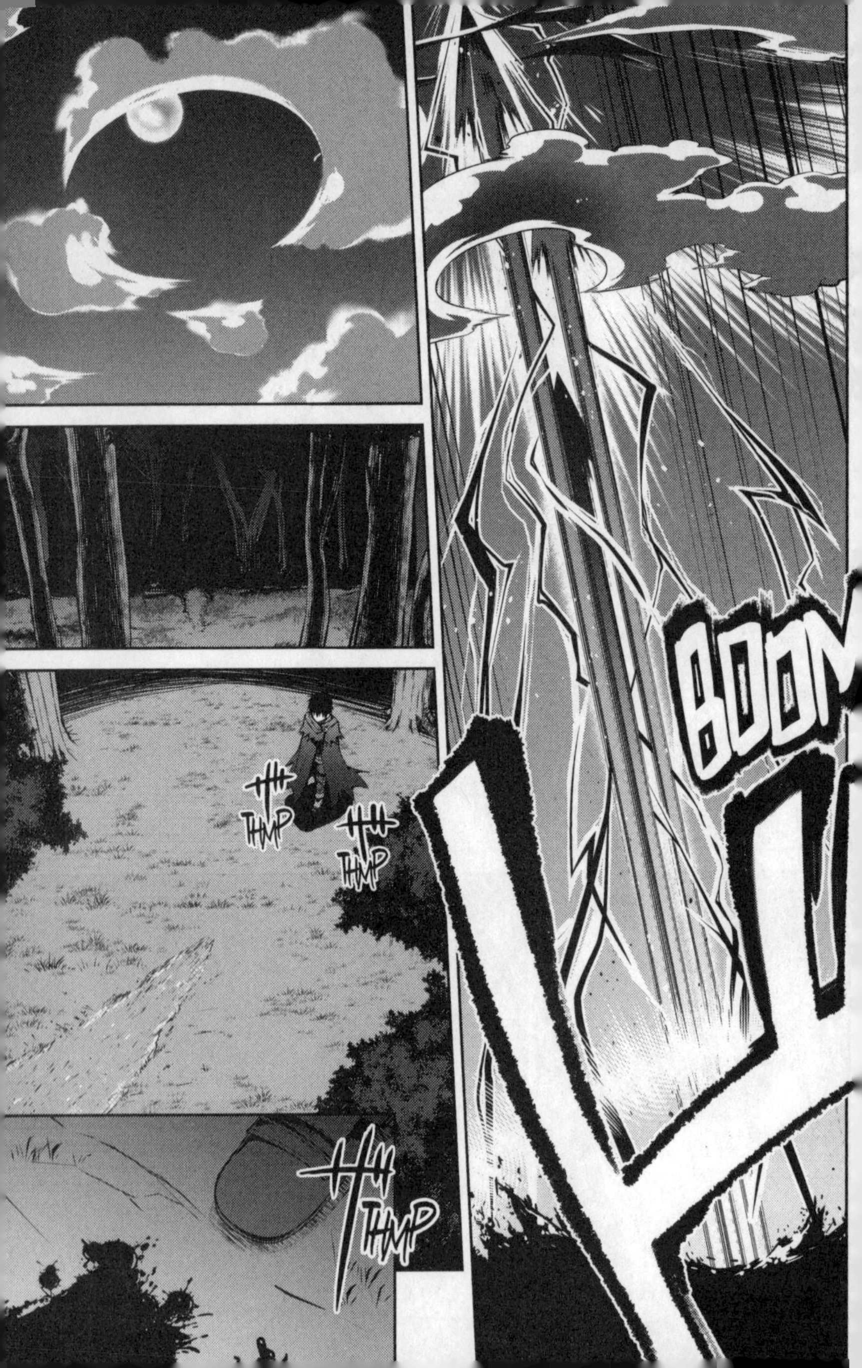
BOOM
THMP
THMP
THMP

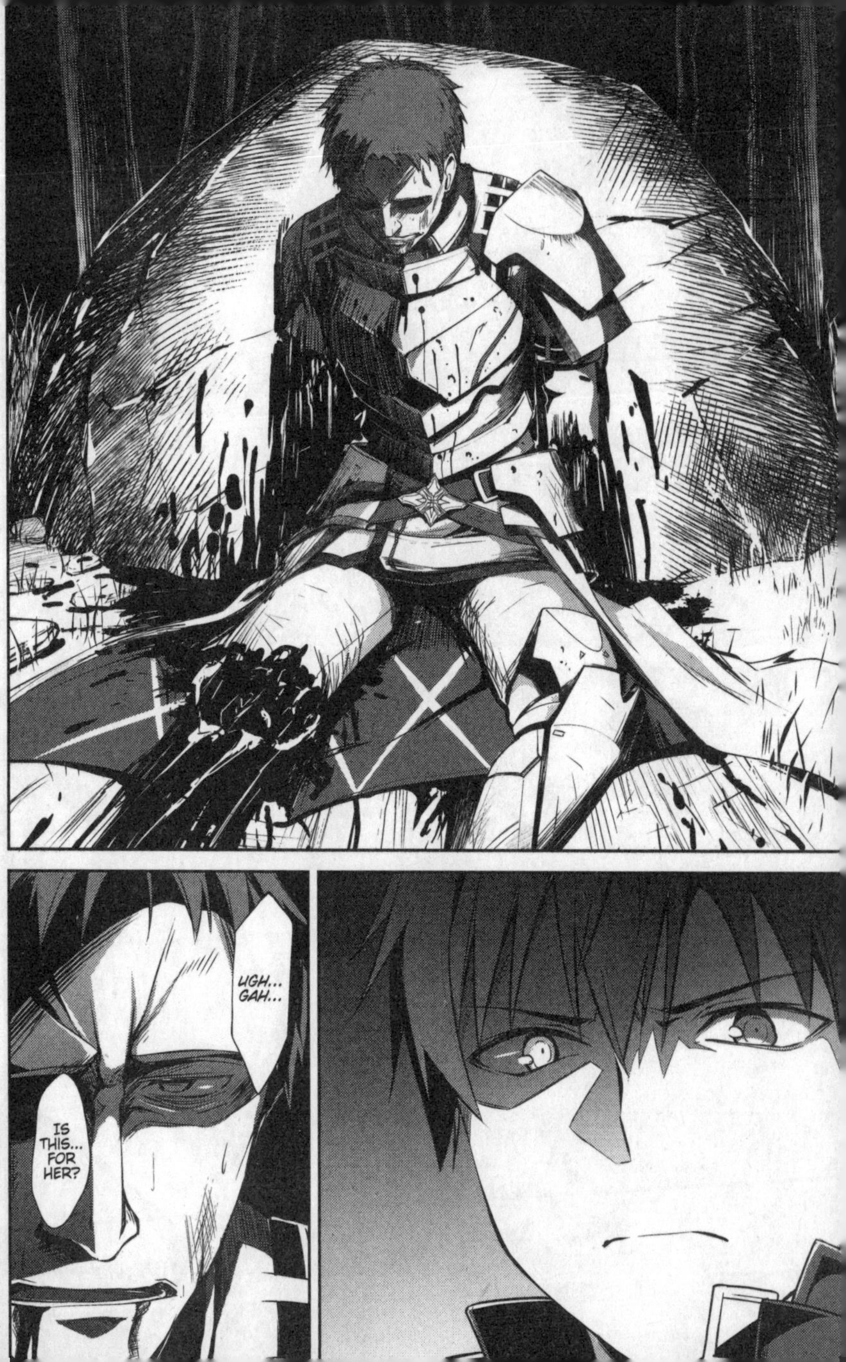
UGH... GAH...
IS THIS... FOR HER?

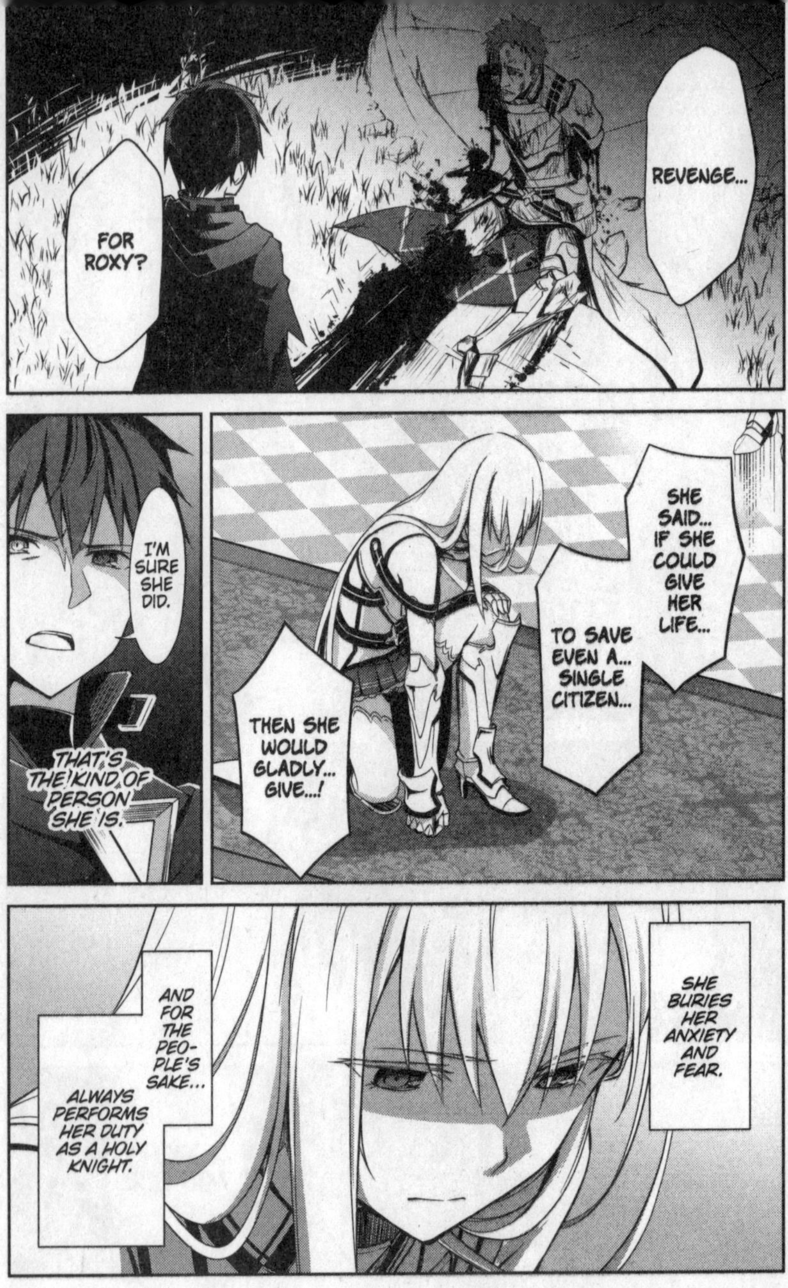
REVENGE...
FOR ROXY?
SHE SAID... IF SHE COULD GIVE HER LIFE...
TO SAVE EVEN A... SINGLE CITIZEN...
THEN SHE WOULD GLADLY... GIVE...!
I'M SURE SHE DID.
THAT'S THE KIND OF PERSON SHE IS.
SHE BURIES HER ANXIETY AND FEAR.
AND FOR THE PEOPLE'S SAKE...
ALWAYS PERFORMS HER DUTY AS A HOLY KNIGHT.

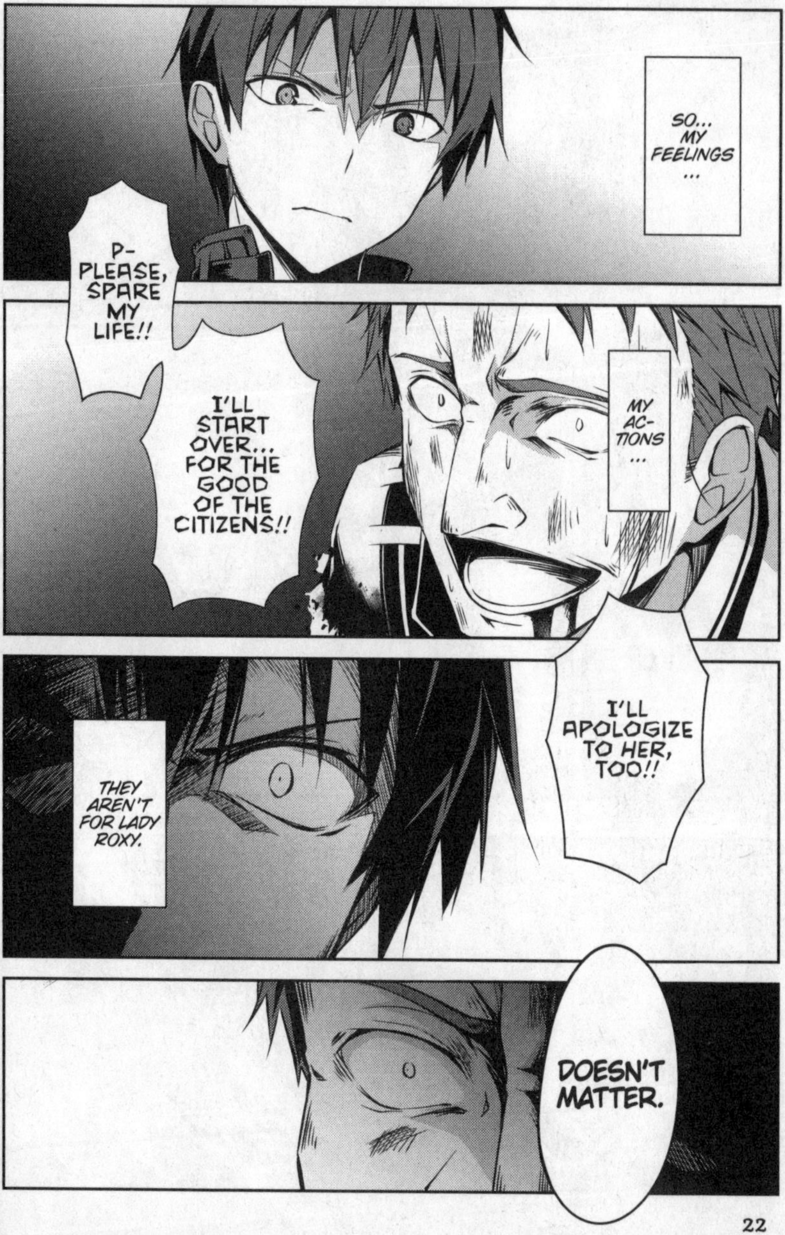
SO... MY FEELINGS ...
P-PLEASE, SPARE MY LIFE!!
MY ACTIONS ...
I'LL START OVER... FOR THE GOOD OF THE CITIZENS!!
I'LL APOLOGIZE TO HER, TOO!!
THEY AREN'T FOR LADY ROXY.
DOESN'T MATTER.

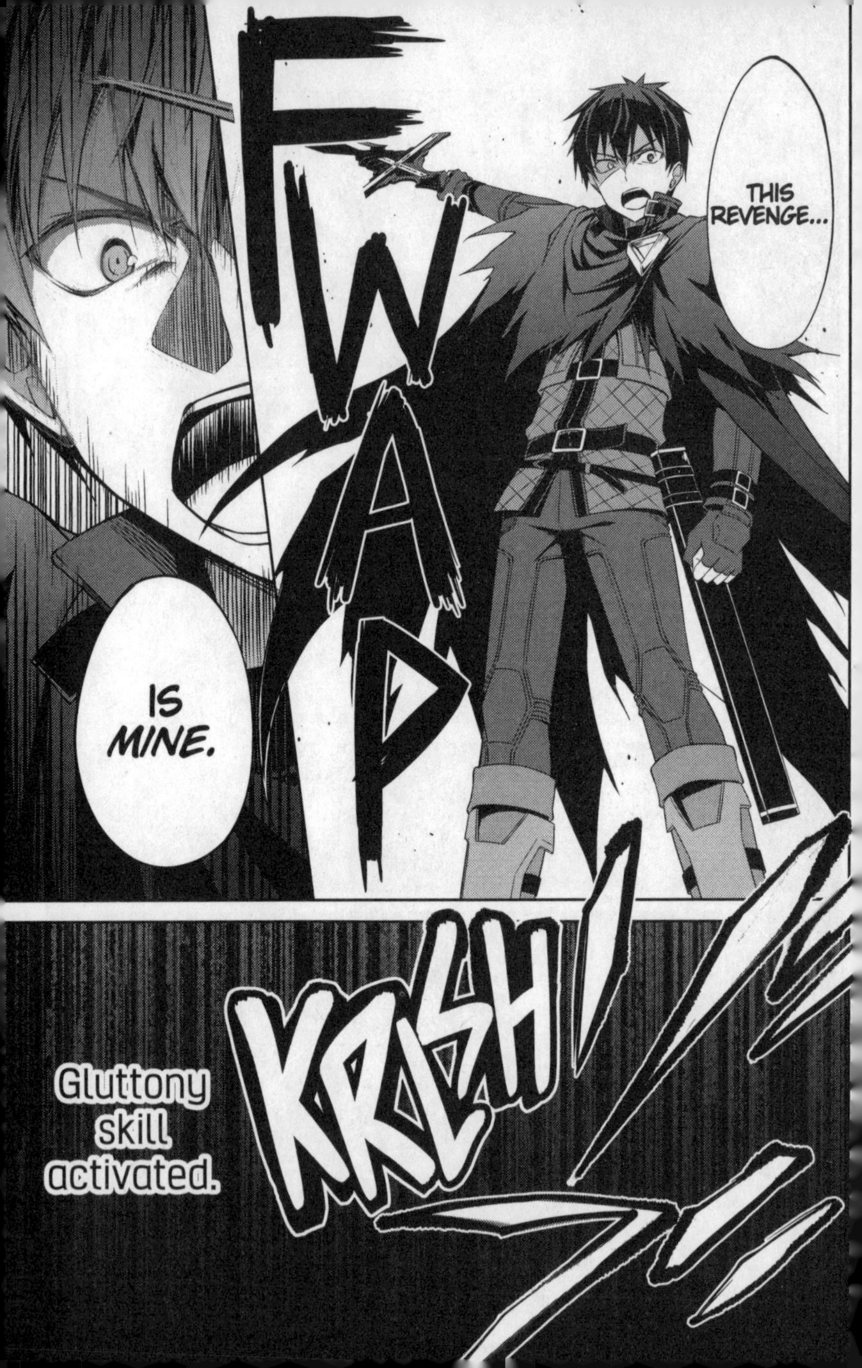
THIS REVENGE...
FWAP
IS MINE.
KRASH
Gluttony skill activated.

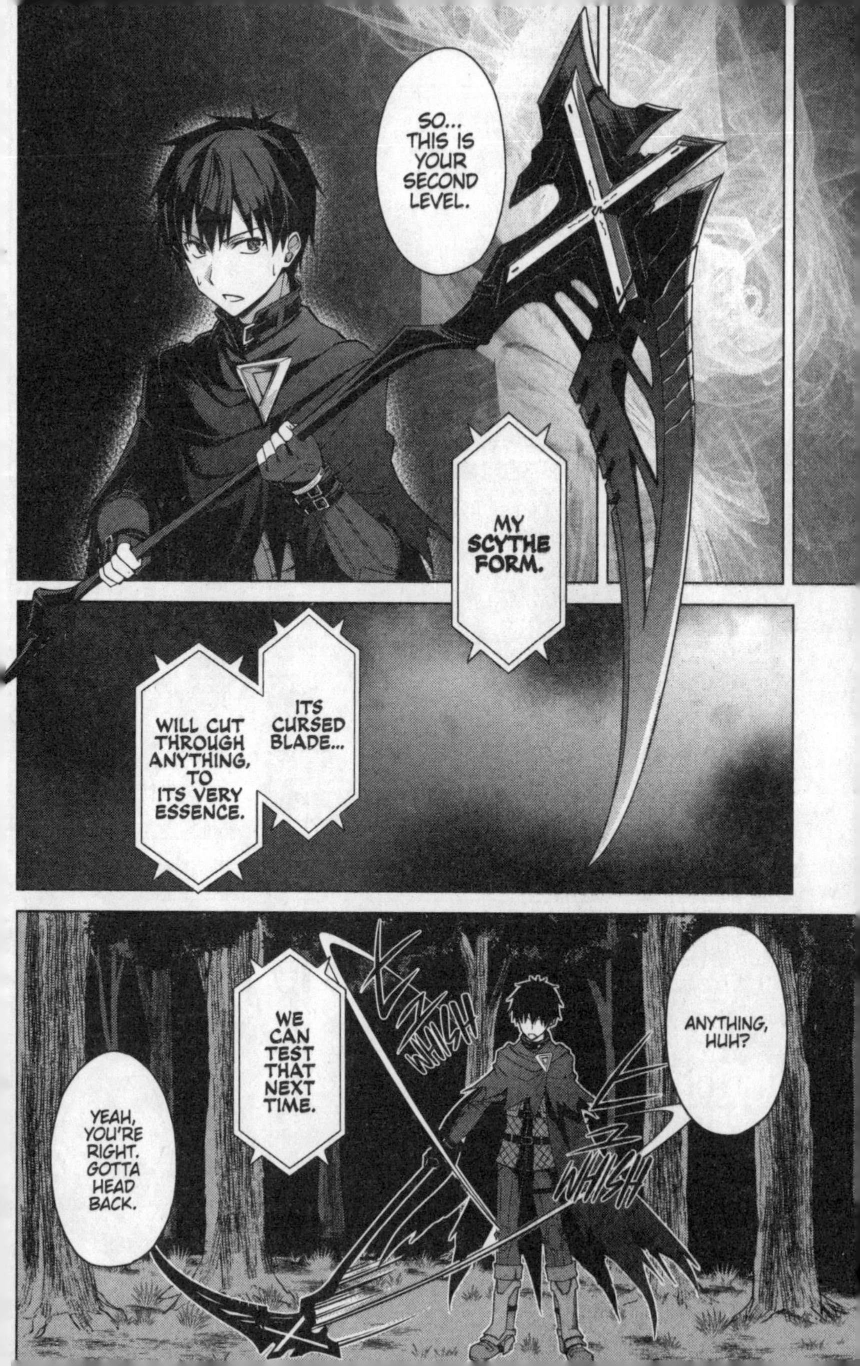
SO... THIS IS YOUR SECOND LEVEL.
MY SCYTHE FORM.
ITS CURSED BLADE...
WILL CUT THROUGH ANYTHING, TO ITS VERY ESSENCE.
ANYTHING, HUH?
WHISH
WHISH
WE CAN TEST THAT NEXT TIME.
YEAH, YOU'RE RIGHT. GOTTA HEAD BACK.

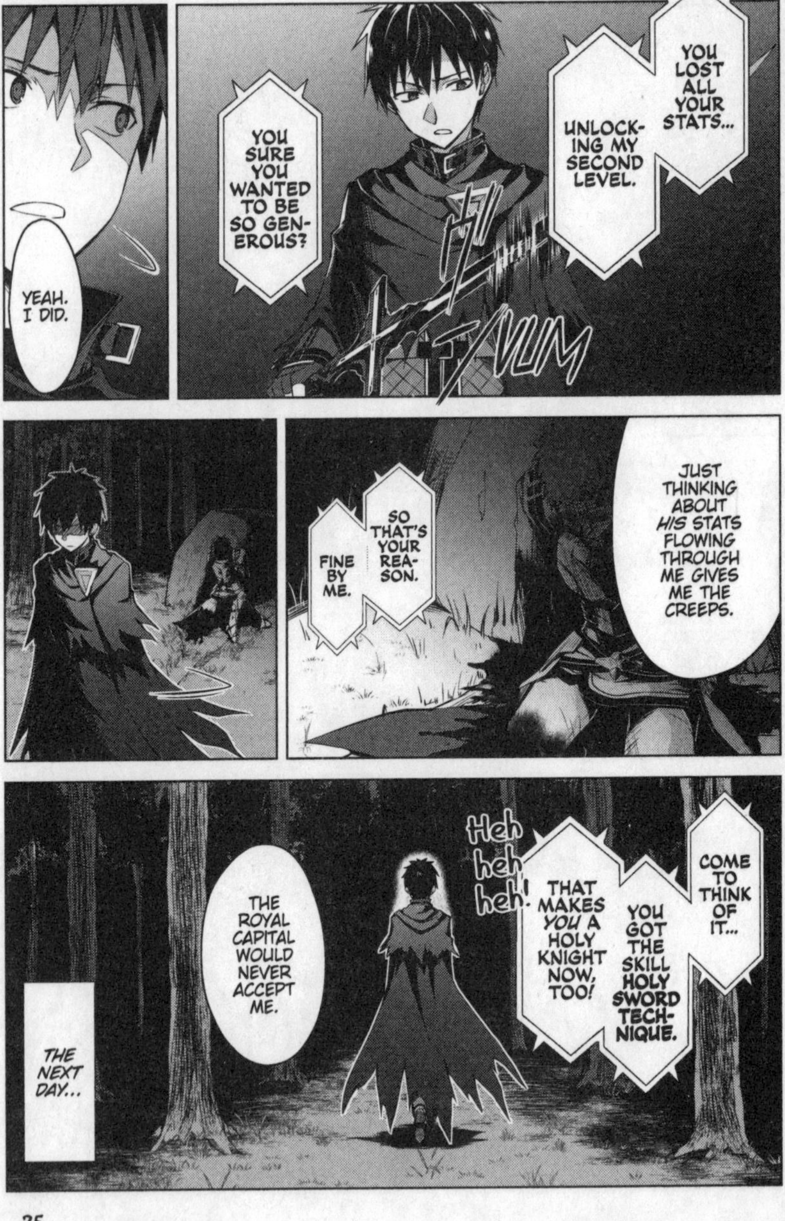
YOU LOST ALL YOUR STATS...
UNLOCKING MY SECOND LEVEL.
YOU SURE YOU WANTED TO BE SO GENEROUS?
YEAH. I DID.
JUST THINKING ABOUT *HIS* STATS FLOWING THROUGH ME GIVES ME THE CREEPS.
SO THAT'S YOUR REASON.
FINE BY ME.
COME TO THINK OF IT...
YOU GOT THE SKILL HOLY SWORD TECHNIQUE.
THAT MAKES *YOU* A HOLY KNIGHT NOW, TOO!
Heh heh heh!
THE ROYAL CAPITAL WOULD NEVER ACCEPT ME.
THE NEXT DAY...

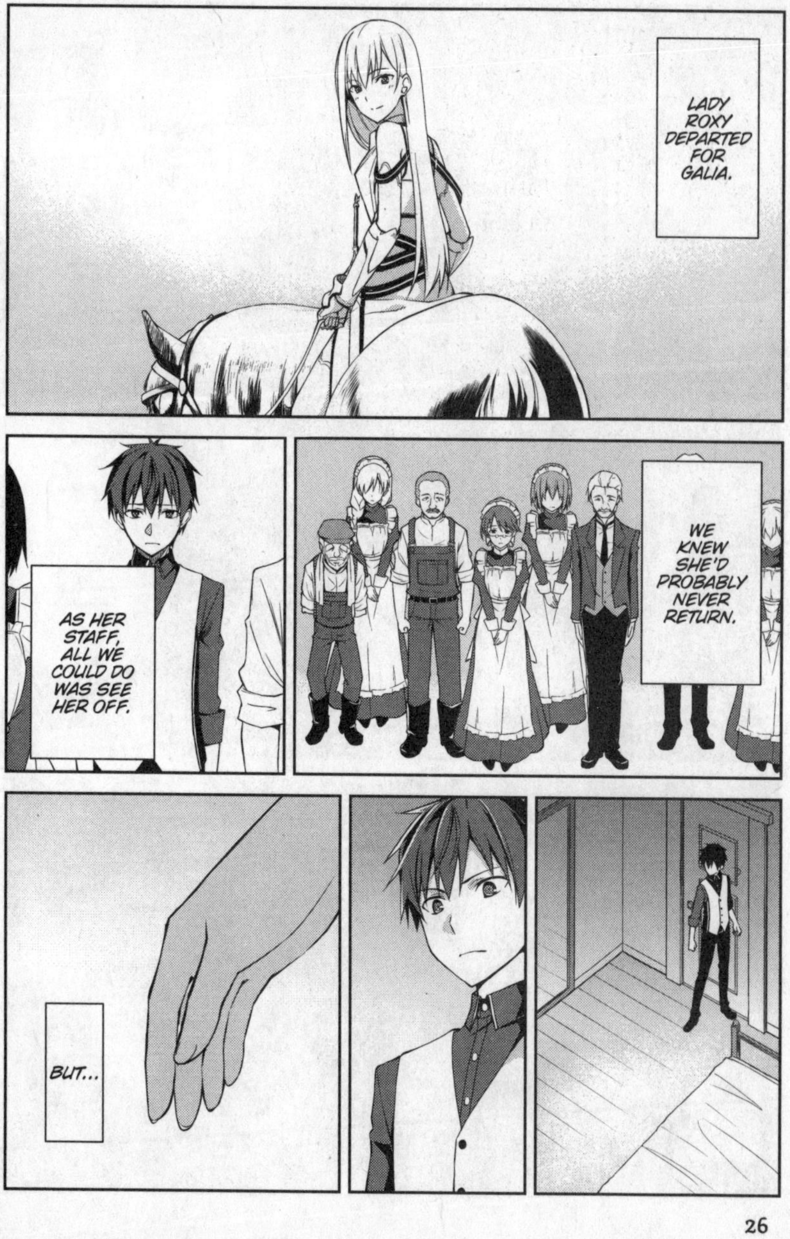
LADY ROXY DEPARTED FOR GALIA.
WE KNEW SHE'D PROBABLY NEVER RETURN.
AS HER STAFF, ALL WE COULD DO WAS SEE HER OFF.
BUT...

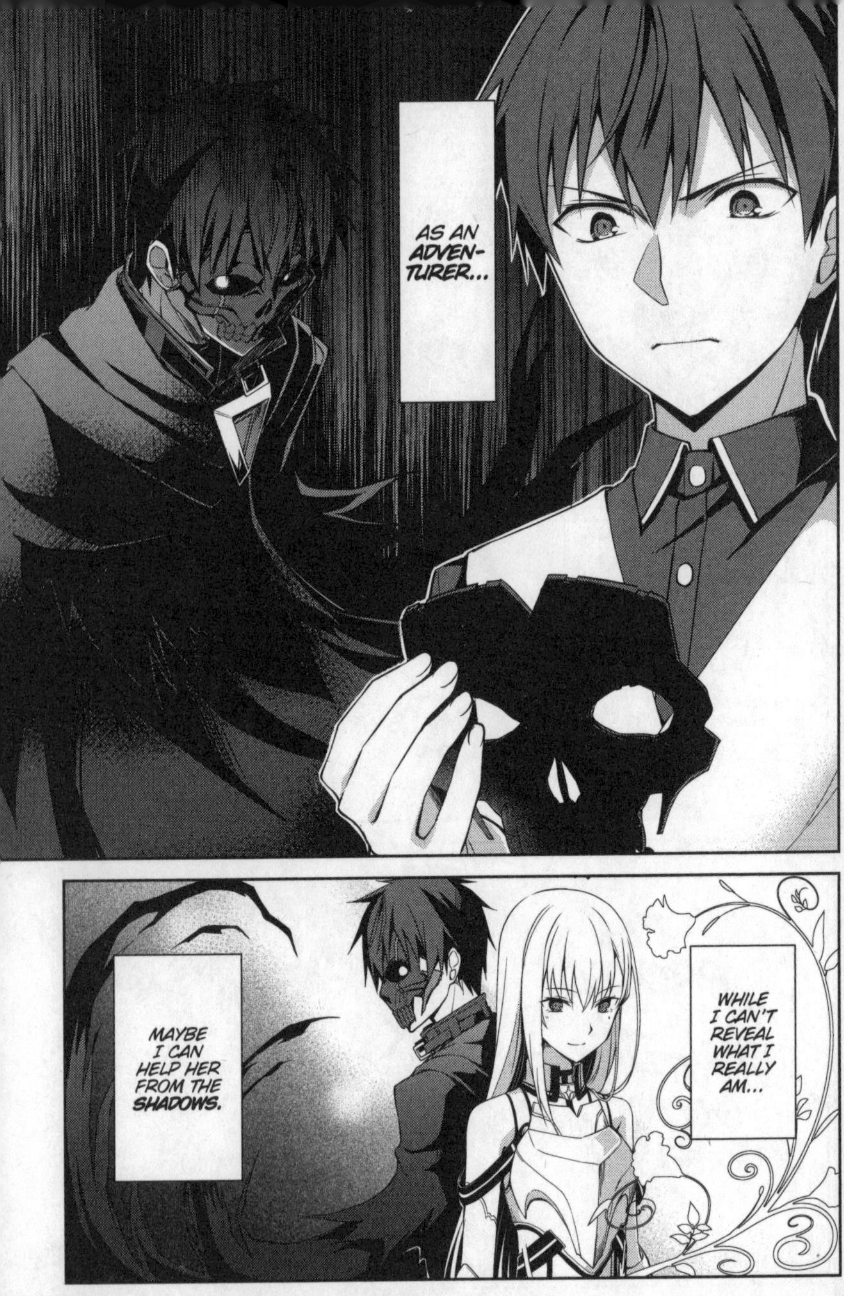
AS AN ADVENTURER...
WHILE I CAN'T REVEAL WHAT I REALLY AM...
MAYBE I CAN HELP HER FROM THE **SHADOWS.**

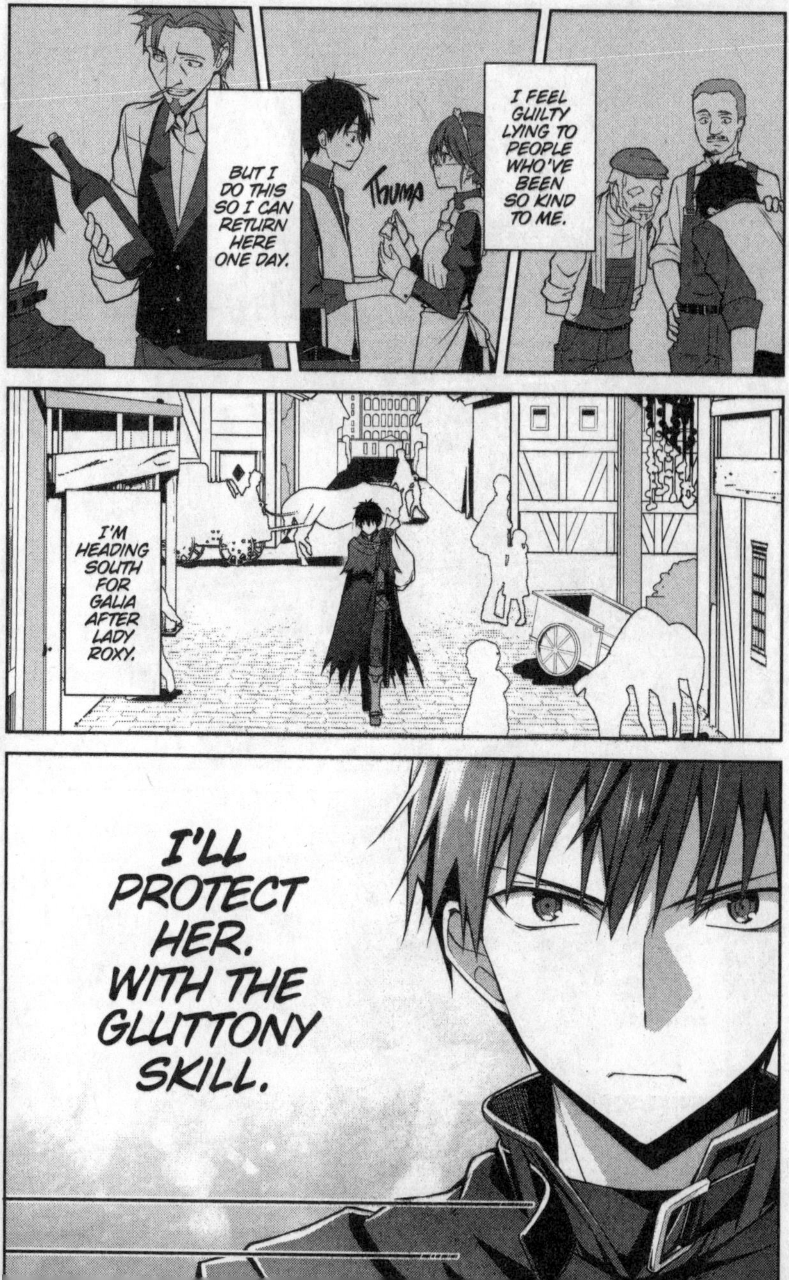

I FEEL GUILTY LYING TO PEOPLE WHO'VE BEEN SO KIND TO ME.
BUT I DO THIS SO I CAN RETURN HERE ONE DAY.
THUMP
I'M HEADING SOUTH FOR GALIA AFTER LADY ROXY.
I'LL PROTECT HER. WITH THE GLUTTONY SKILL.

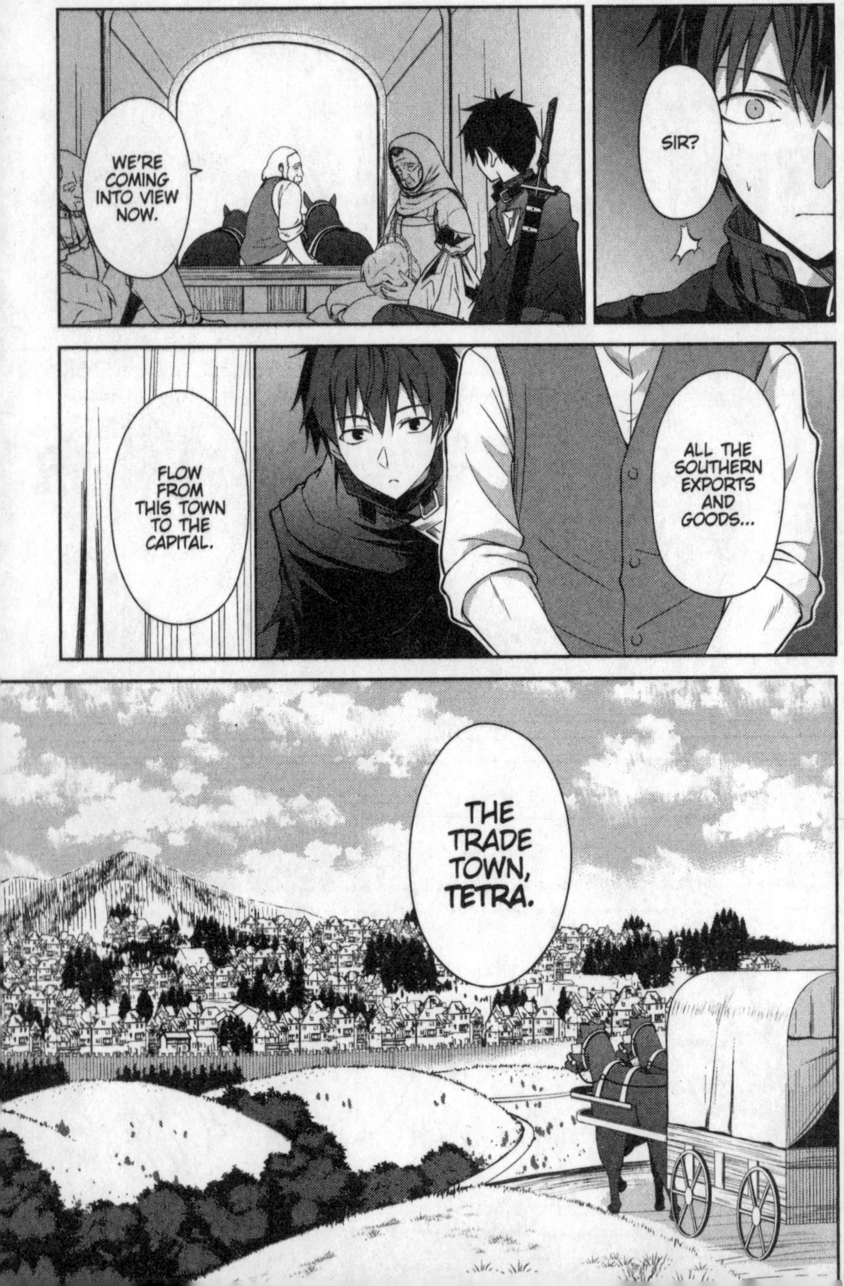
SIR?
WE'RE COMING INTO VIEW NOW.
ALL THE SOUTHERN EXPORTS AND GOODS...
FLOW FROM THIS TOWN TO THE CAPITAL.
THE TRADE TOWN, TETRA.

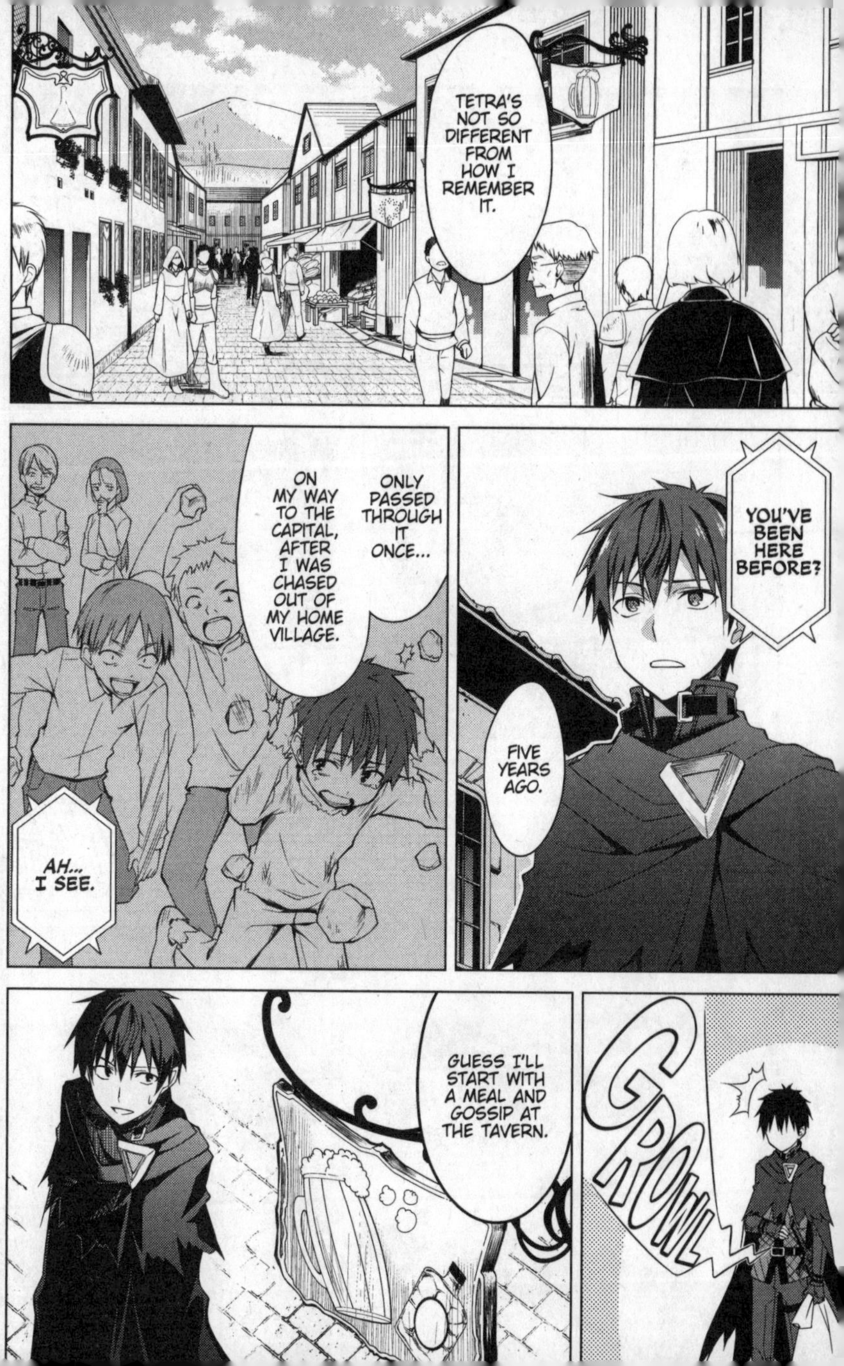
TETRA'S NOT SO DIFFERENT FROM HOW I REMEMBER IT.
YOU'VE BEEN HERE BEFORE?
FIVE YEARS AGO.
ONLY PASSED THROUGH IT ONCE...
ON MY WAY TO THE CAPITAL, AFTER I WAS CHASED OUT OF MY HOME VILLAGE.
AH... I SEE.
GROWL
GUESS I'LL START WITH A MEAL AND GOSSIP AT THE TAVERN.

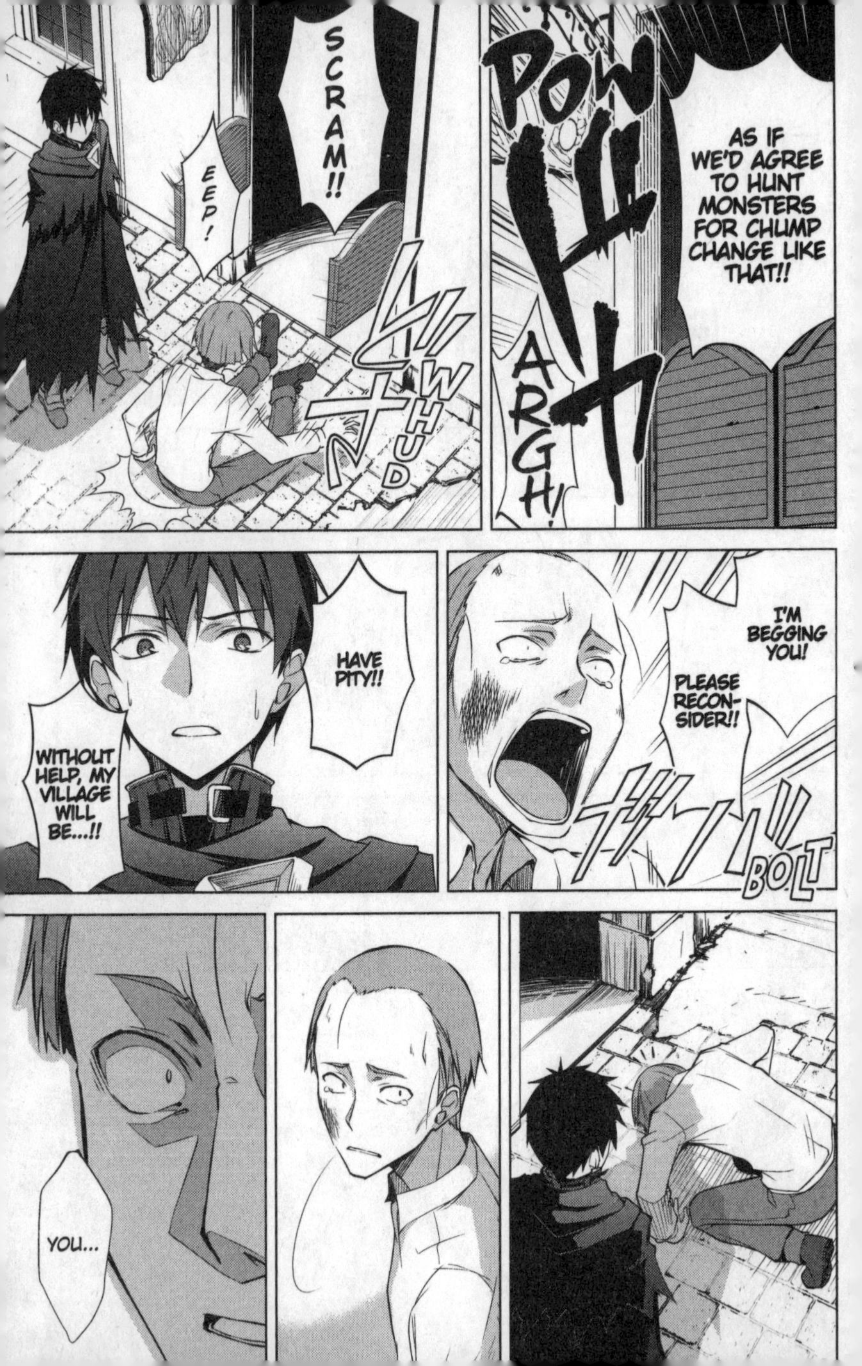
POW
AS IF WE'D AGREE TO HUNT MONSTERS FOR CHUMP CHANGE LIKE THAT!!
ARGH!
SCRAM!!
EEP!
WHUD
I'M BEGGING YOU!
PLEASE RECONSIDER!!
BOLT
HAVE PITY!!
WITHOUT HELP, MY VILLAGE WILL BE...!!
YOU...

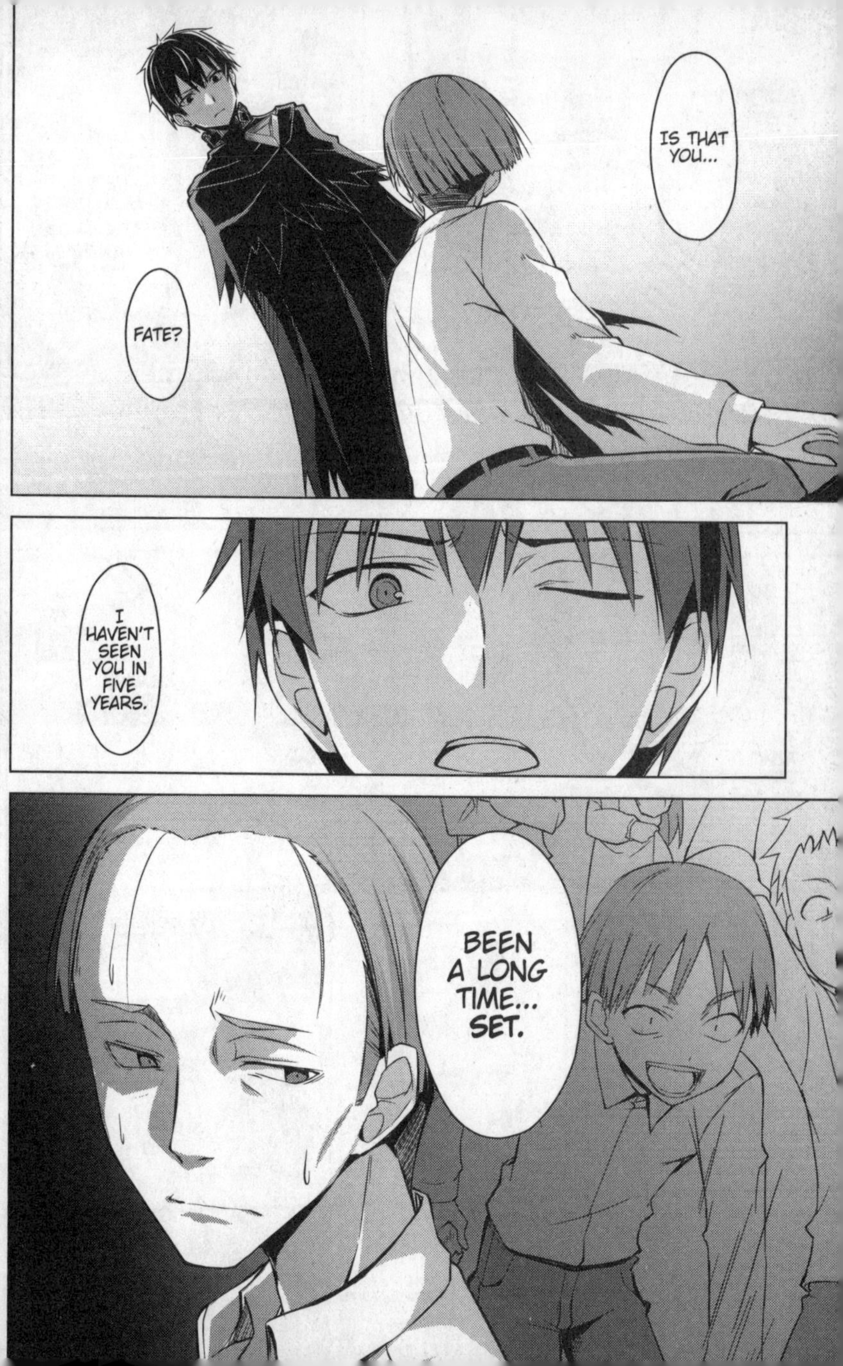
IS THAT YOU...
FATE?
I HAVEN'T SEEN YOU IN FIVE YEARS.
BEEN A LONG TIME... SET.

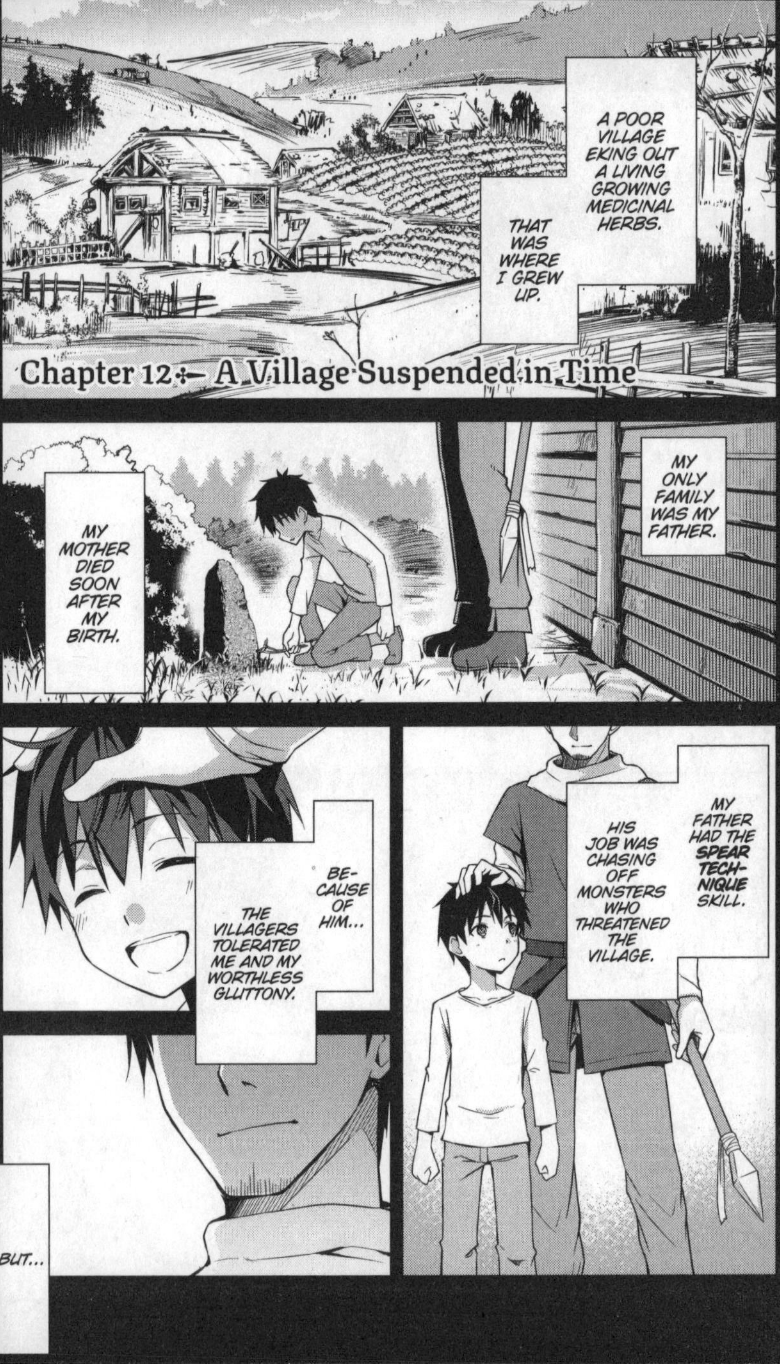
A POOR VILLAGE EKING OUT A LIVING GROWING MEDICINAL HERBS.
THAT WAS WHERE I GREW UP.
Chapter 12 ✣ A Village Suspended in Time
MY ONLY FAMILY WAS MY FATHER.
MY MOTHER DIED SOON AFTER MY BIRTH.
MY FATHER HAD THE SPEAR TECHNIQUE SKILL.
HIS JOB WAS CHASING OFF MONSTERS WHO THREATENED THE VILLAGE.
BECAUSE OF HIM...
THE VILLAGERS TOLERATED ME AND MY WORTHLESS GLUTTONY.
BUT...

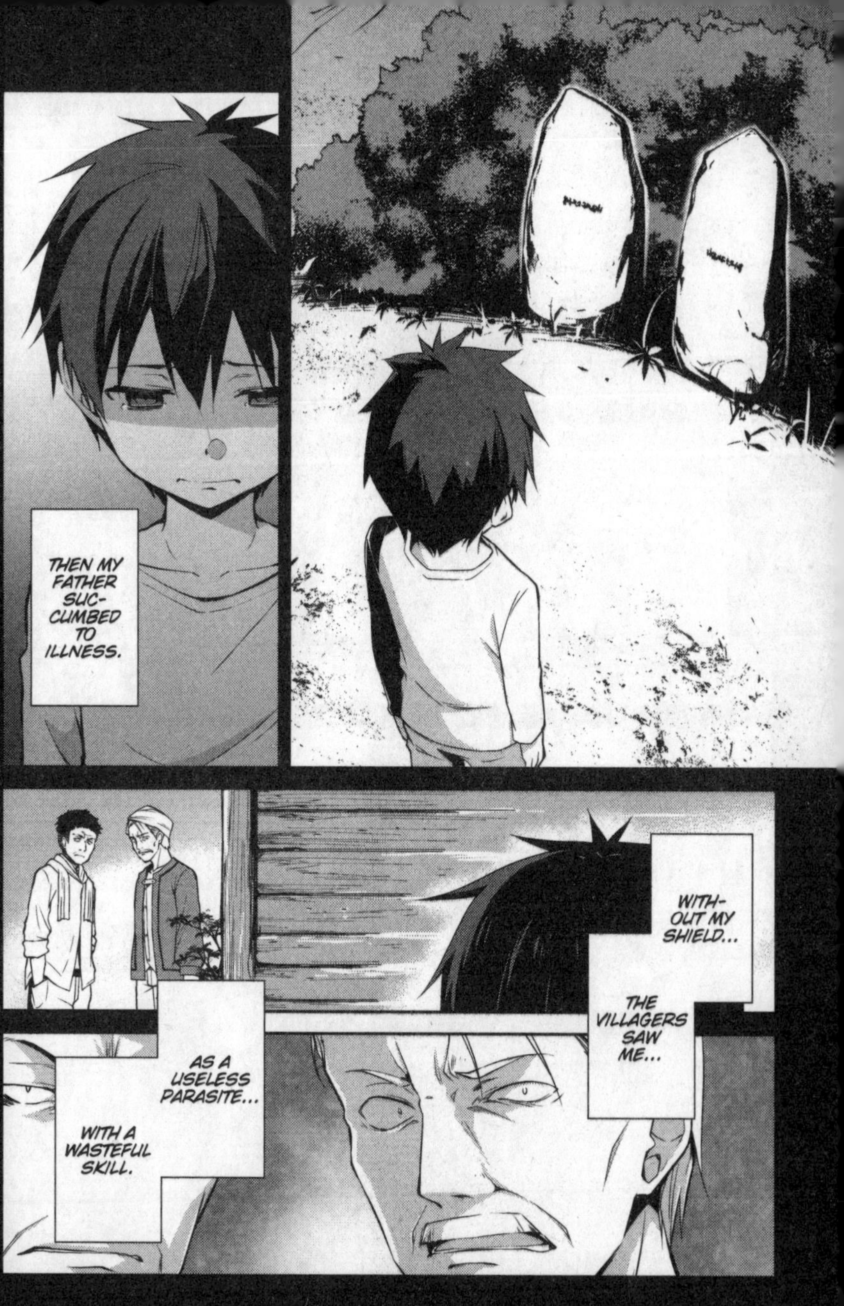
THEN MY FATHER SUCCUMBED TO ILLNESS.
WITHOUT MY SHIELD...
THE VILLAGERS SAW ME...
AS A USELESS PARASITE...
WITH A WASTEFUL SKILL.

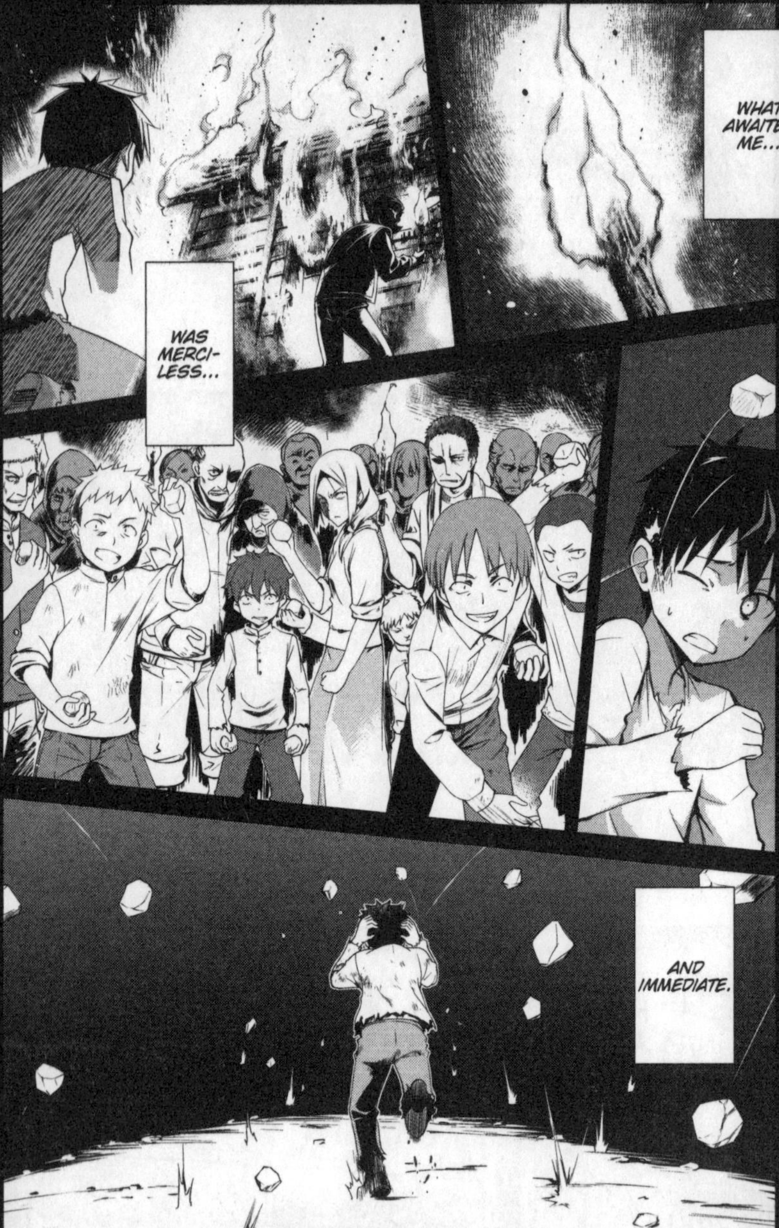
WHAT AWAITED ME...
WAS MERCI-LESS...
AND IMMEDIATE.

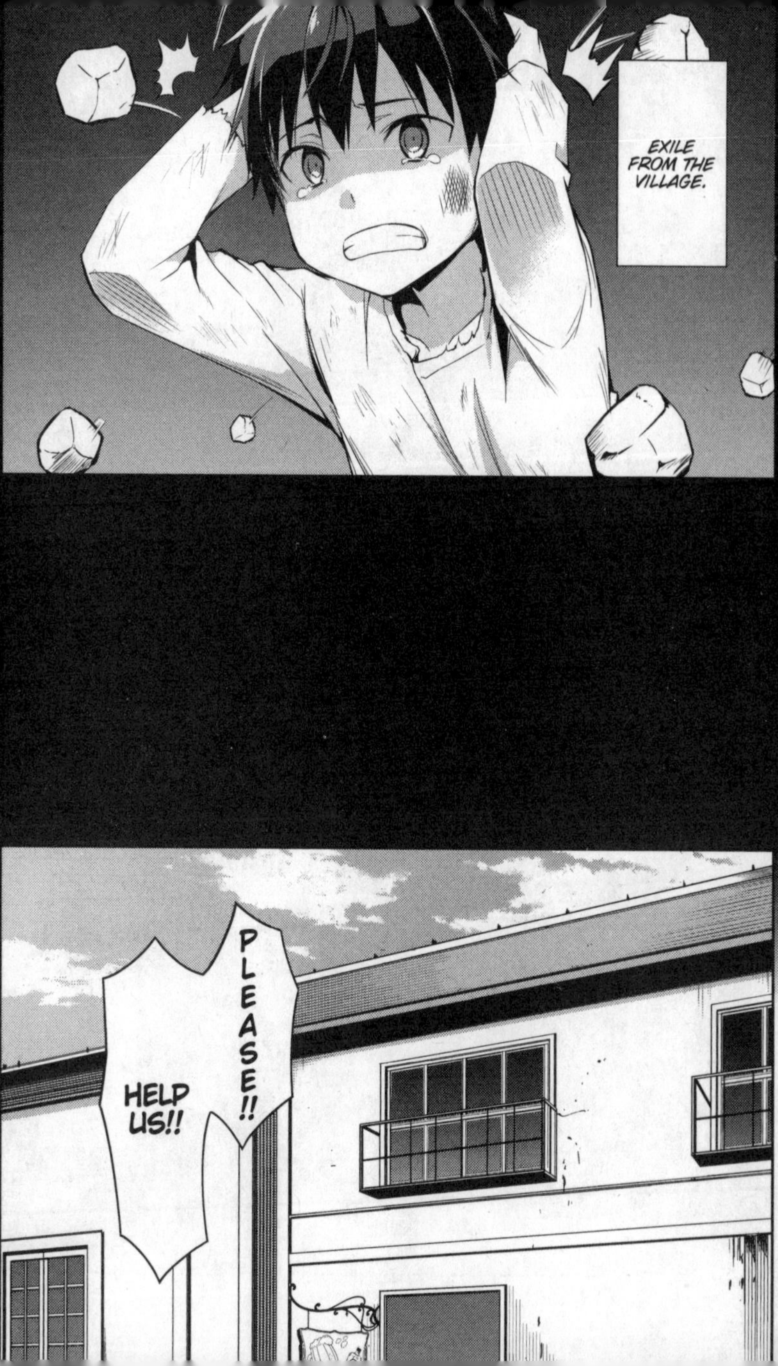
EXILE FROM THE VILLAGE.
PLEASE!! HELP US!!

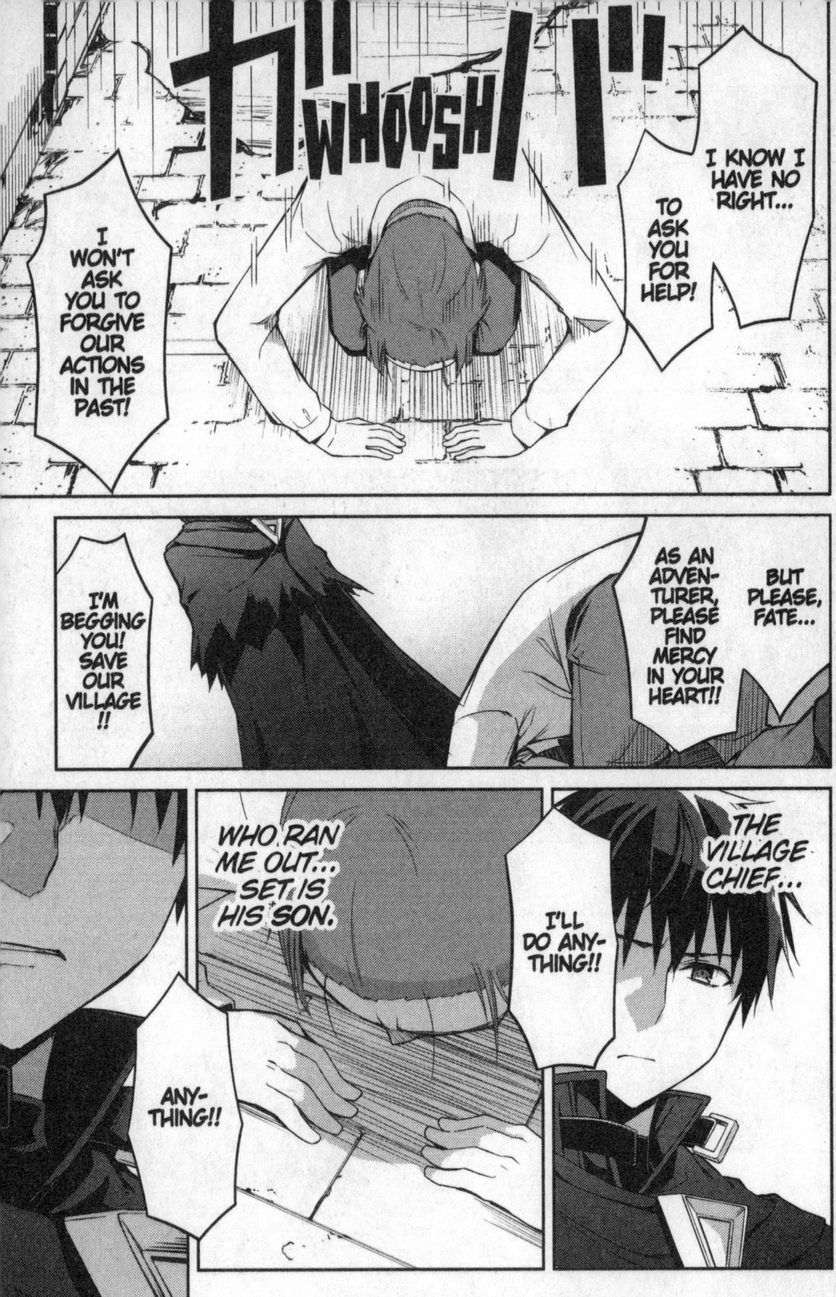
I KNOW I HAVE NO RIGHT...
TO ASK YOU FOR HELP!
WHOOSH
I WON'T ASK YOU TO FORGIVE OUR ACTIONS IN THE PAST!
BUT PLEASE, FATE...
AS AN ADVENTURER, PLEASE FIND MERCY IN YOUR HEART!!
I'M BEGGING YOU! SAVE OUR VILLAGE!!
THE VILLAGE CHIEF...
I'LL DO ANYTHING!!
WHO RAN ME OUT... SET IS HIS SON.
ANYTHING!!

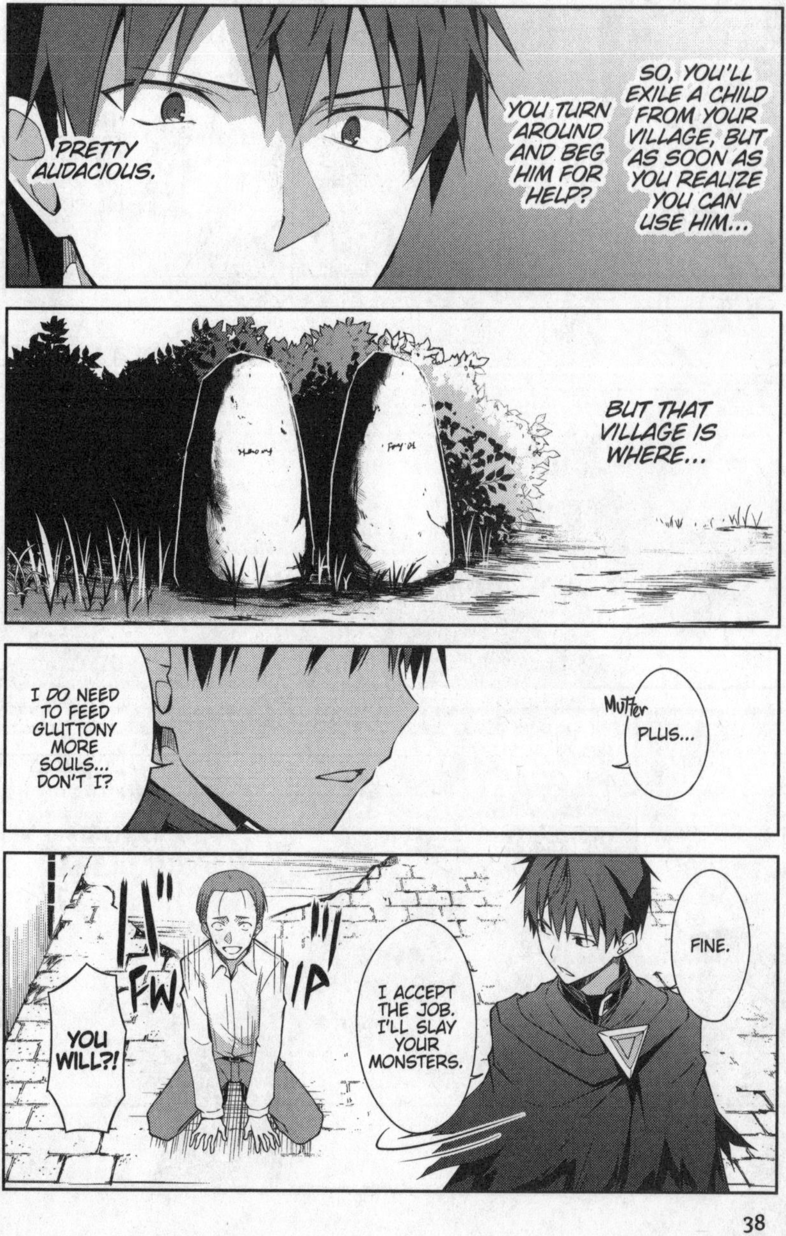
SO, YOU'LL EXILE A CHILD FROM YOUR VILLAGE, BUT AS SOON AS YOU REALIZE YOU CAN USE HIM...
YOU TURN AROUND AND BEG HIM FOR HELP?
PRETTY AUDACIOUS.
BUT THAT VILLAGE IS WHERE...
Mutter
PLUS...
I DO NEED TO FEED GLUTTONY MORE SOULS... DON'T I?
FINE.
I ACCEPT THE JOB. I'LL SLAY YOUR MONSTERS.
FWIP
YOU WILL?!

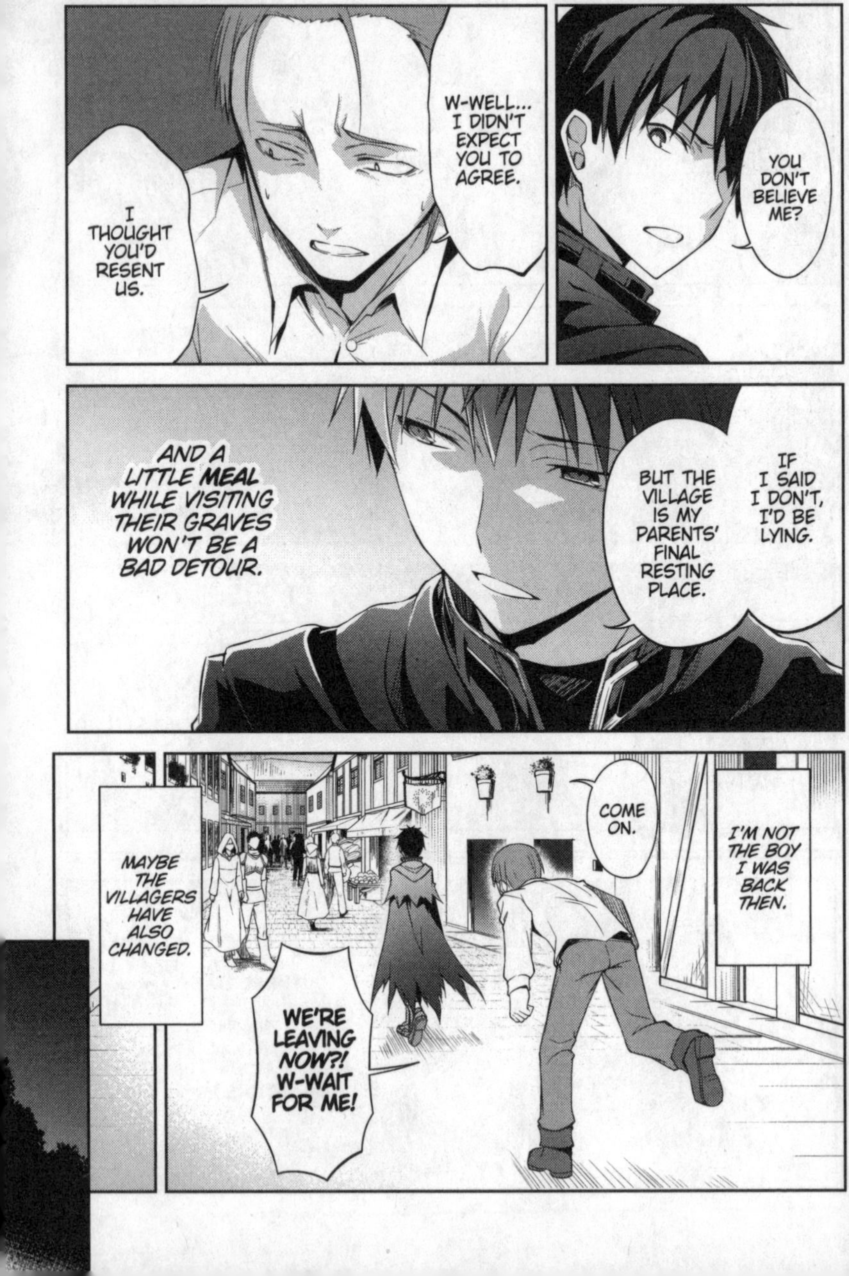
YOU DON'T BELIEVE ME?
W-WELL... I DIDN'T EXPECT YOU TO AGREE.
I THOUGHT YOU'D RESENT US.
IF I SAID I DON'T, I'D BE LYING.
BUT THE VILLAGE IS MY PARENTS' FINAL RESTING PLACE.
AND A LITTLE MEAL WHILE VISITING THEIR GRAVES WON'T BE A BAD DETOUR.
I'M NOT THE BOY I WAS BACK THEN.
COME ON.
MAYBE THE VILLAGERS HAVE ALSO CHANGED.
WE'RE LEAVING NOW?! W-WAIT FOR ME!

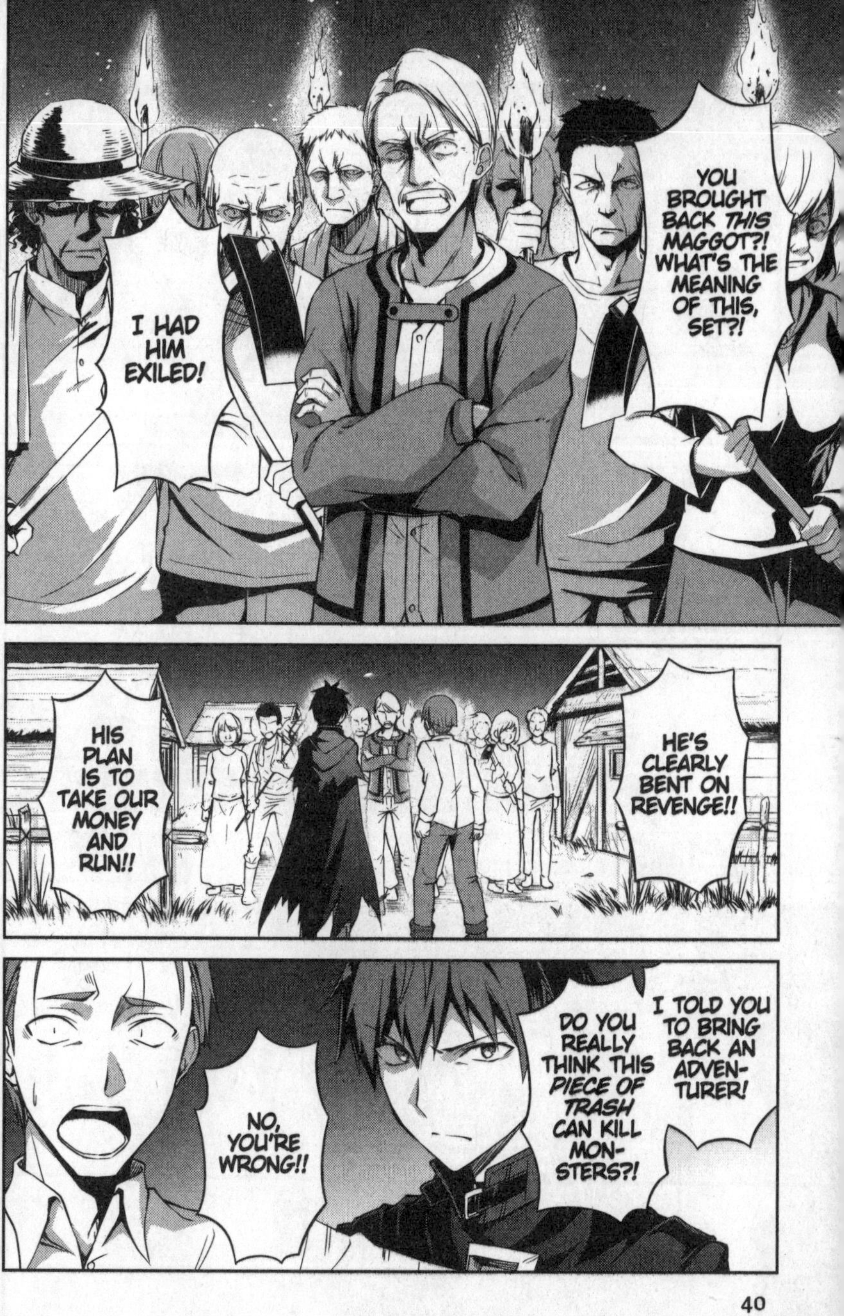
YOU BROUGHT BACK *THIS* MAGGOT?! WHAT'S THE MEANING OF THIS, SET?!
I HAD HIM EXILED!
HE'S CLEARLY BENT ON REVENGE!!
HIS PLAN IS TO TAKE OUR MONEY AND RUN!!
I TOLD YOU TO BRING BACK AN ADVEN-TURER!
DO YOU REALLY THINK THIS *PIECE OF TRASH* CAN KILL MON-STERS?!
NO, YOU'RE WRONG!!

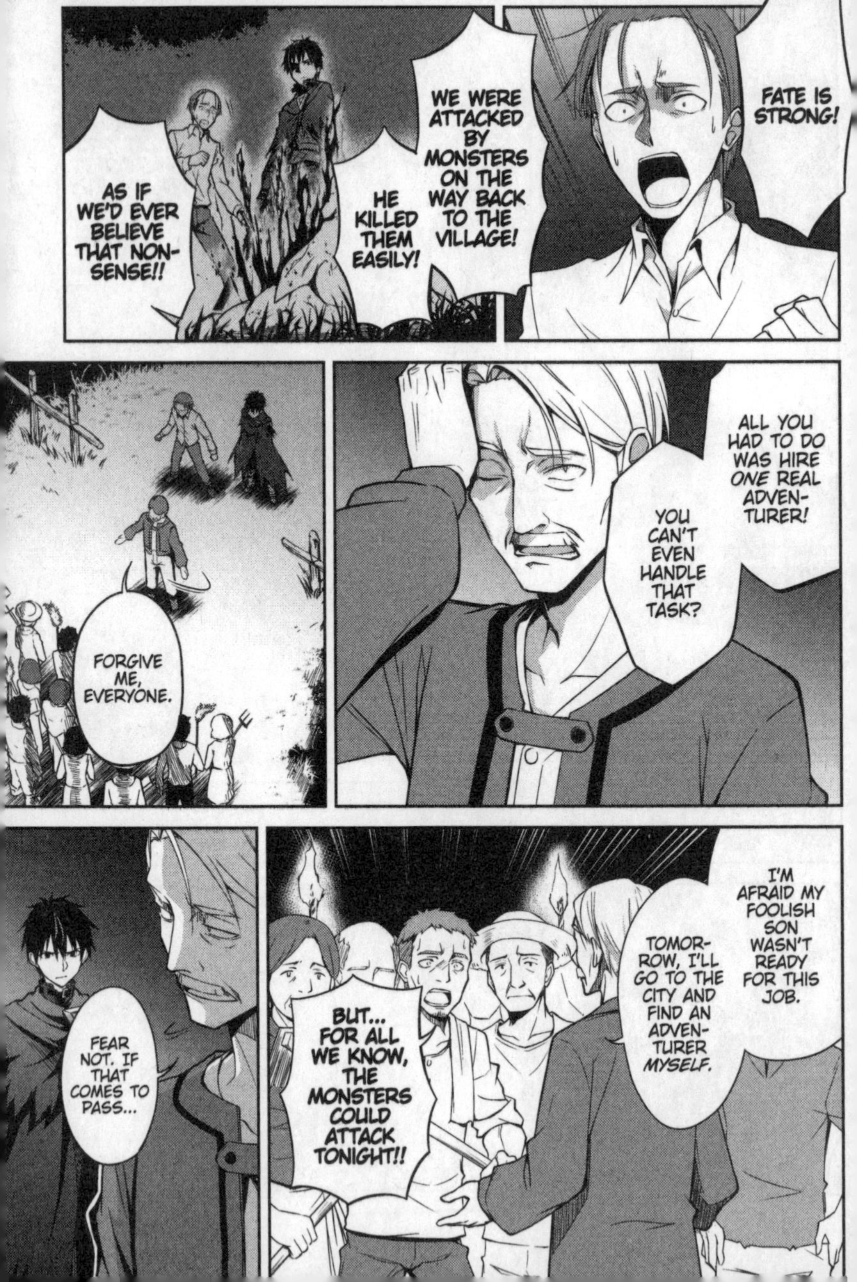
FATE IS STRONG!
WE WERE ATTACKED BY MONSTERS ON THE WAY BACK TO THE VILLAGE!
HE KILLED THEM EASILY!
AS IF WE'D EVER BELIEVE THAT NON-SENSE!!
ALL YOU HAD TO DO WAS HIRE *ONE* REAL ADVEN-TURER!
YOU CAN'T EVEN HANDLE THAT TASK?
FORGIVE ME, EVERYONE.
I'M AFRAID MY FOOLISH SON WASN'T READY FOR THIS JOB.
TOMOR-ROW, I'LL GO TO THE CITY AND FIND AN ADVEN-TURER *MYSELF*.
BUT... FOR ALL WE KNOW, THE MONSTERS COULD ATTACK TONIGHT!!
FEAR NOT. IF THAT COMES TO PASS...

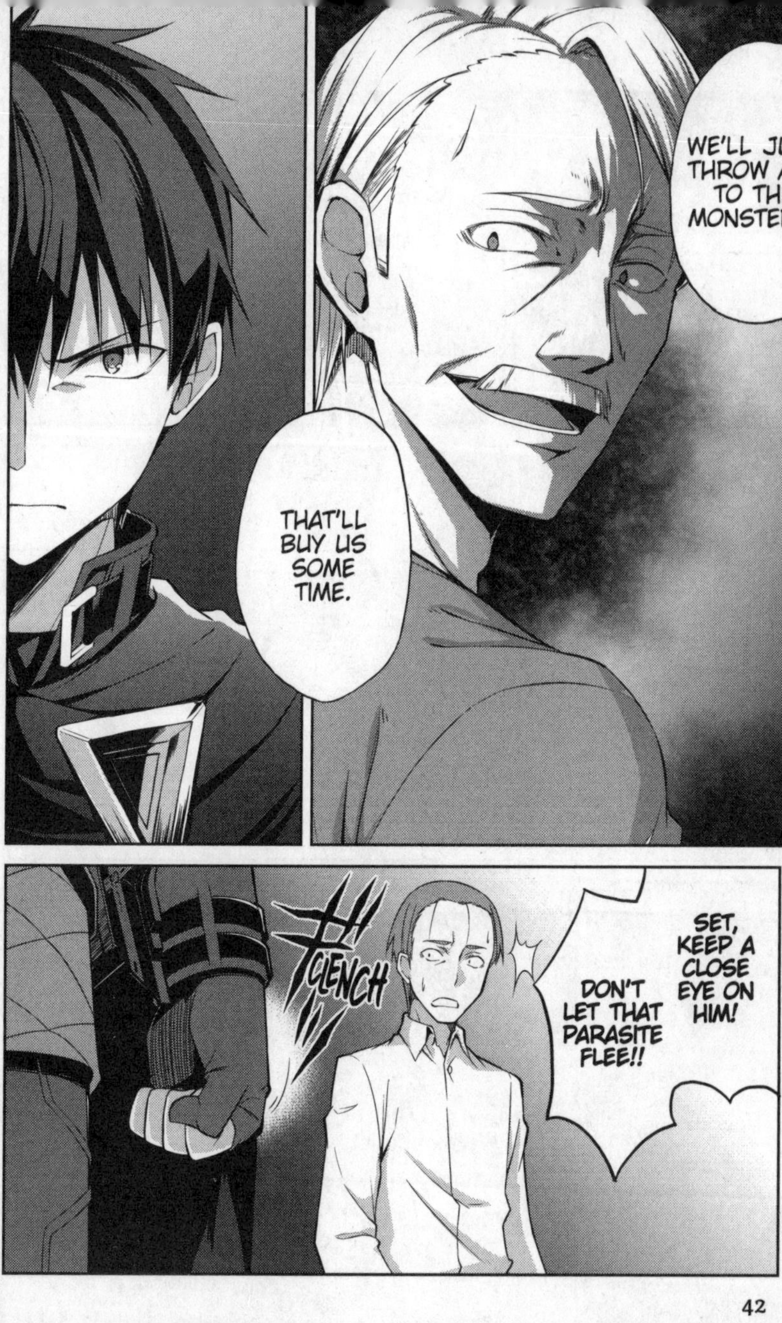
WE'LL JUST THROW *HIM* TO THE MONSTERS.
THAT'LL BUY US SOME TIME.
SET, KEEP A CLOSE EYE ON HIM!
DON'T LET THAT PARASITE FLEE!!
CLENCH

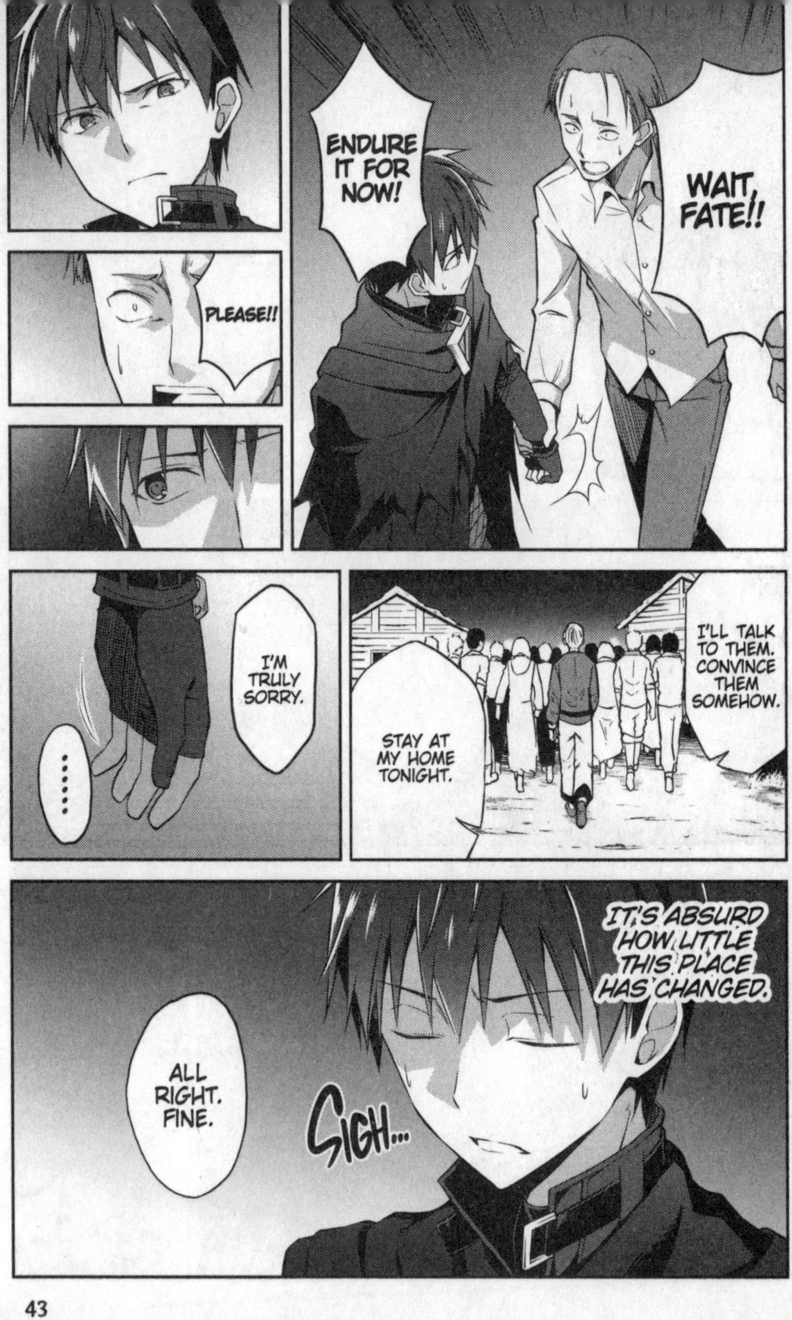
WAIT, FATE!!
ENDURE IT FOR NOW!
PLEASE!!
I'LL TALK TO THEM. CONVINCE THEM SOMEHOW.
STAY AT MY HOME TONIGHT.
I'M TRULY SORRY.
......
IT'S ABSURD HOW LITTLE THIS PLACE HAS CHANGED.
SIGH...
ALL RIGHT. FINE.

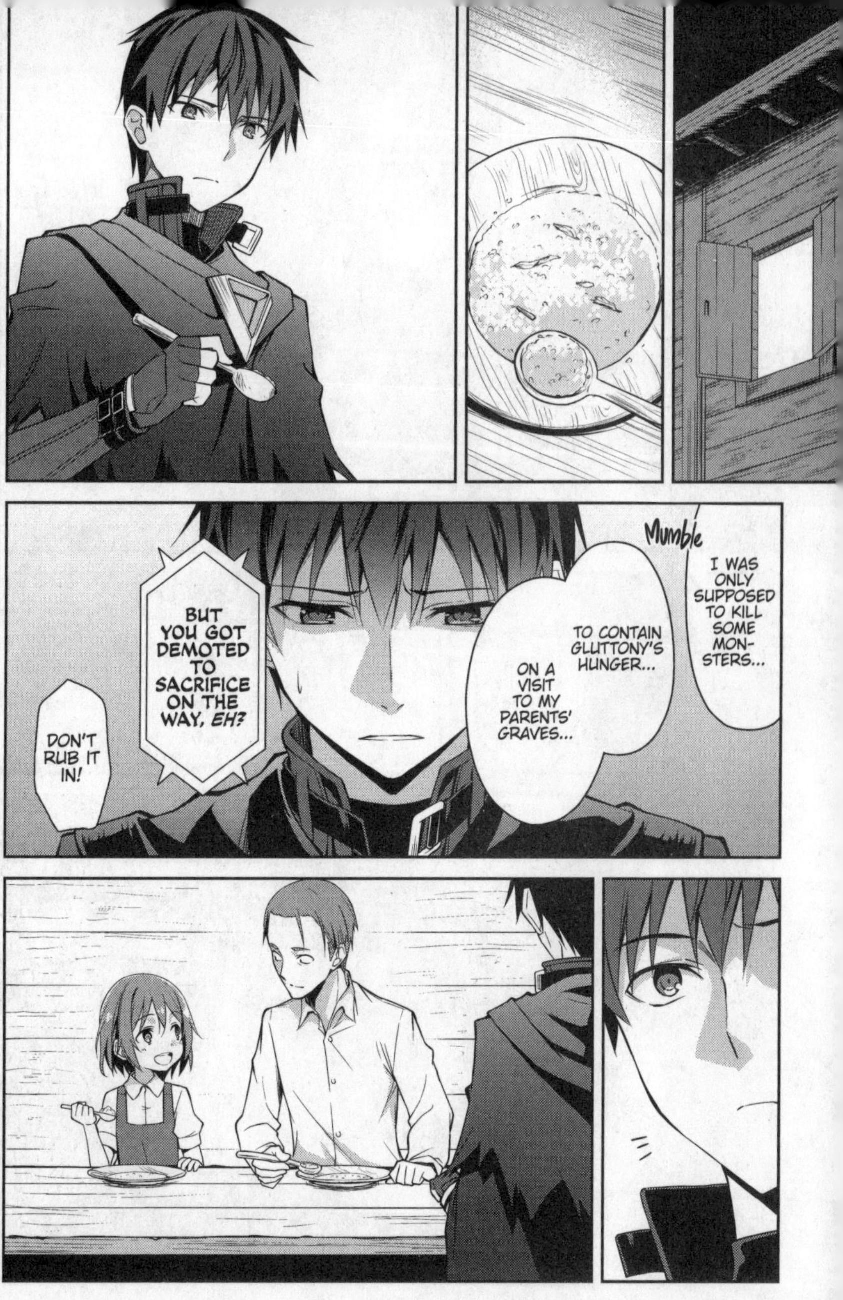
Mumble
I WAS ONLY SUPPOSED TO KILL SOME MON-STERS...
TO CONTAIN GLUTTONY'S HUNGER...
ON A VISIT TO MY PARENTS' GRAVES...
BUT YOU GOT DEMOTED TO SACRIFICE ON THE WAY, *EH?*
DON'T RUB IT IN!

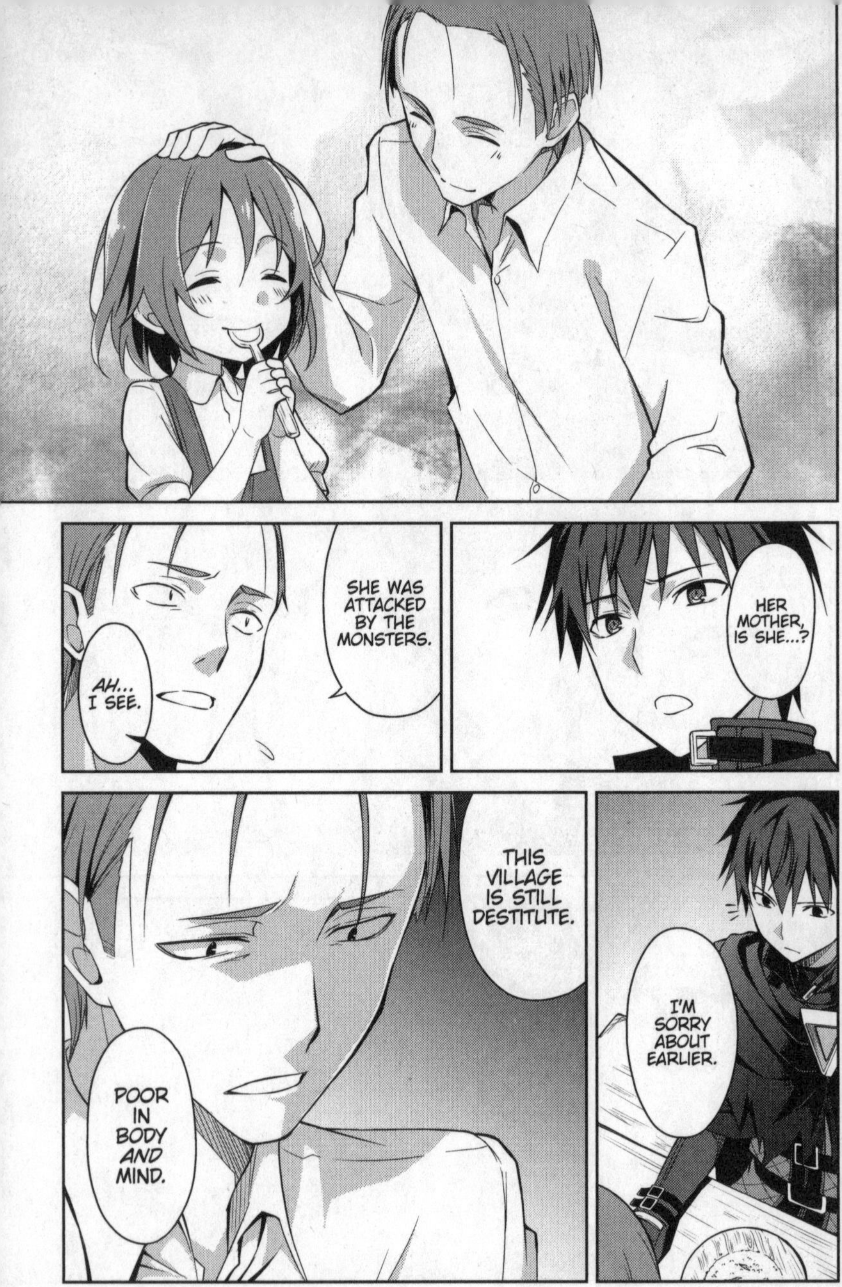
HER MOTHER, IS SHE...?
SHE WAS ATTACKED BY THE MONSTERS.
AH... I SEE.
I'M SORRY ABOUT EARLIER.
THIS VILLAGE IS STILL DESTITUTE.
POOR IN BODY AND MIND.

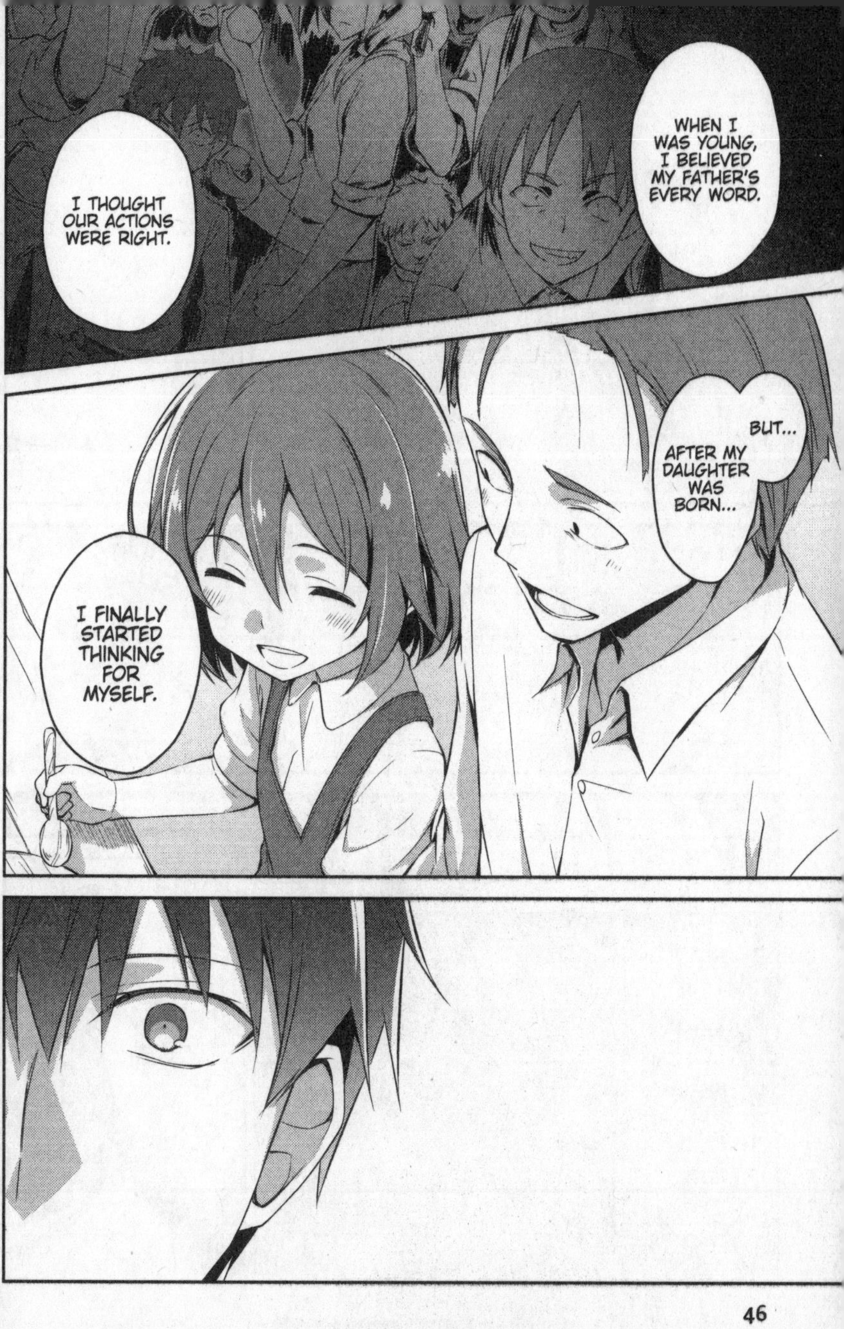
WHEN I WAS YOUNG, I BELIEVED MY FATHER'S EVERY WORD.
I THOUGHT OUR ACTIONS WERE RIGHT.
BUT... AFTER MY DAUGHTER WAS BORN...
I FINALLY STARTED THINKING FOR MYSELF.

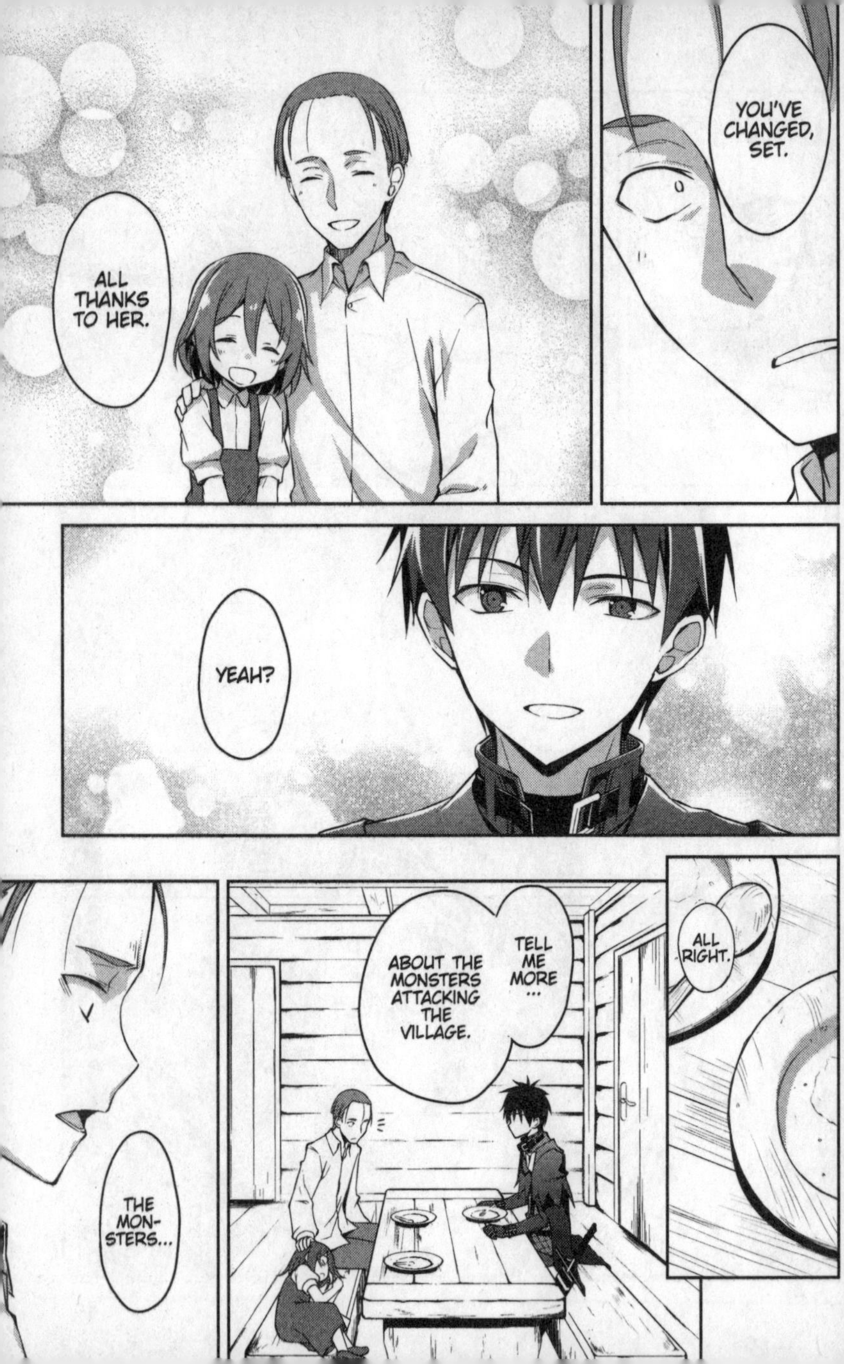
YOU'VE CHANGED, SET.
ALL THANKS TO HER.
YEAH?
ALL RIGHT.
TELL ME MORE...
ABOUT THE MONSTERS ATTACKING THE VILLAGE.
THE MON-STERS...

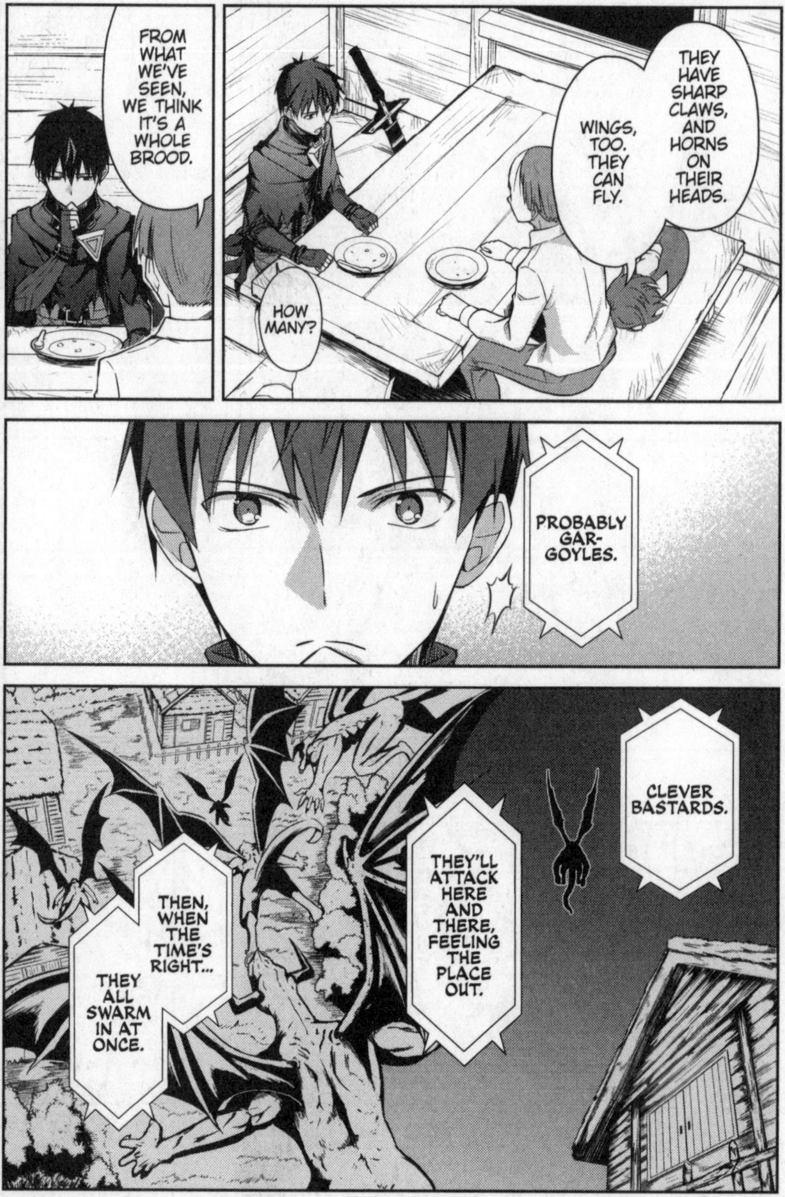
THEY HAVE SHARP CLAWS, AND HORNS ON THEIR HEADS.
WINGS, TOO. THEY CAN FLY.
HOW MANY?
FROM WHAT WE'VE SEEN, WE THINK IT'S A WHOLE BROOD.
PROBABLY GAR-GOYLES.
CLEVER BASTARDS.
THEY'LL ATTACK HERE AND THERE, FEELING THE PLACE OUT.
THEN, WHEN THE TIME'S RIGHT...
THEY ALL SWARM IN AT ONCE.

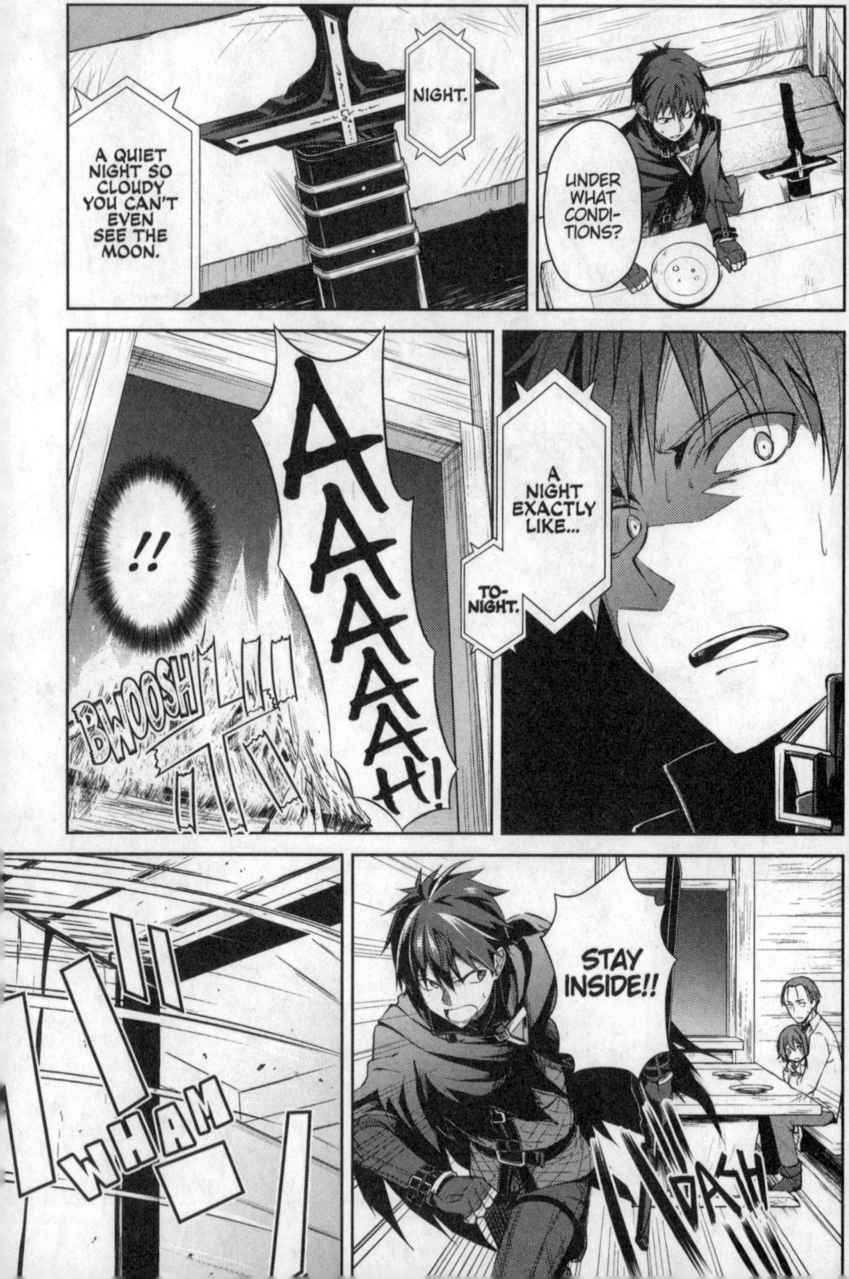
UNDER WHAT CONDITIONS?
NIGHT.
A QUIET NIGHT SO CLOUDY YOU CAN'T EVEN SEE THE MOON.
A NIGHT EXACTLY LIKE...
TO-NIGHT.
AAAAAH!
!!
BWOOSH
STAY INSIDE!!
DASH
WHAM

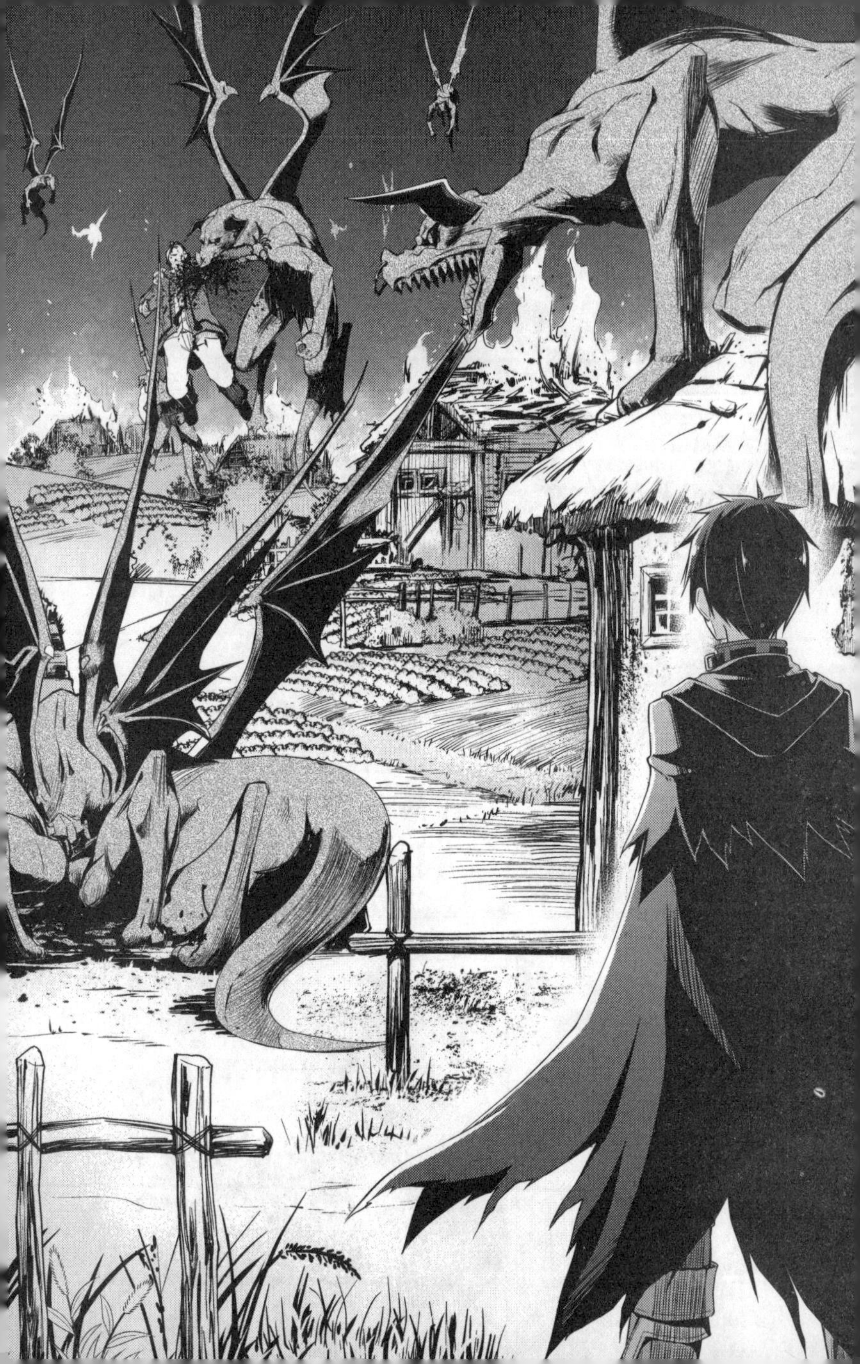

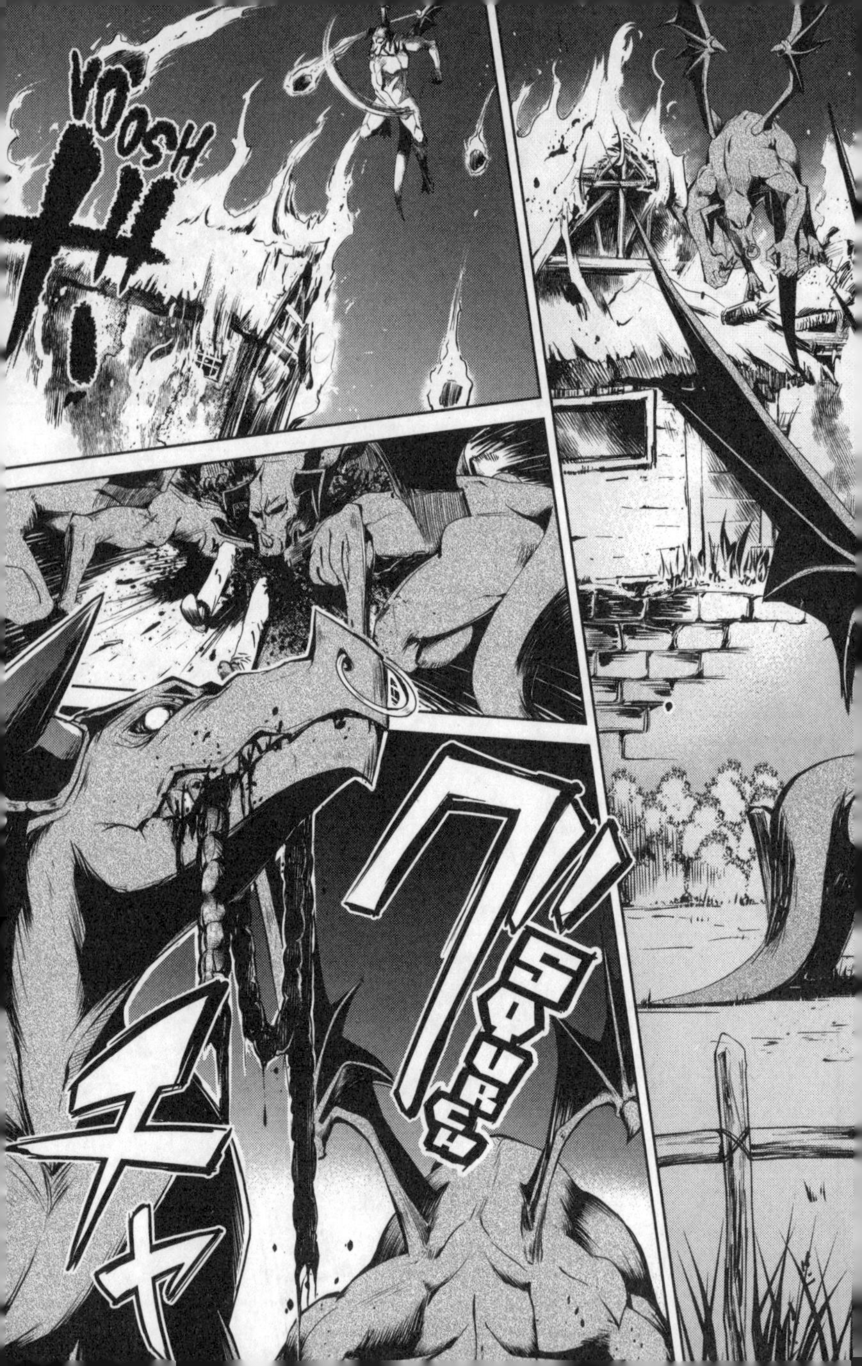
VOOSH
SQUASH

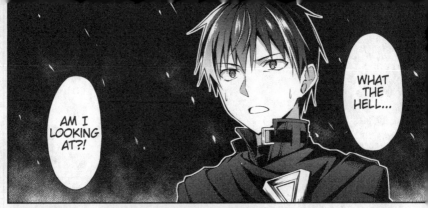

WHAT THE HELL...

AM I LOOKING AT?!

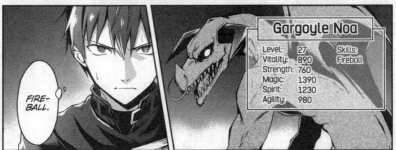

FIRE-BALL.

Gargoyle Noa

Level:	27	Skills:	
Vitality:	890	Fireball	
Strength:	760		
Magic:	1390		
Spirit:	1230		
Agility:	980		

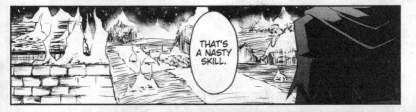

THAT'S A NASTY SKILL.

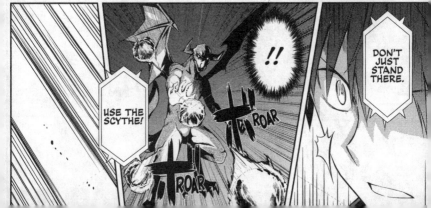

DON'T JUST STAND THERE.

USE THE SCYTHE!

!!

ROAR

ROAR

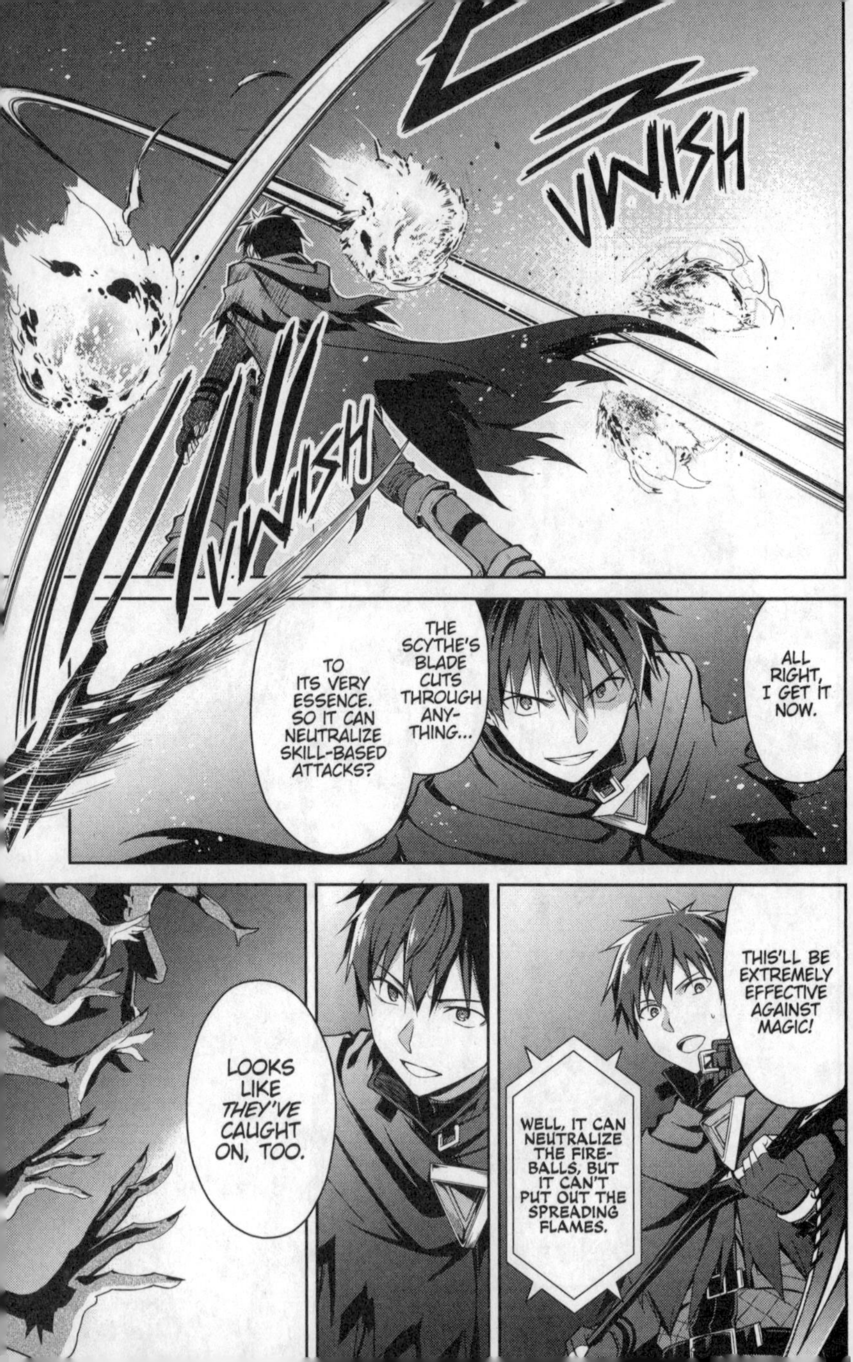
VWISH
VWISH
ALL RIGHT, I GET IT NOW.
THE SCYTHE'S BLADE CUTS THROUGH ANY-THING...
TO ITS VERY ESSENCE. SO IT CAN NEUTRALIZE SKILL-BASED ATTACKS?
THIS'LL BE EXTREMELY EFFECTIVE AGAINST MAGIC!
WELL, IT CAN NEUTRALIZE THE FIRE-BALLS, BUT IT CAN'T PUT OUT THE SPREADING FLAMES.
LOOKS LIKE *THEY'VE* CAUGHT ON, TOO.

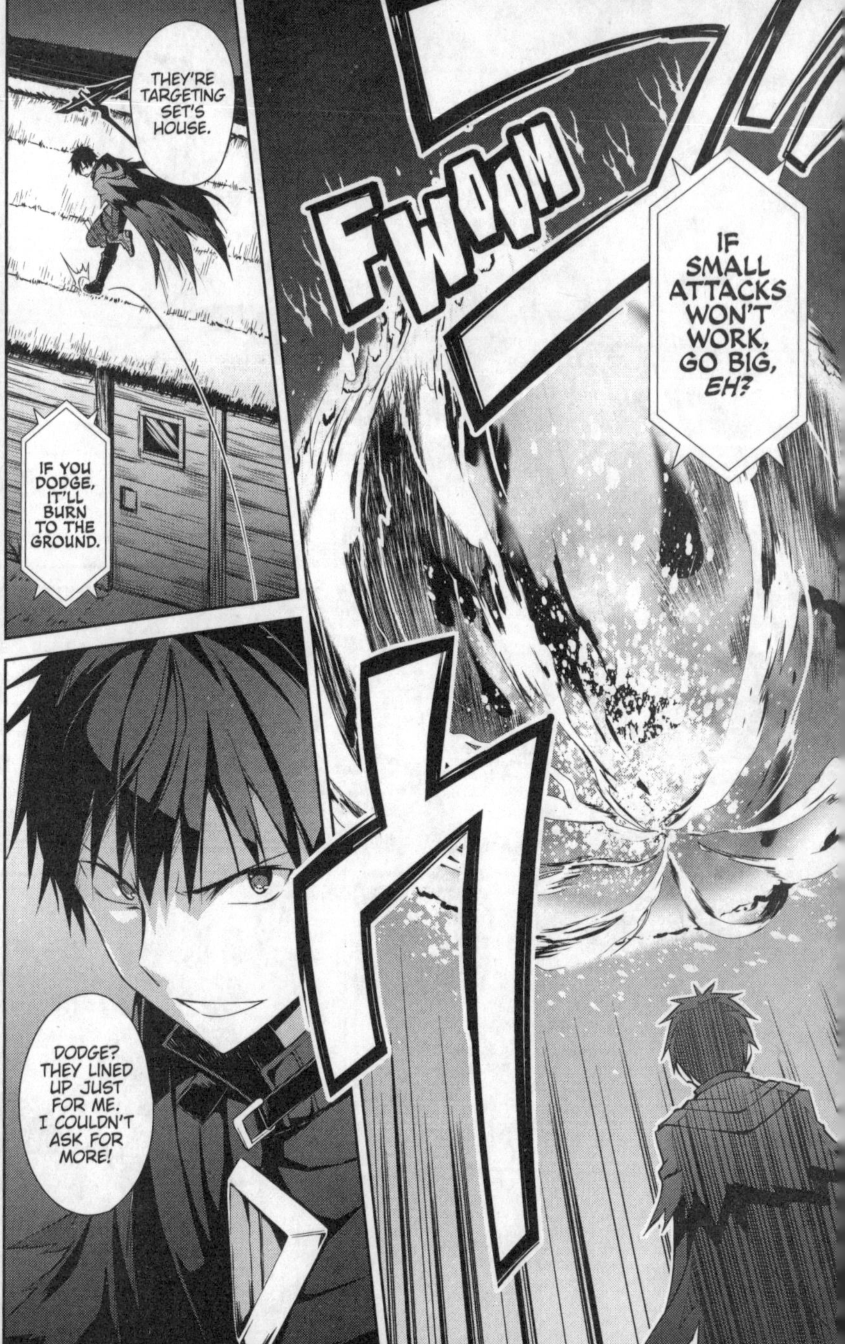
FWOOM
IF SMALL ATTACKS WON'T WORK, GO BIG, *EH?*
THEY'RE TARGETING SET'S HOUSE.
IF YOU DODGE, IT'LL BURN TO THE GROUND.
DODGE? THEY LINED UP JUST FOR ME. I COULDN'T ASK FOR MORE!

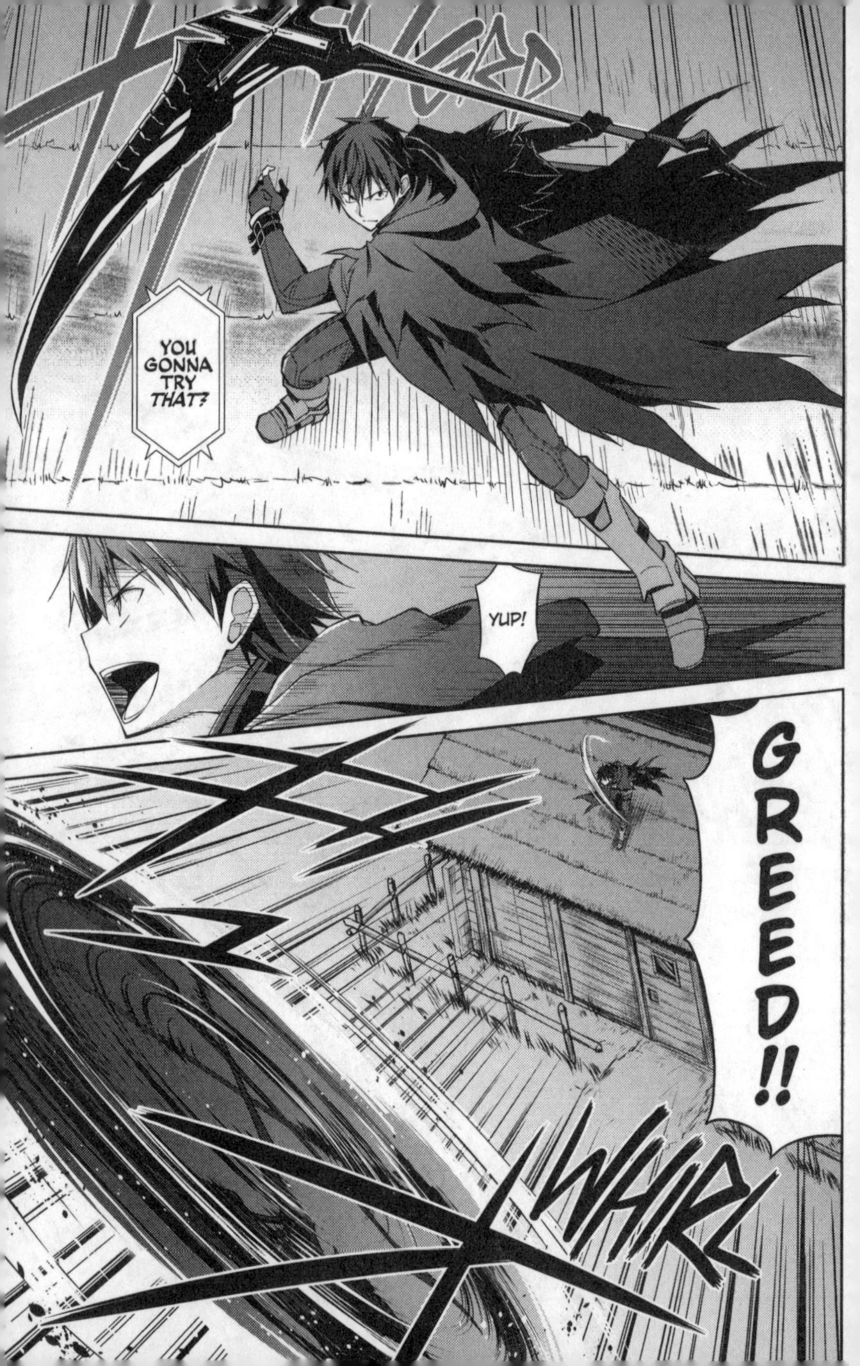
YOU GONNA TRY THAT?
YUP!
GREED!!
WHIRL

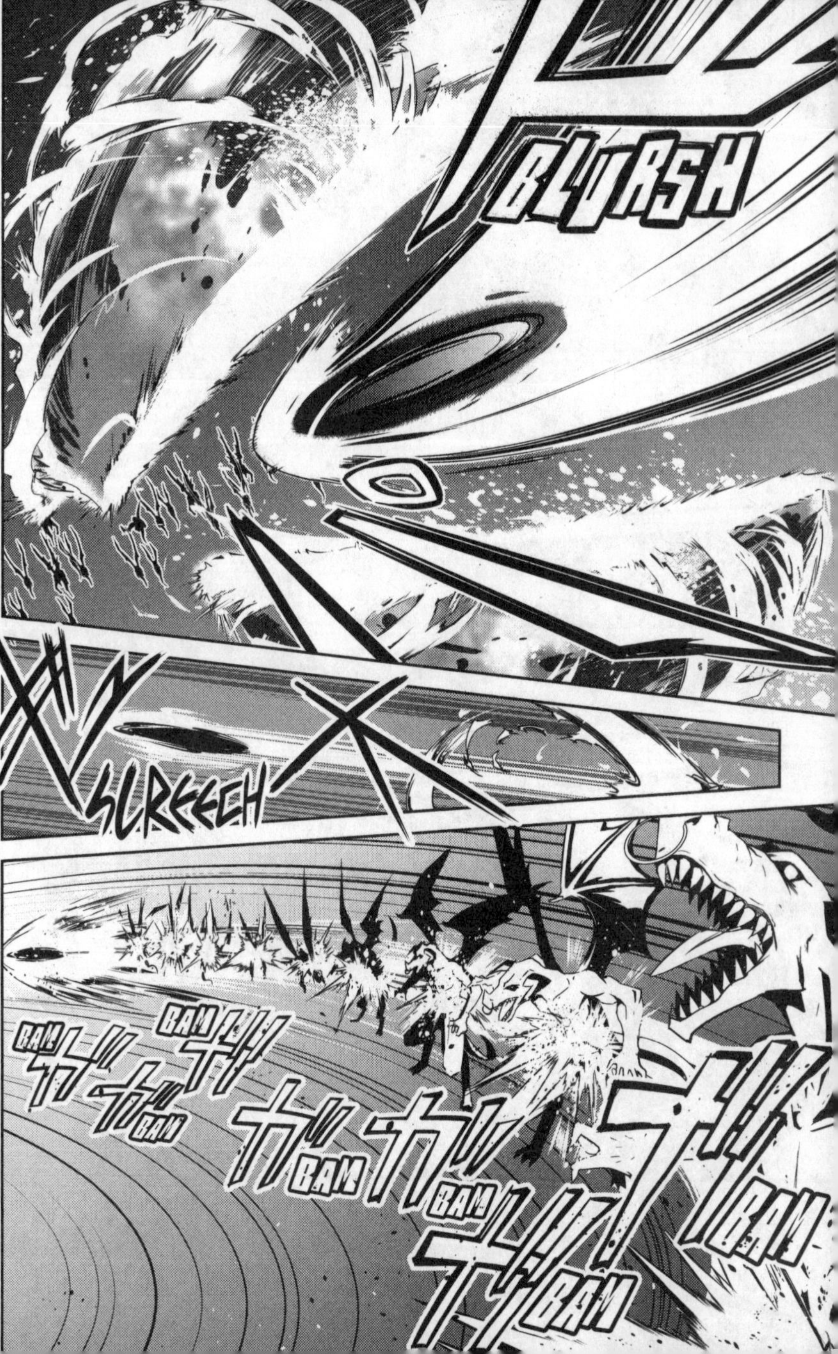
BLURSH
SCREECH
BAM
BAM
BAM
BAM
BAM
BAM
BAM
BAM

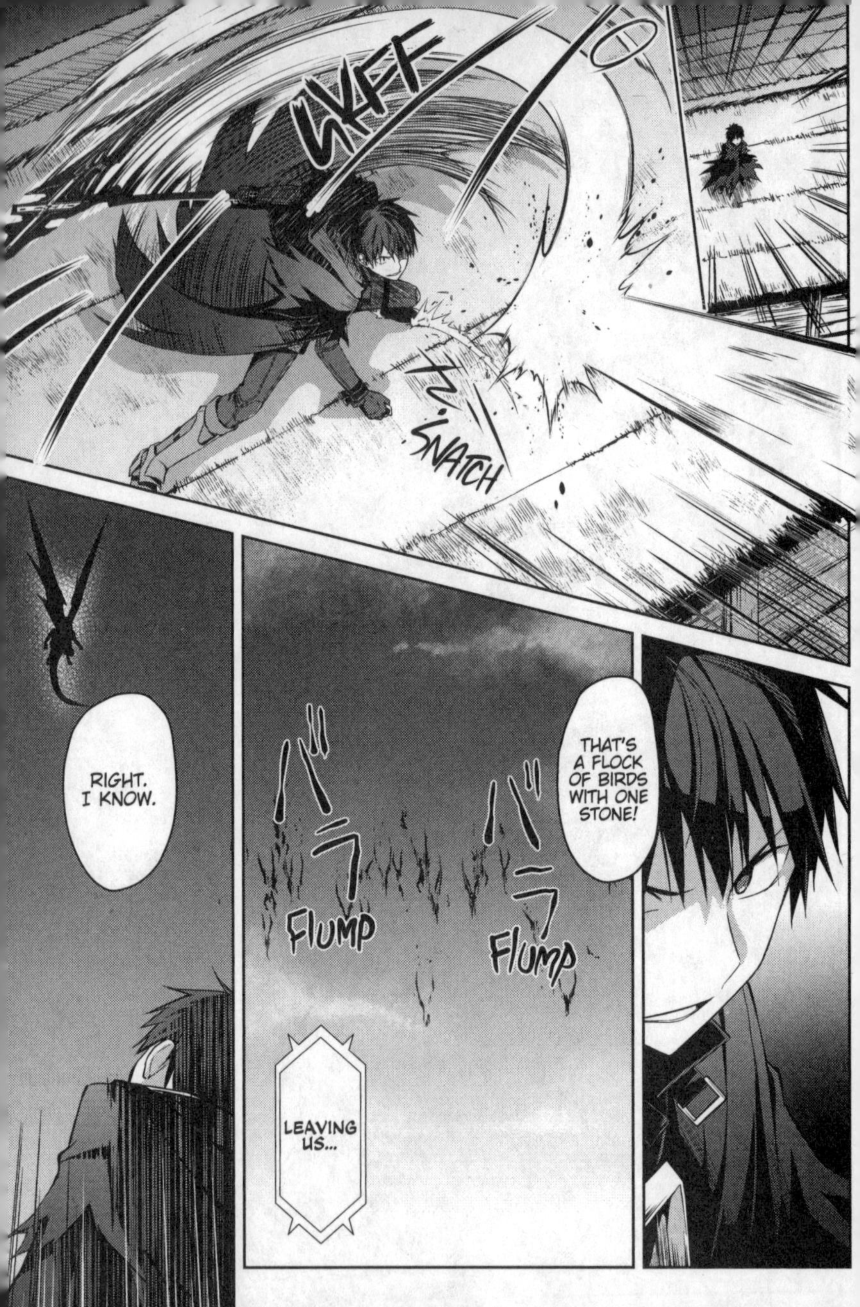
SKFF
SNATCH
THAT'S A FLOCK OF BIRDS WITH ONE STONE!
バラ
FLUMP
バラ
FLUMP
LEAVING US...
RIGHT. I KNOW.

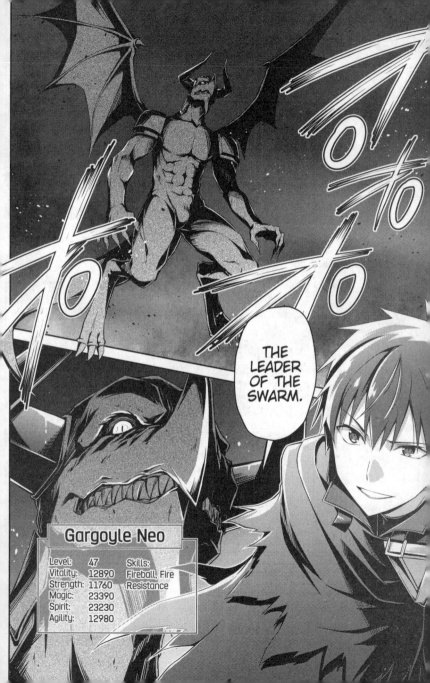

THE LEADER OF THE SWARM.

Gargoyle Neo

Level:	47	Skills:
Vitality:	12890	Fireball, Fire
Strength:	11760	Resistance
Magic:	23390	
Spirit:	23230	
Agility:	12980	

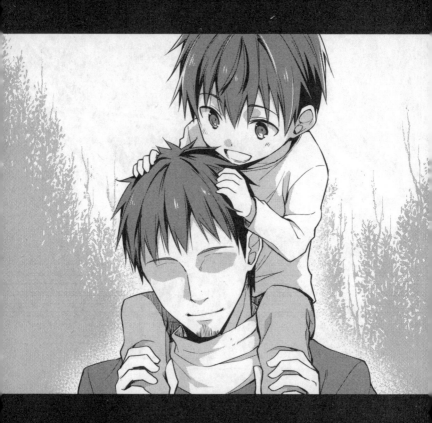

Chapter 13 ✦ The Weight of a Fist

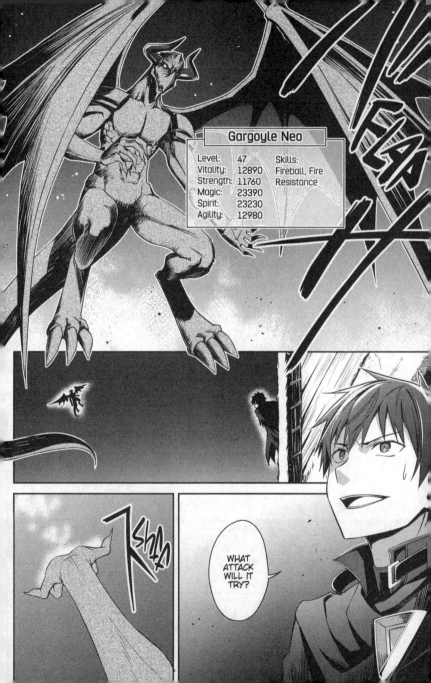

Gargoyle Neo

Level:	47	Skills:
Vitality:	12890	Fireball, Fire
Strength:	11760	Resistance
Magic:	23390	
Spirit:	23230	
Agility:	12980	

WHAT ATTACK WILL IT TRY?

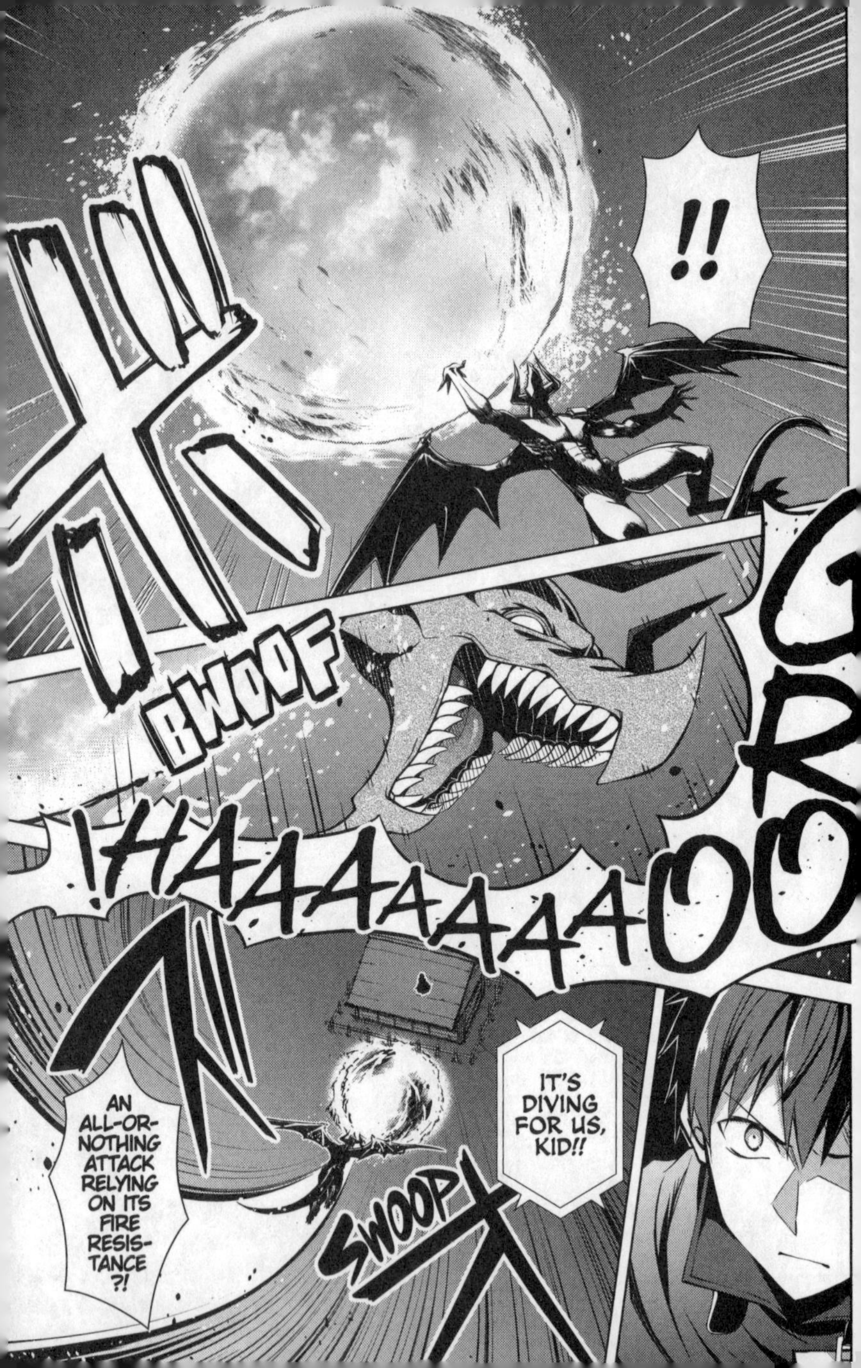
!!
BWOOF
GROOOAAAAAAAH!
IT'S DIVING FOR US, KID!!
SWOOP
AN ALL-OR-NOTHING ATTACK RELYING ON ITS FIRE RESISTANCE?!

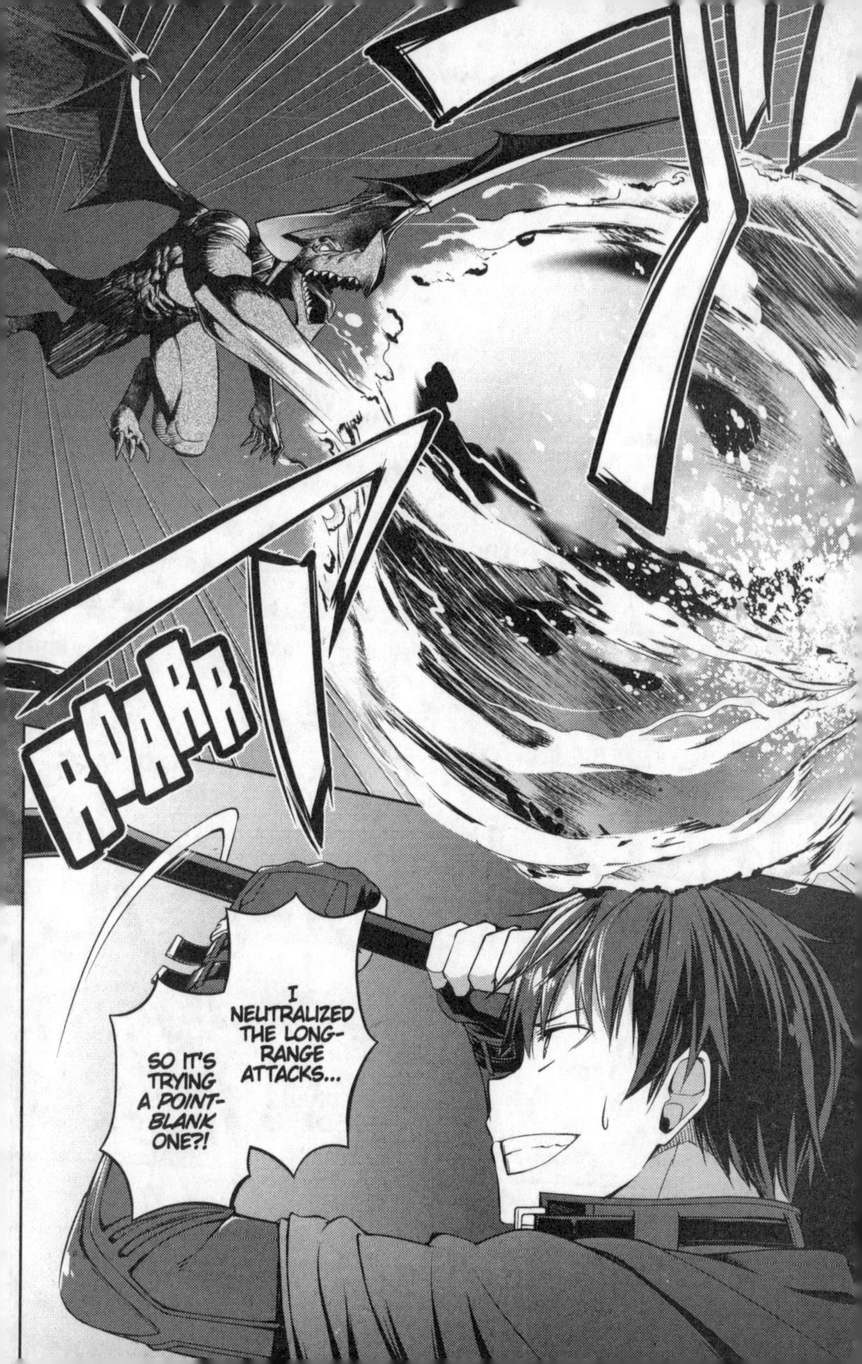
ROARR
I NEUTRALIZED THE LONG-RANGE ATTACKS...
SO IT'S TRYING A POINT-BLANK ONE?!

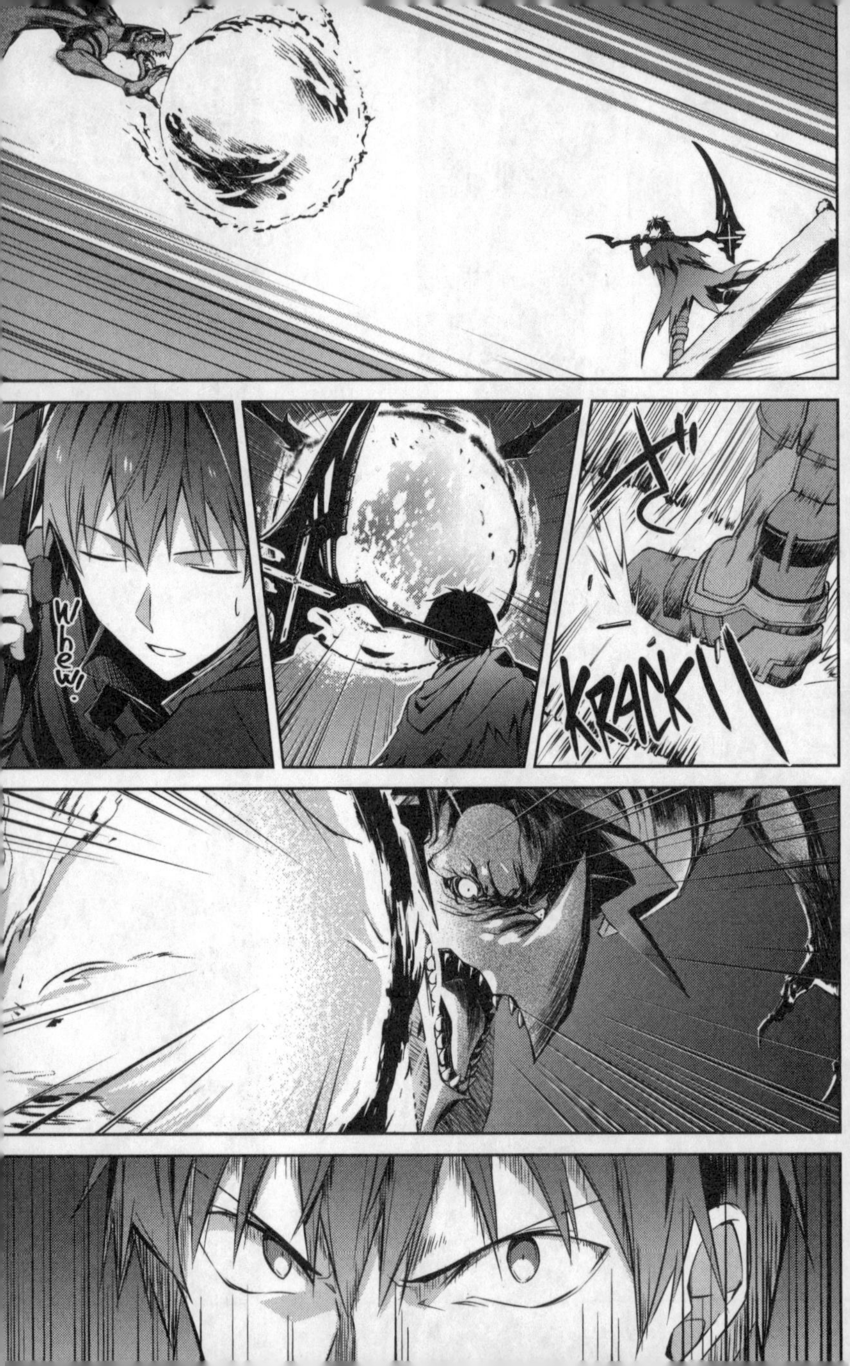
KRACK!
Whew!

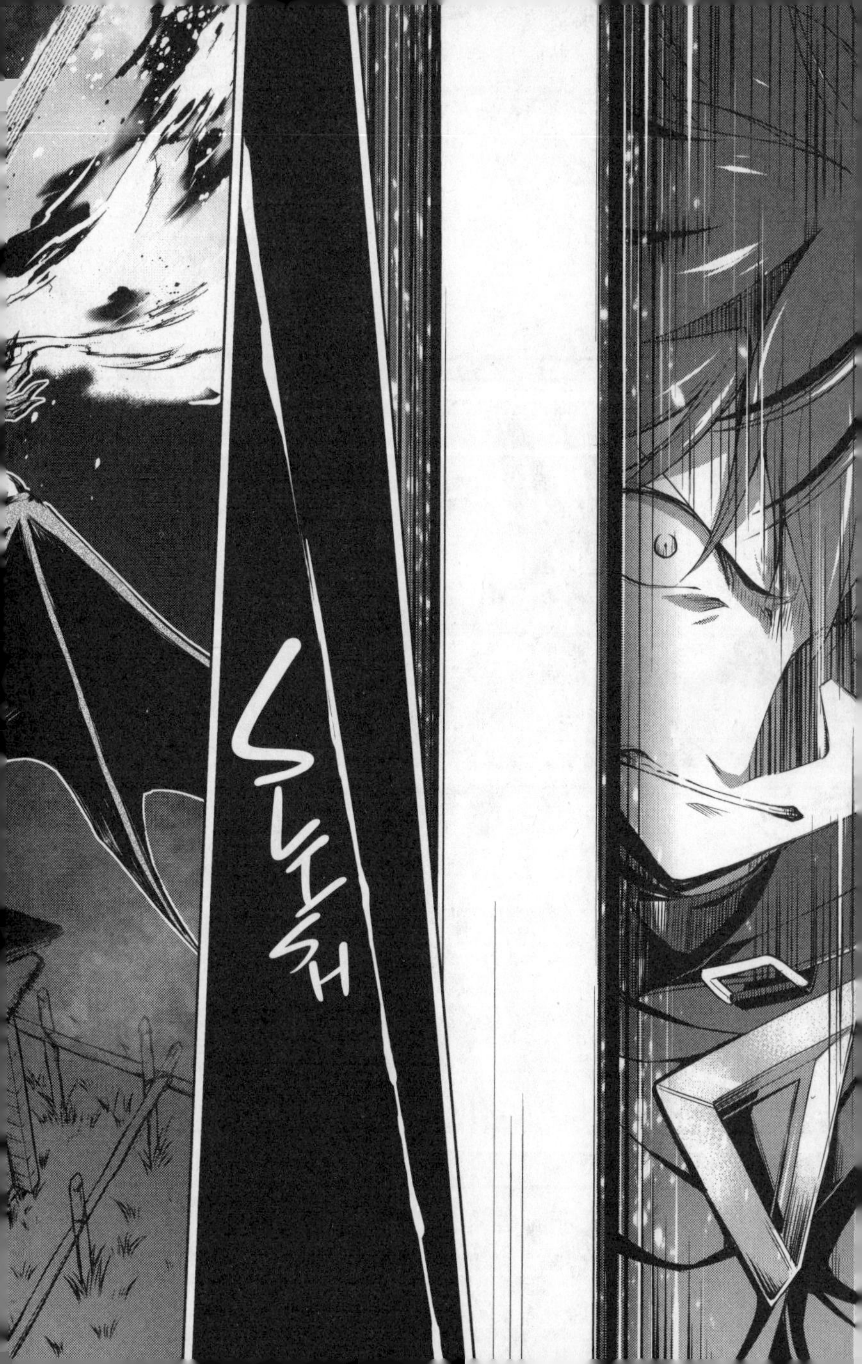
SLISH

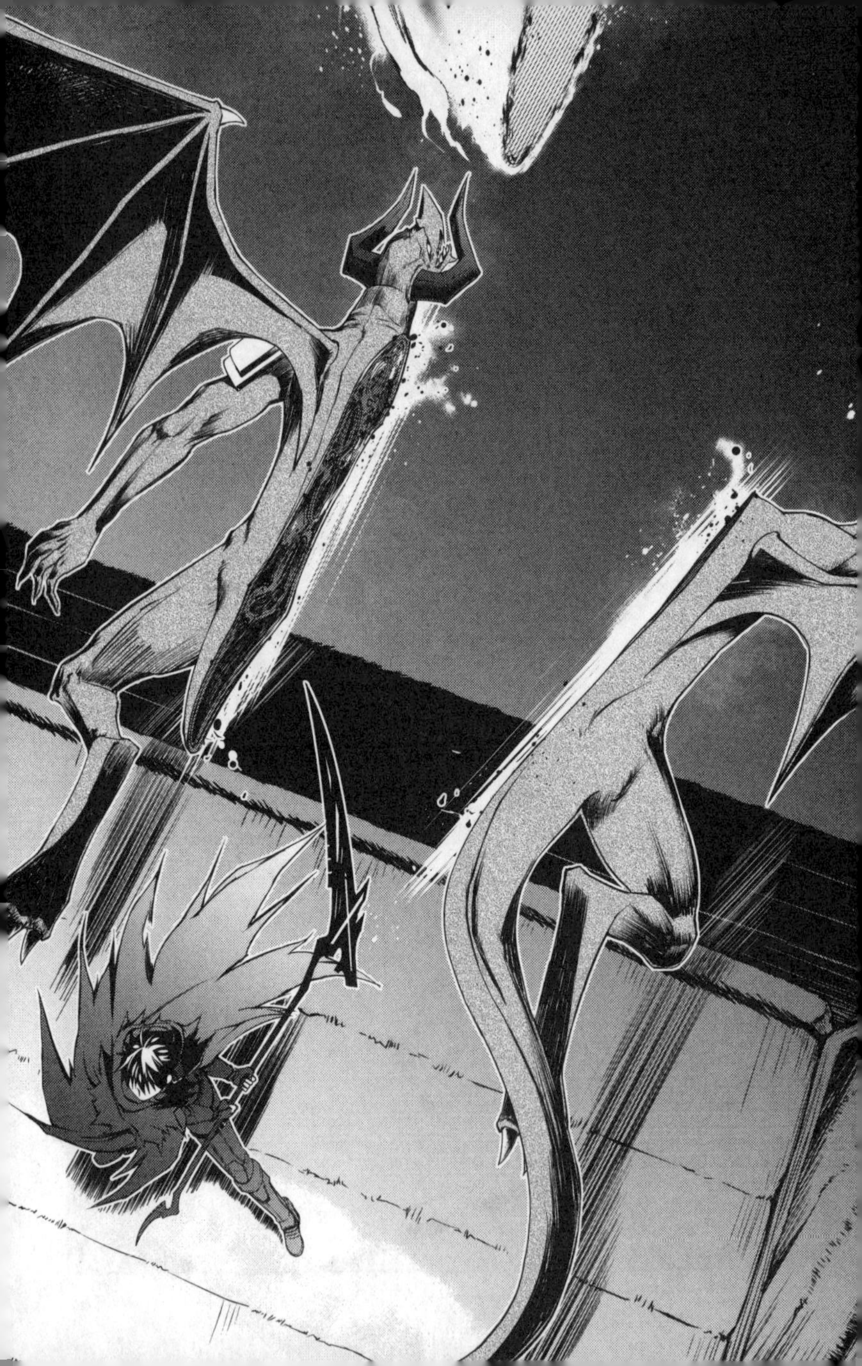

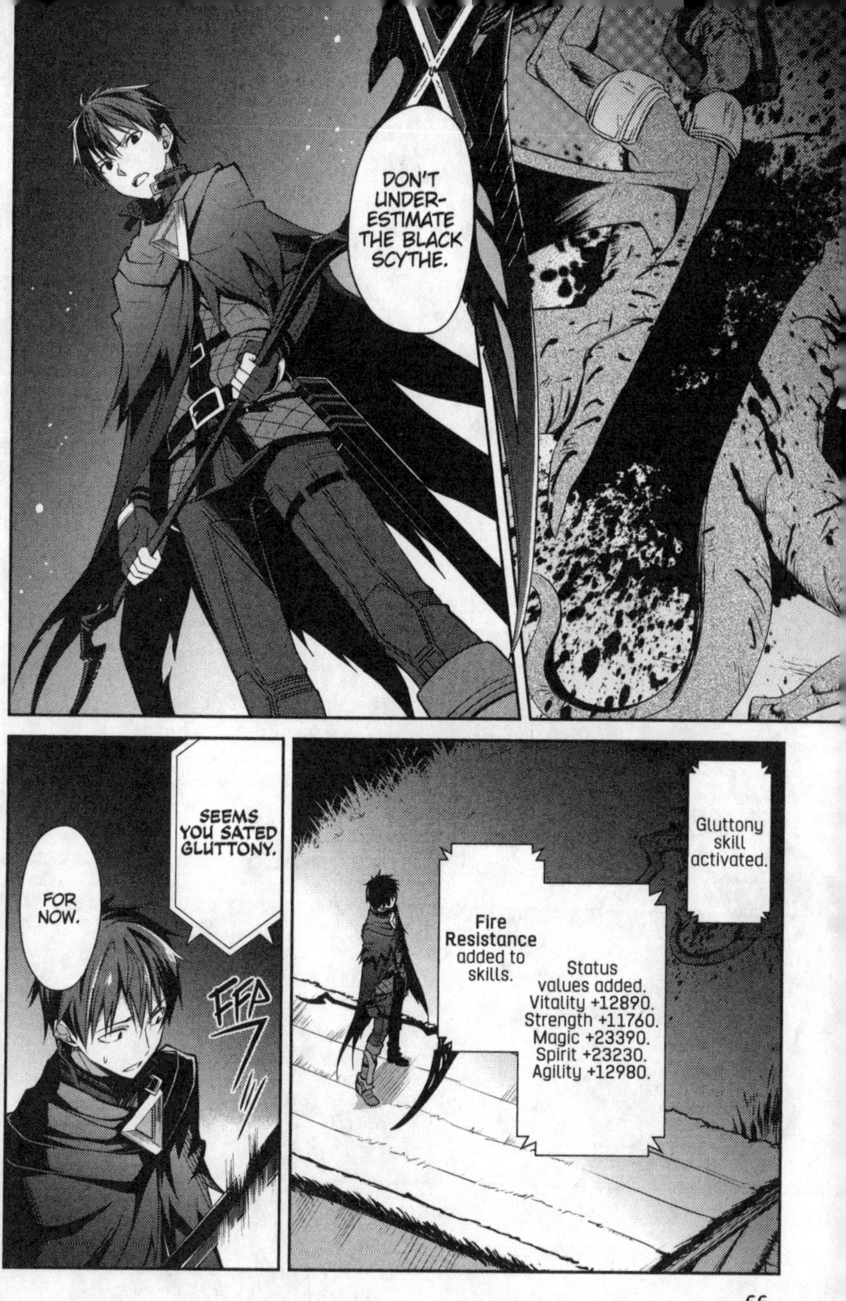
DON'T UNDER-ESTIMATE THE BLACK SCYTHE.
Gluttony skill activated.
Fire Resistance added to skills.
Status values added. Vitality +12890. Strength +11760. Magic +23390. Spirit +23230. Agility +12980.
SEEMS YOU SATED GLUTTONY.
FOR NOW.
FFP

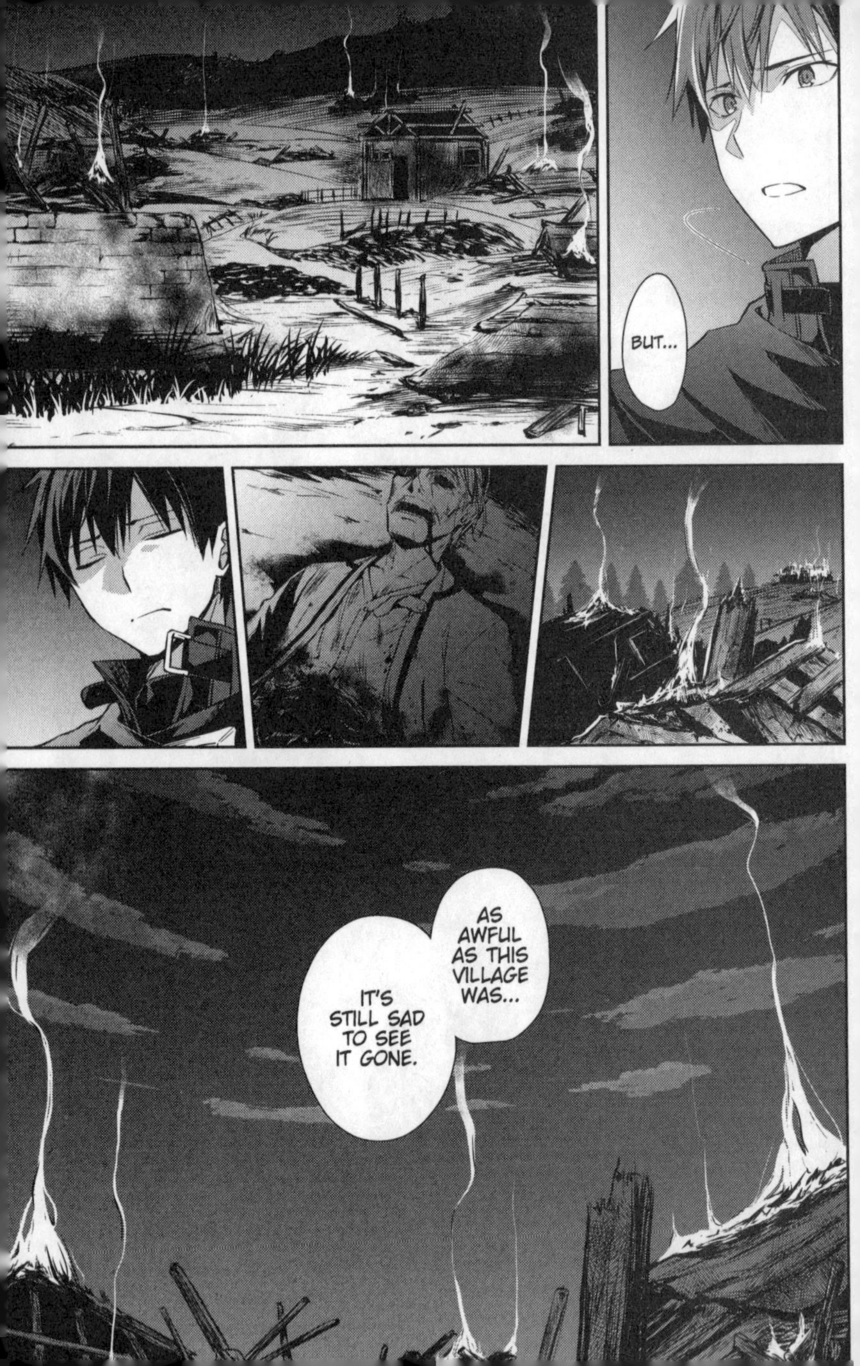
BUT...
AS AWFUL AS THIS VILLAGE WAS...
IT'S STILL SAD TO SEE IT GONE.

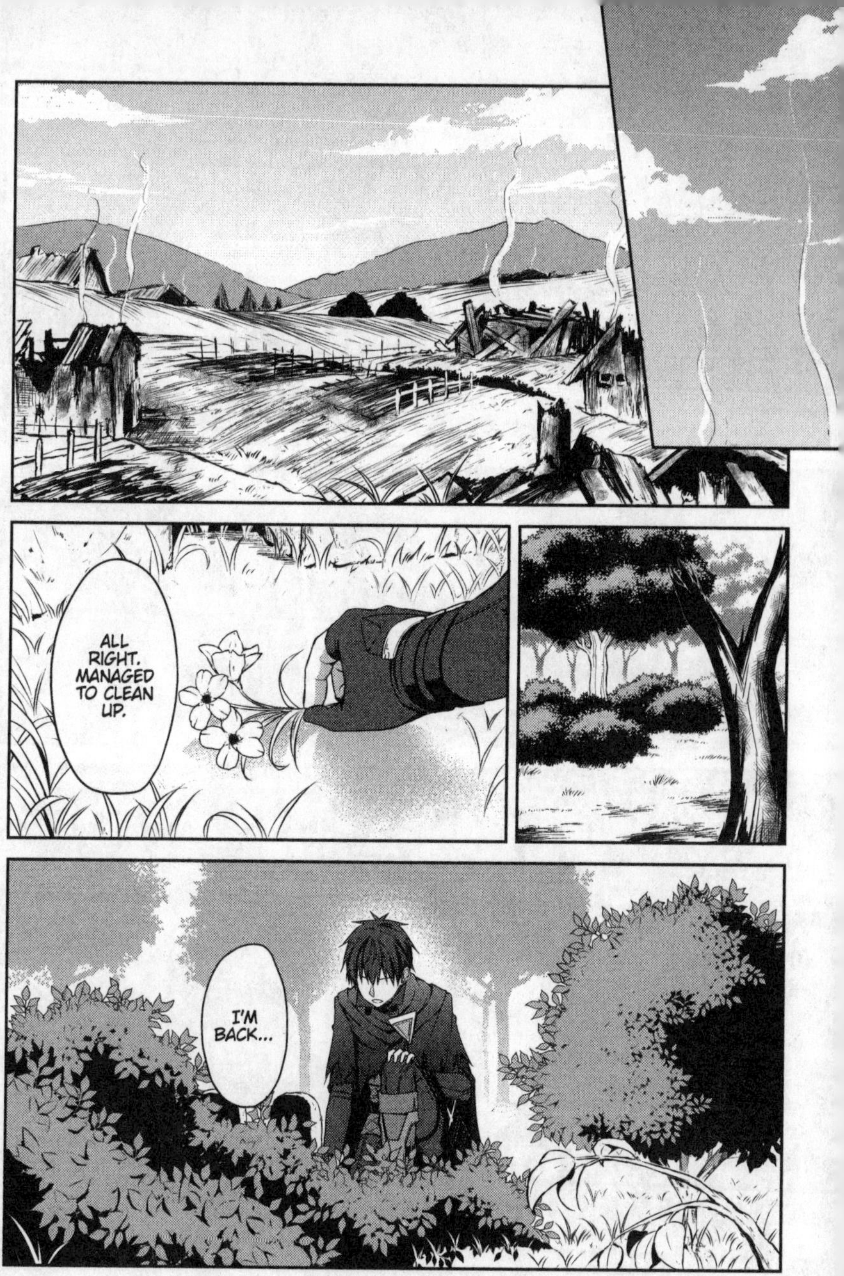
ALL RIGHT. MANAGED TO CLEAN UP.
I'M BACK...

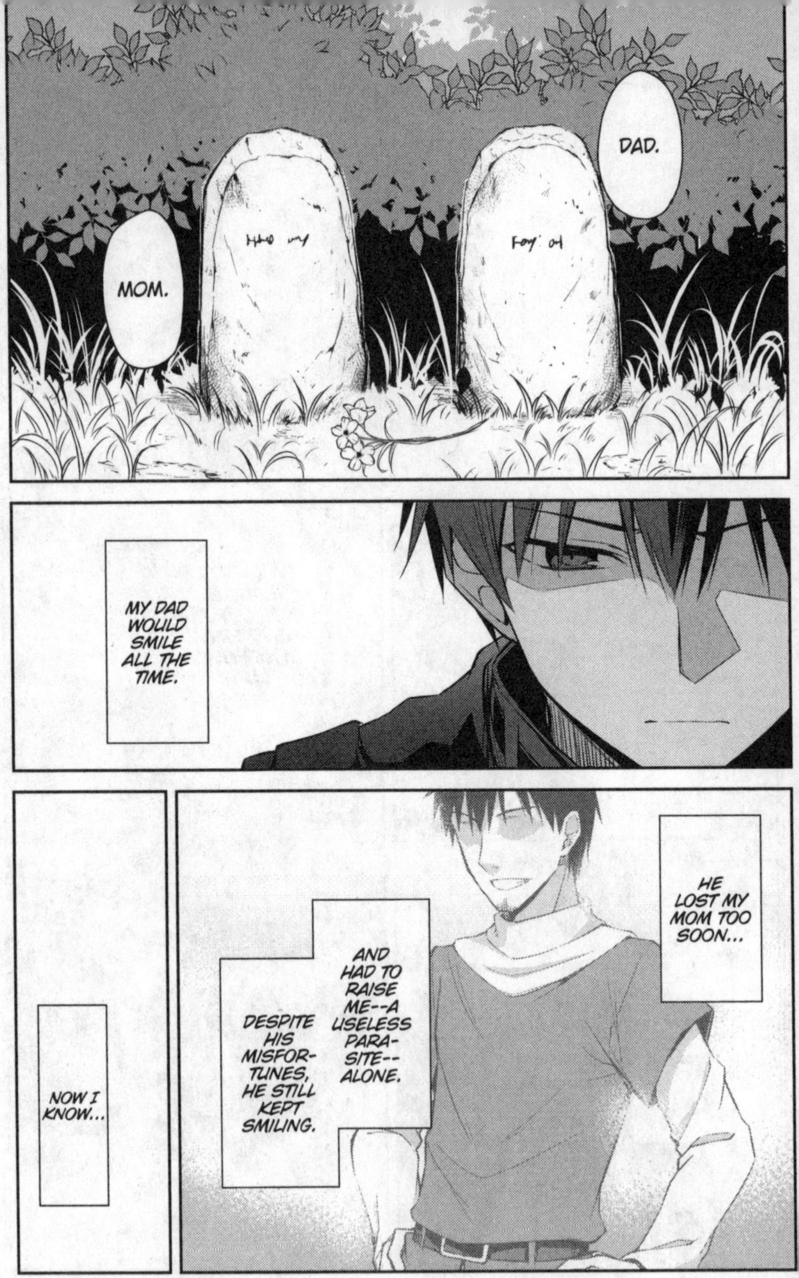
DAD.
MOM.
MY DAD WOULD SMILE ALL THE TIME.
HE LOST MY MOM TOO SOON...
AND HAD TO RAISE ME--A USELESS PARA-SITE--ALONE.
DESPITE HIS MISFOR-TUNES, HE STILL KEPT SMILING.
NOW I KNOW...

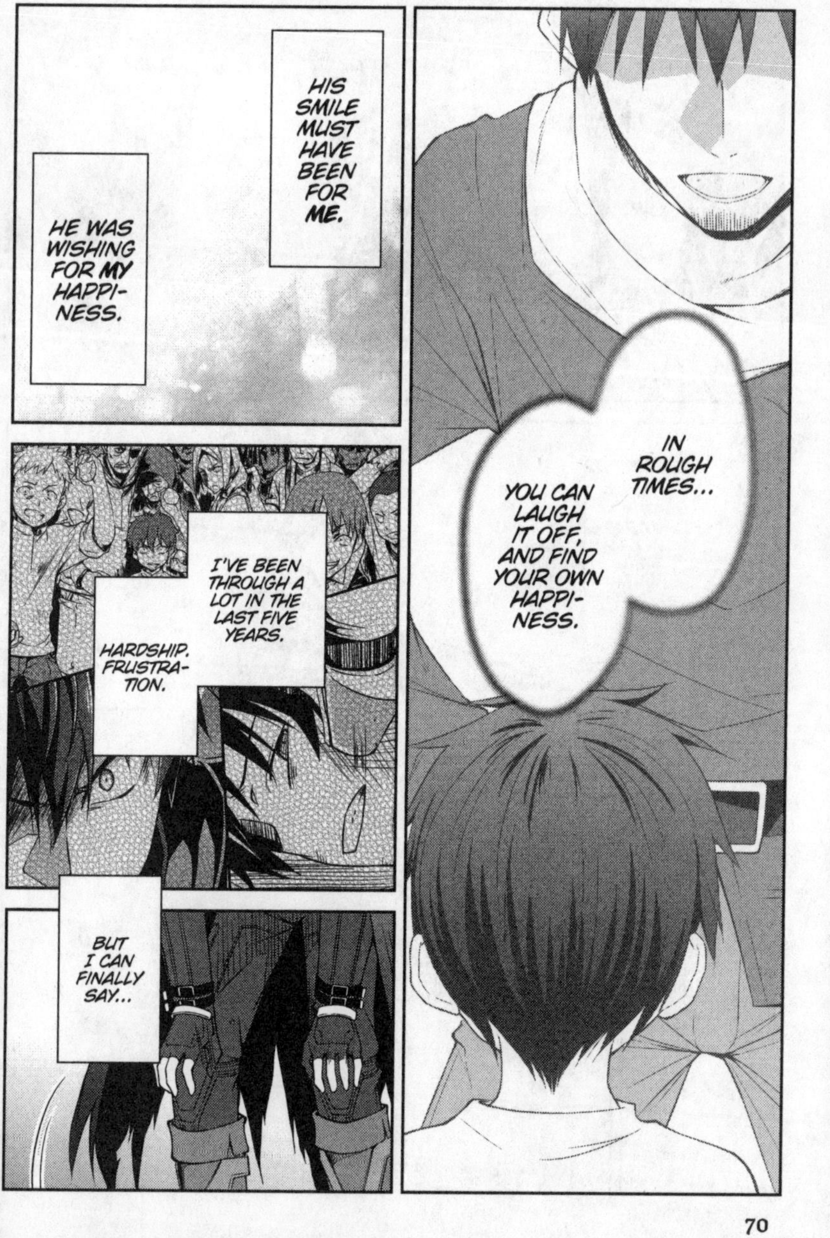
IN ROUGH TIMES...
YOU CAN LAUGH IT OFF, AND FIND YOUR OWN HAPPINESS.
HIS SMILE MUST HAVE BEEN FOR ME.
HE WAS WISHING FOR MY HAPPINESS.
I'VE BEEN THROUGH A LOT IN THE LAST FIVE YEARS.
HARDSHIP. FRUSTRATION.
BUT I CAN FINALLY SAY...

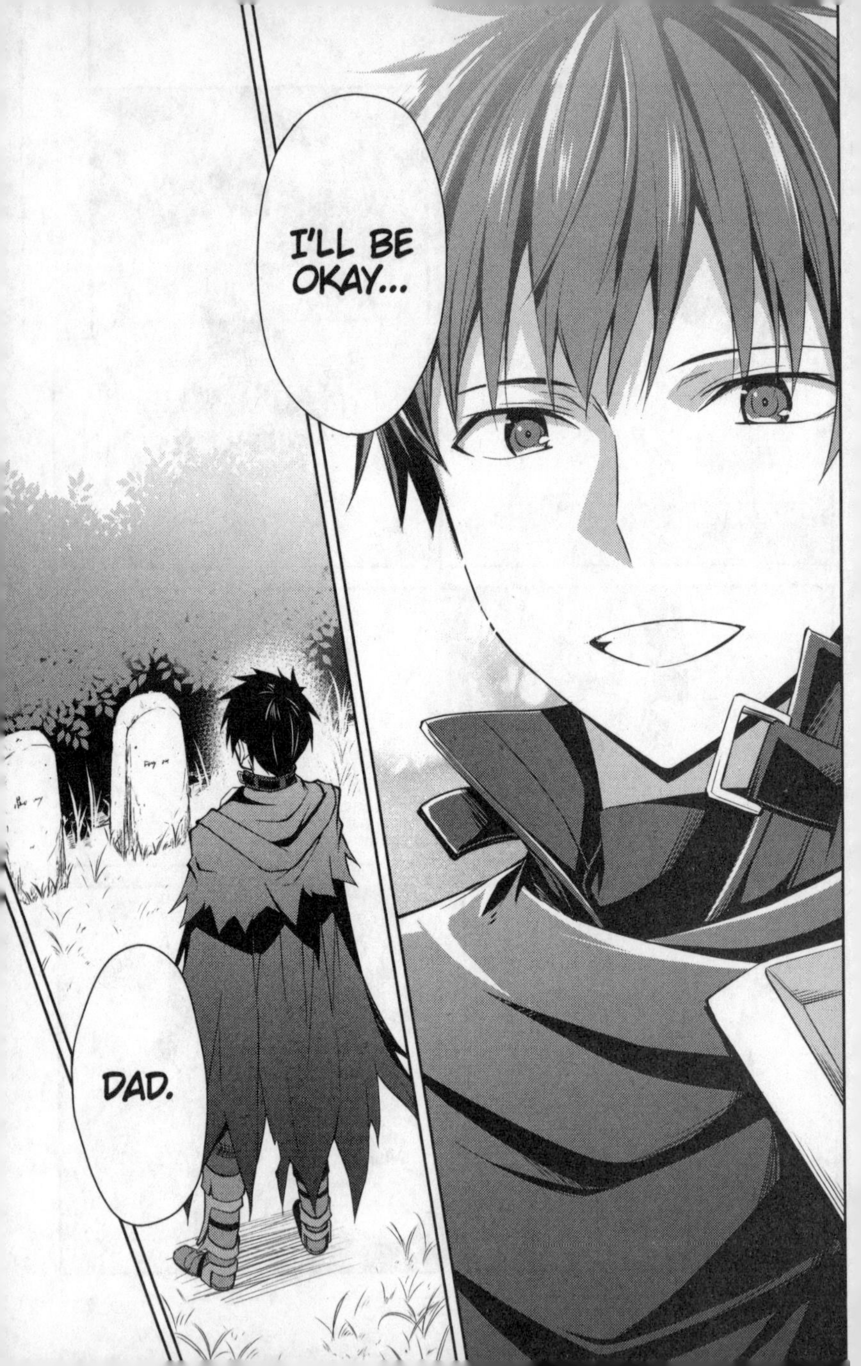
I'LL BE OKAY...
DAD.

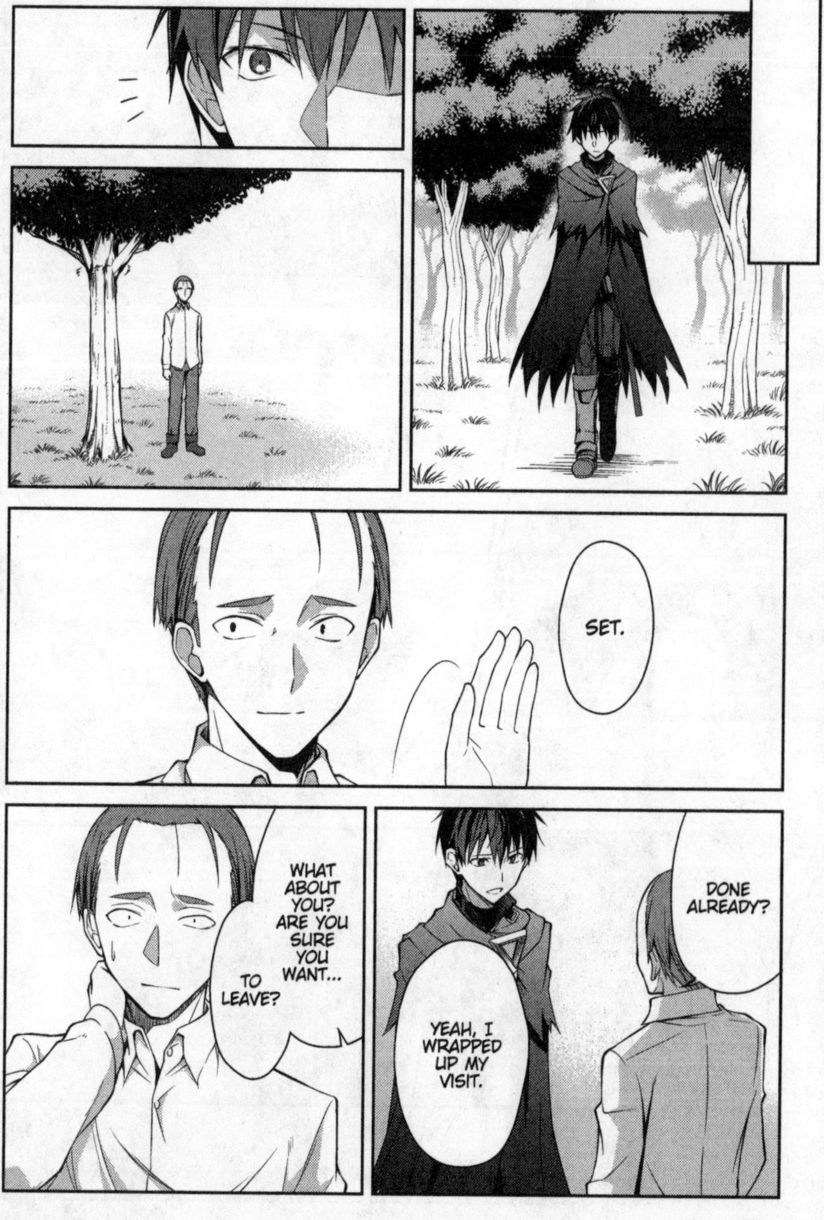
SET.
DONE ALREADY?
YEAH, I WRAPPED UP MY VISIT.
WHAT ABOUT YOU? ARE YOU SURE YOU WANT...
TO LEAVE?

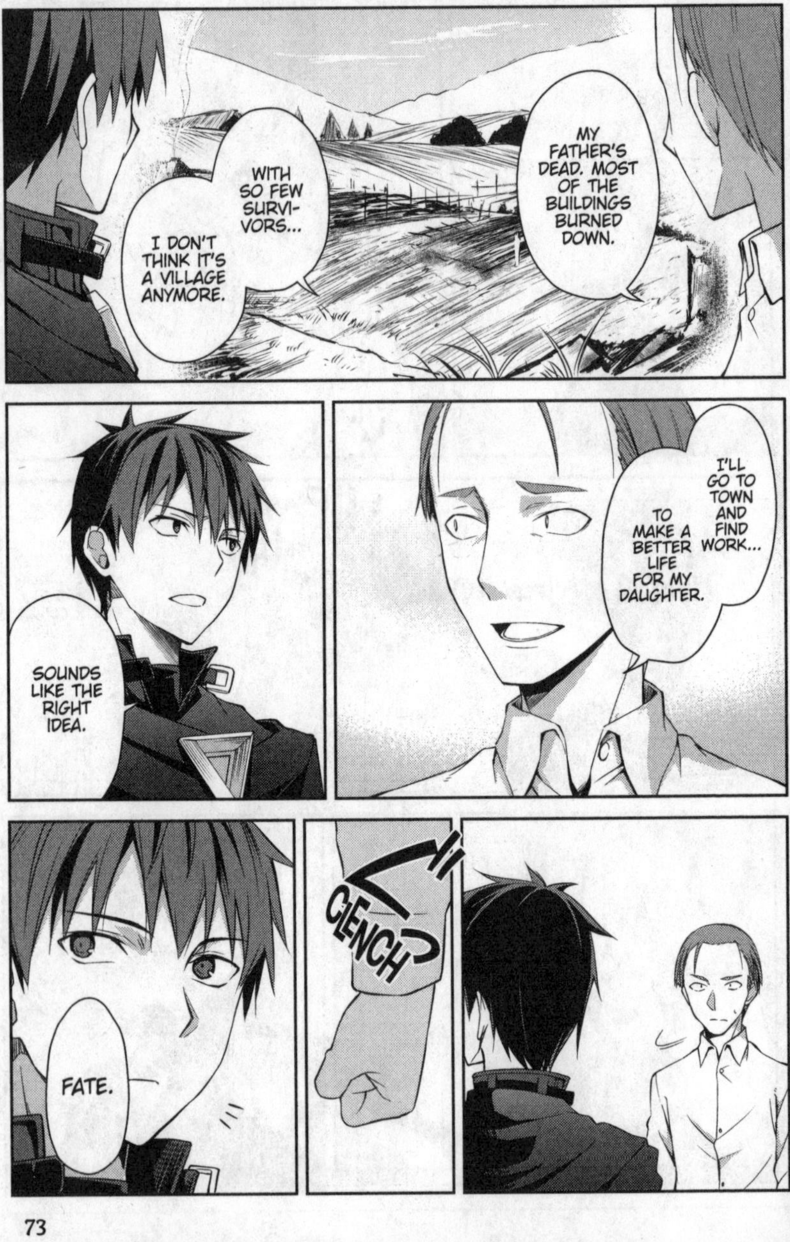
MY FATHER'S DEAD. MOST OF THE BUILDINGS BURNED DOWN.
WITH SO FEW SURVIVORS...
I DON'T THINK IT'S A VILLAGE ANYMORE.
I'LL GO TO TOWN AND FIND WORK...
TO MAKE A BETTER LIFE FOR MY DAUGHTER.
SOUNDS LIKE THE RIGHT IDEA.
CLENCH
FATE.

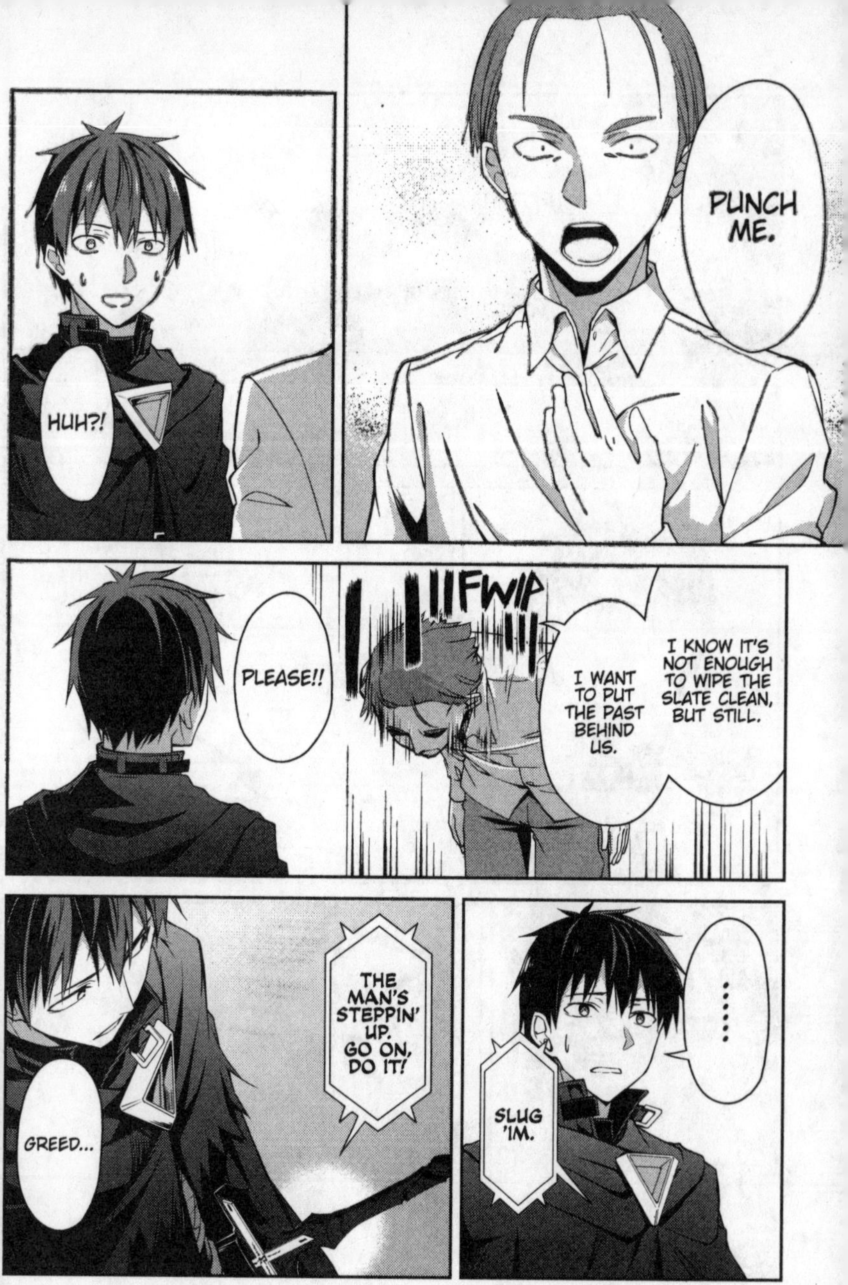
PUNCH ME.
HUH?!
I KNOW IT'S NOT ENOUGH TO WIPE THE SLATE CLEAN, BUT STILL.
I WANT TO PUT THE PAST BEHIND US.
FWIP
PLEASE!!
......
SLUG 'IM.
THE MAN'S STEPPIN' UP. GO ON, DO IT!
GREED...

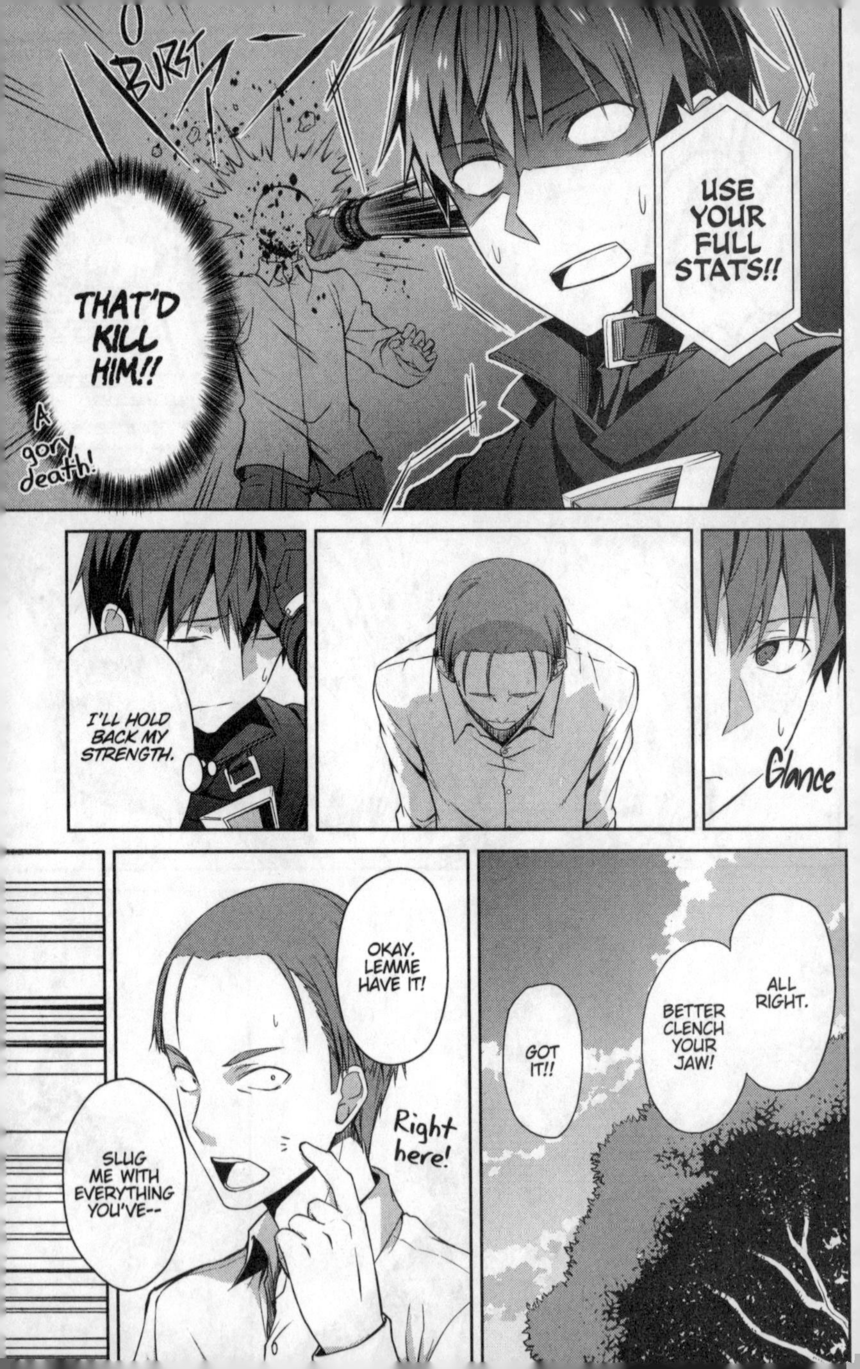
USE YOUR FULL STATS!!
BURST
THAT'D KILL HIM!!
A gory death!
Glance
I'LL HOLD BACK MY STRENGTH.
ALL RIGHT.
BETTER CLENCH YOUR JAW!
GOT IT!!
OKAY. LEMME HAVE IT!
Right here!
SLUG ME WITH EVERYTHING YOU'VE--

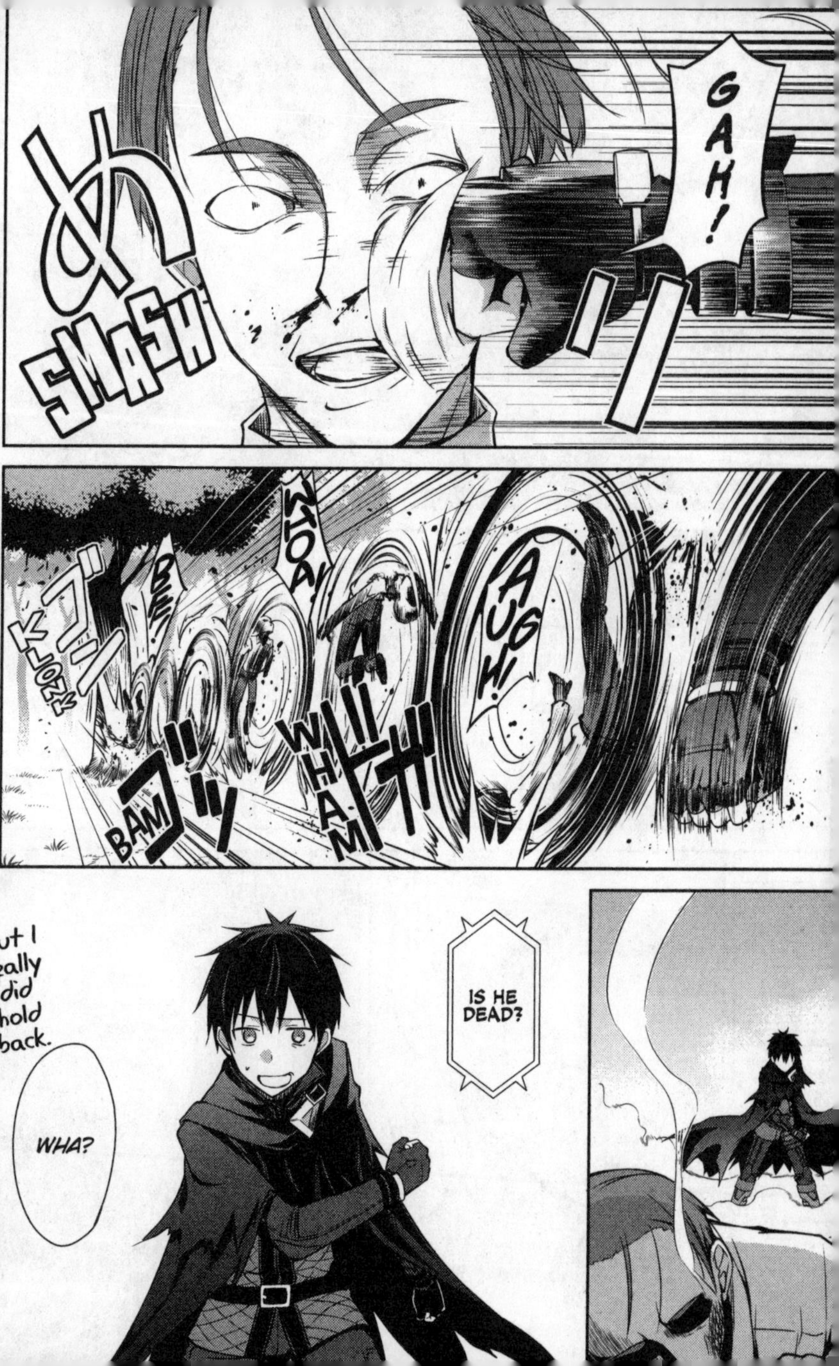
GAH!
SMASH
AUGH!
WHAM
WHOA!
BE!
BAM
KLONK
IS HE DEAD?
But I really did hold back.
WHA?

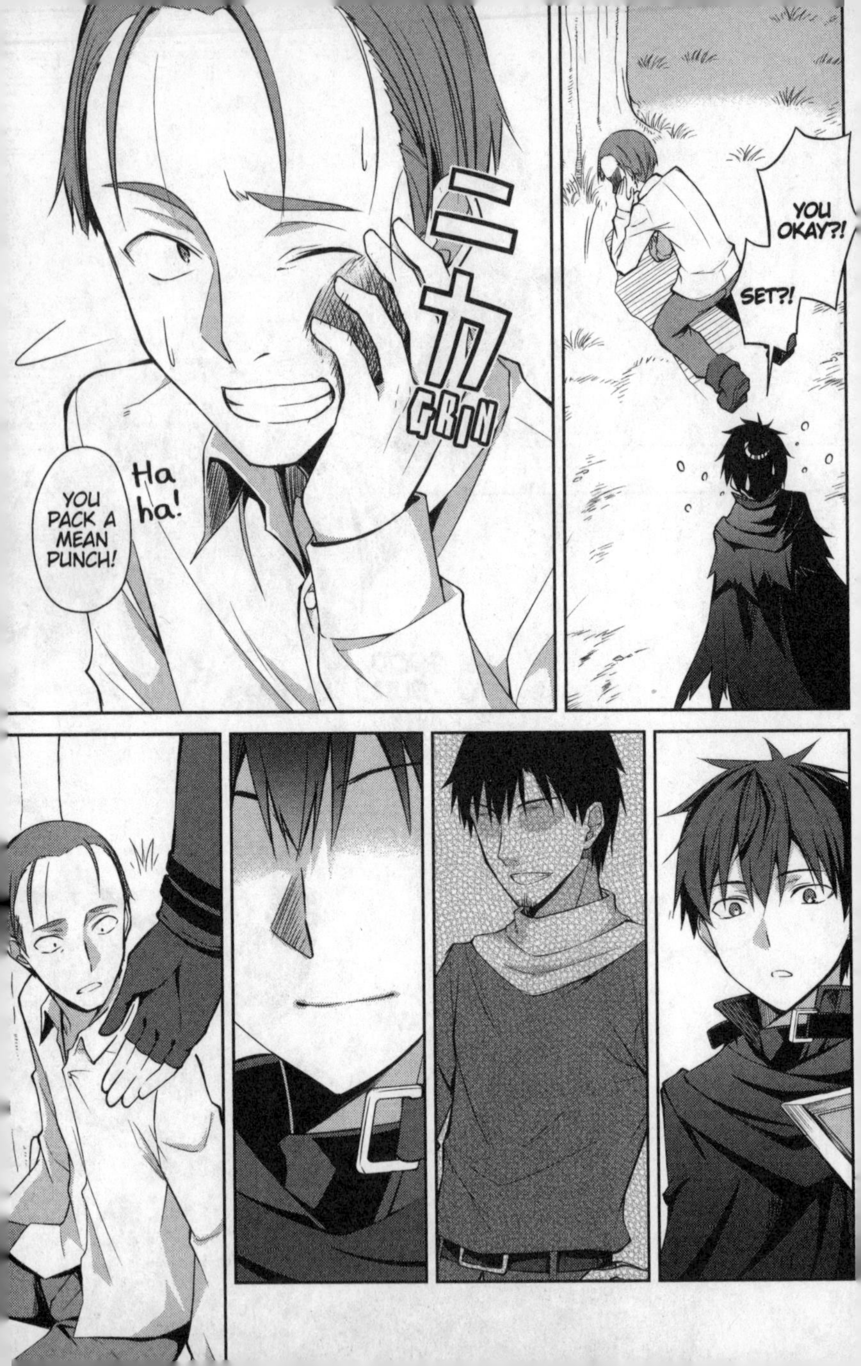
YOU OKAY?!
SET?!
ニカ
GRIN
YOU PACK A MEAN PUNCH!
Ha ha!

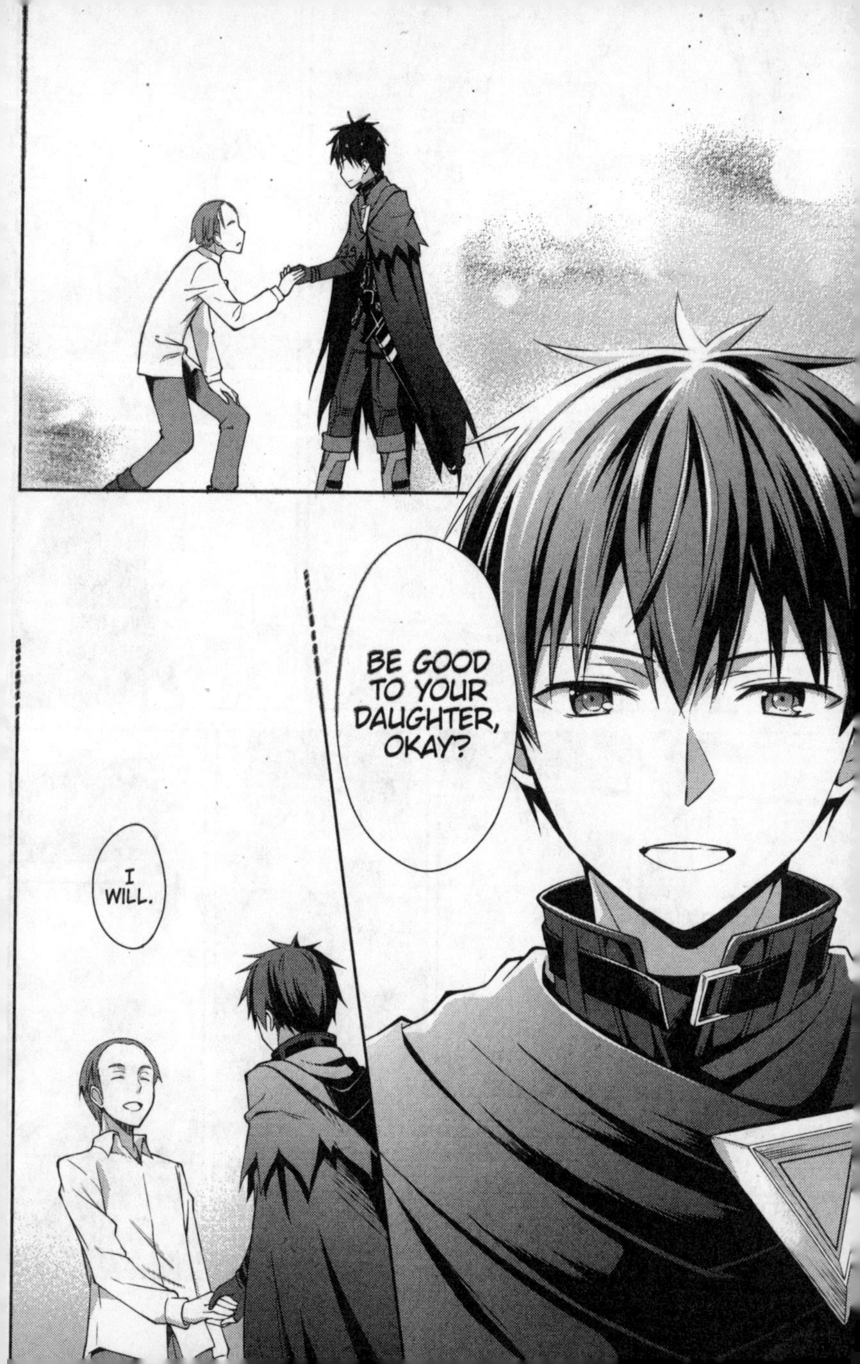
BE GOOD TO YOUR DAUGHTER, OKAY?
I WILL.

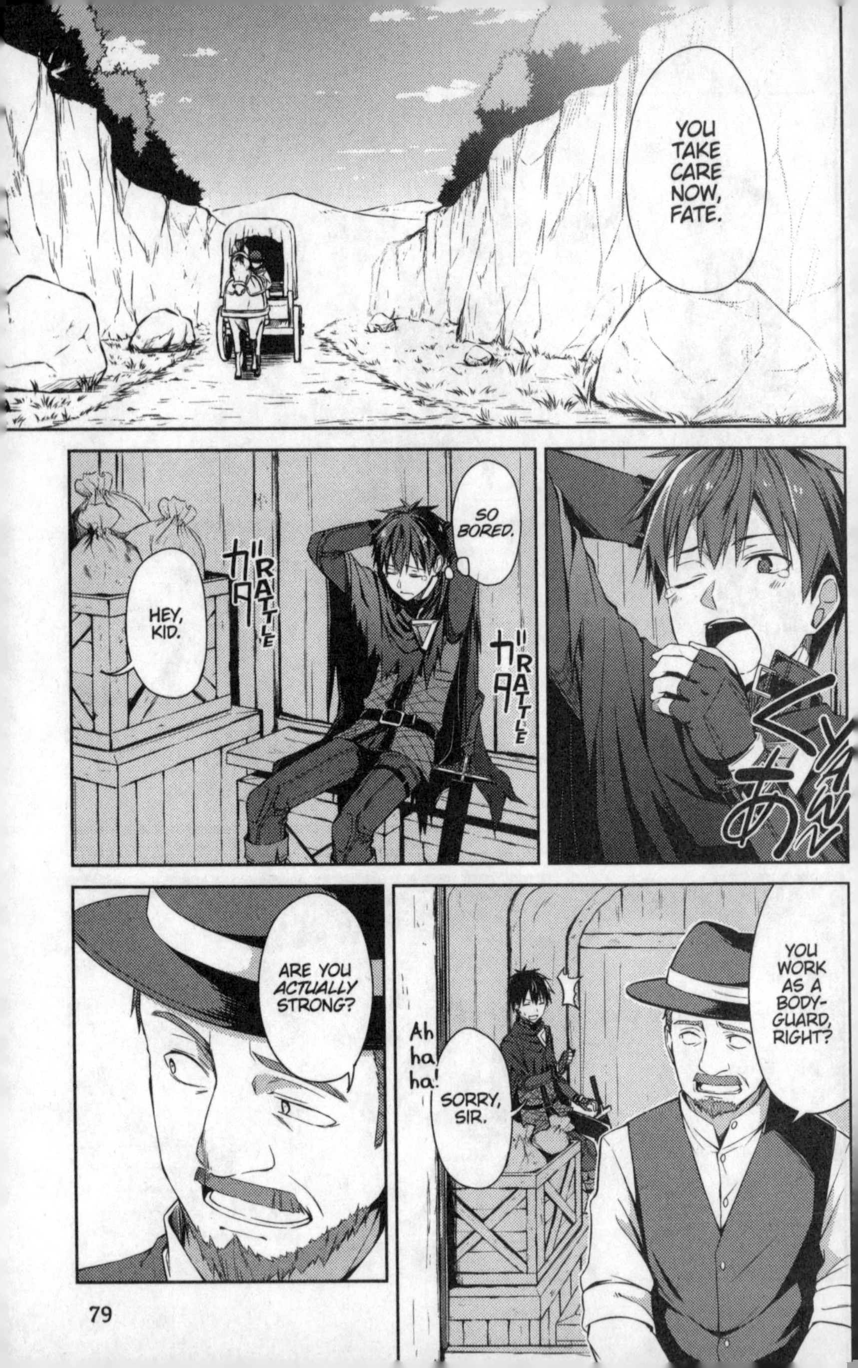
YOU TAKE CARE NOW, FATE.
ガタ RATTLE
SO BORED.
ガタ RATTLE
HEY, KID.
YOU WORK AS A BODY-GUARD, RIGHT?
Ah ha ha!
SORRY, SIR.
ARE YOU ACTUALLY STRONG?

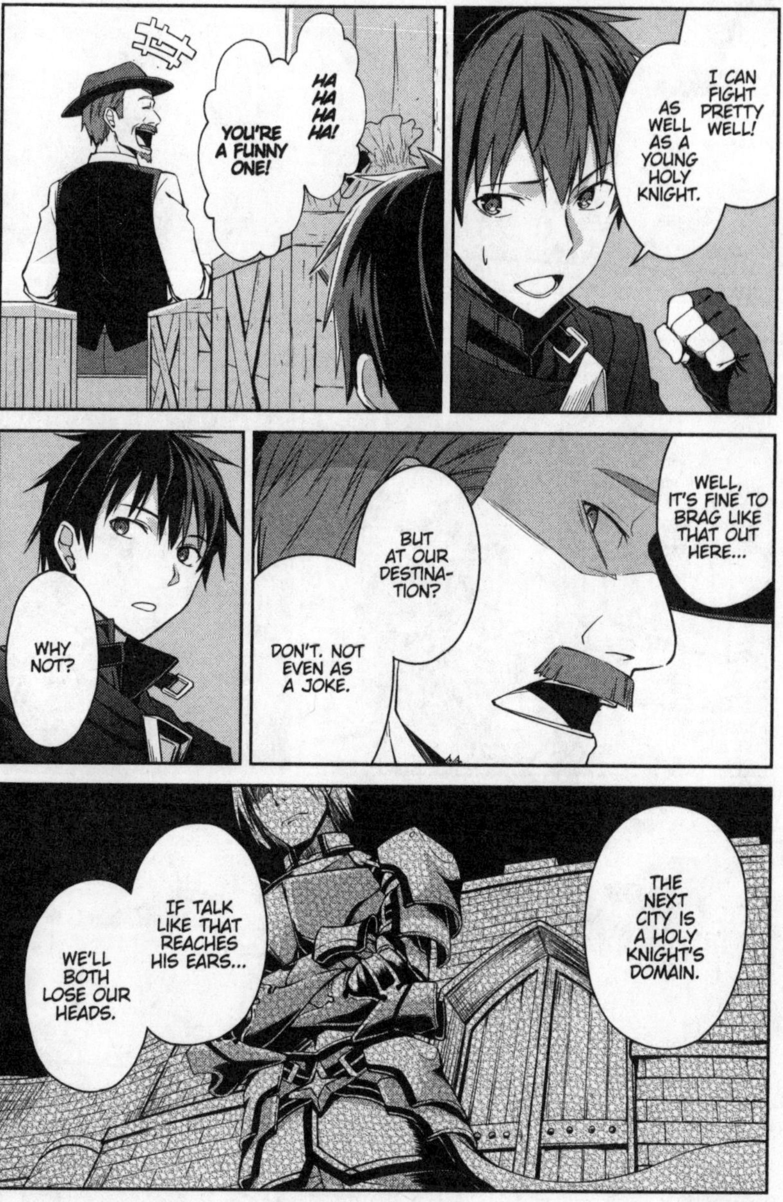
I CAN FIGHT PRETTY WELL!
AS WELL AS A YOUNG HOLY KNIGHT.
HA HA HA HA!
YOU'RE A FUNNY ONE!
WELL, IT'S FINE TO BRAG LIKE THAT OUT HERE...
BUT AT OUR DESTINA-TION?
DON'T. NOT EVEN AS A JOKE.
WHY NOT?
THE NEXT CITY IS A HOLY KNIGHT'S DOMAIN.
IF TALK LIKE THAT REACHES HIS EARS...
WE'LL BOTH LOSE OUR HEADS.

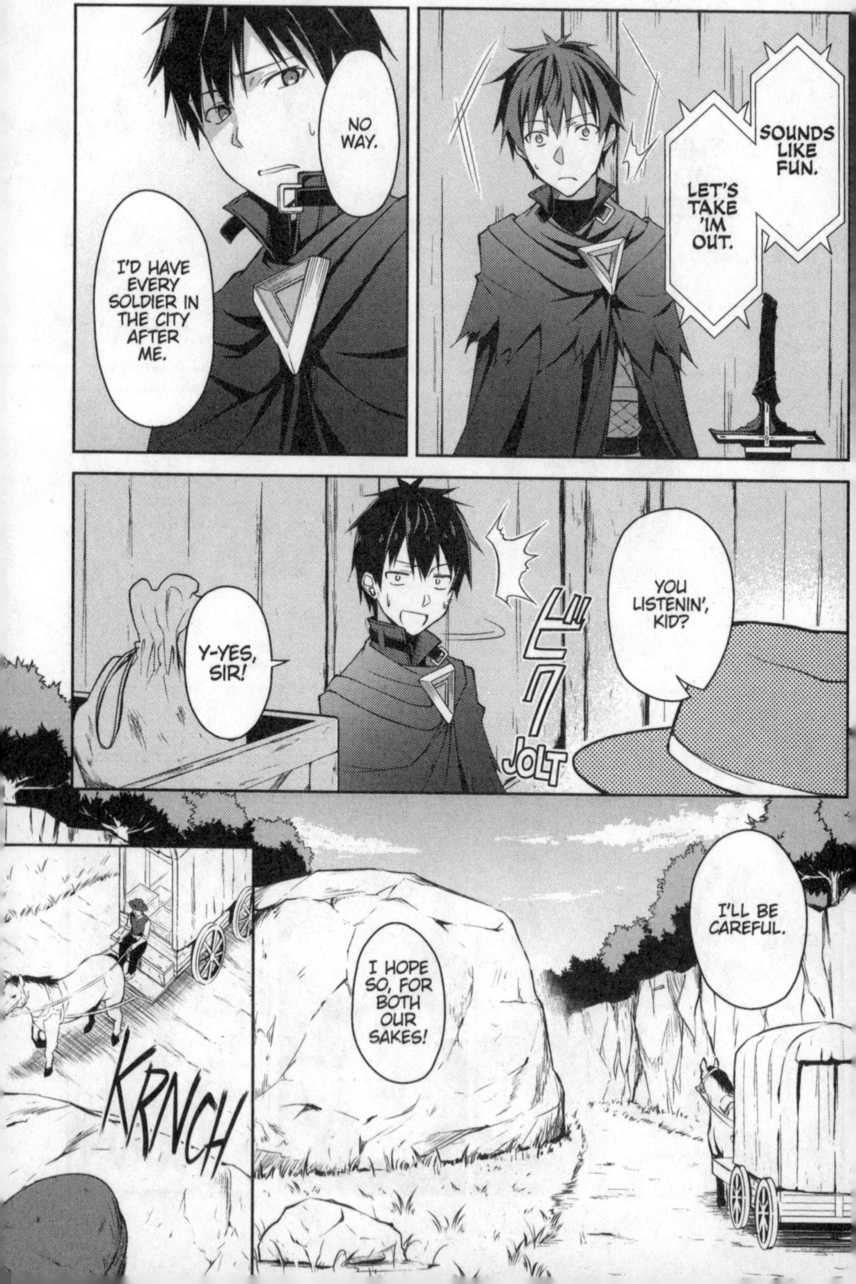
SOUNDS LIKE FUN.
LET'S TAKE 'IM OUT.
NO WAY.
I'D HAVE EVERY SOLDIER IN THE CITY AFTER ME.
YOU LISTENIN', KID?
ビク
JOLT
Y-YES, SIR!
I'LL BE CAREFUL.
I HOPE SO, FOR BOTH OUR SAKES!
KRNCH

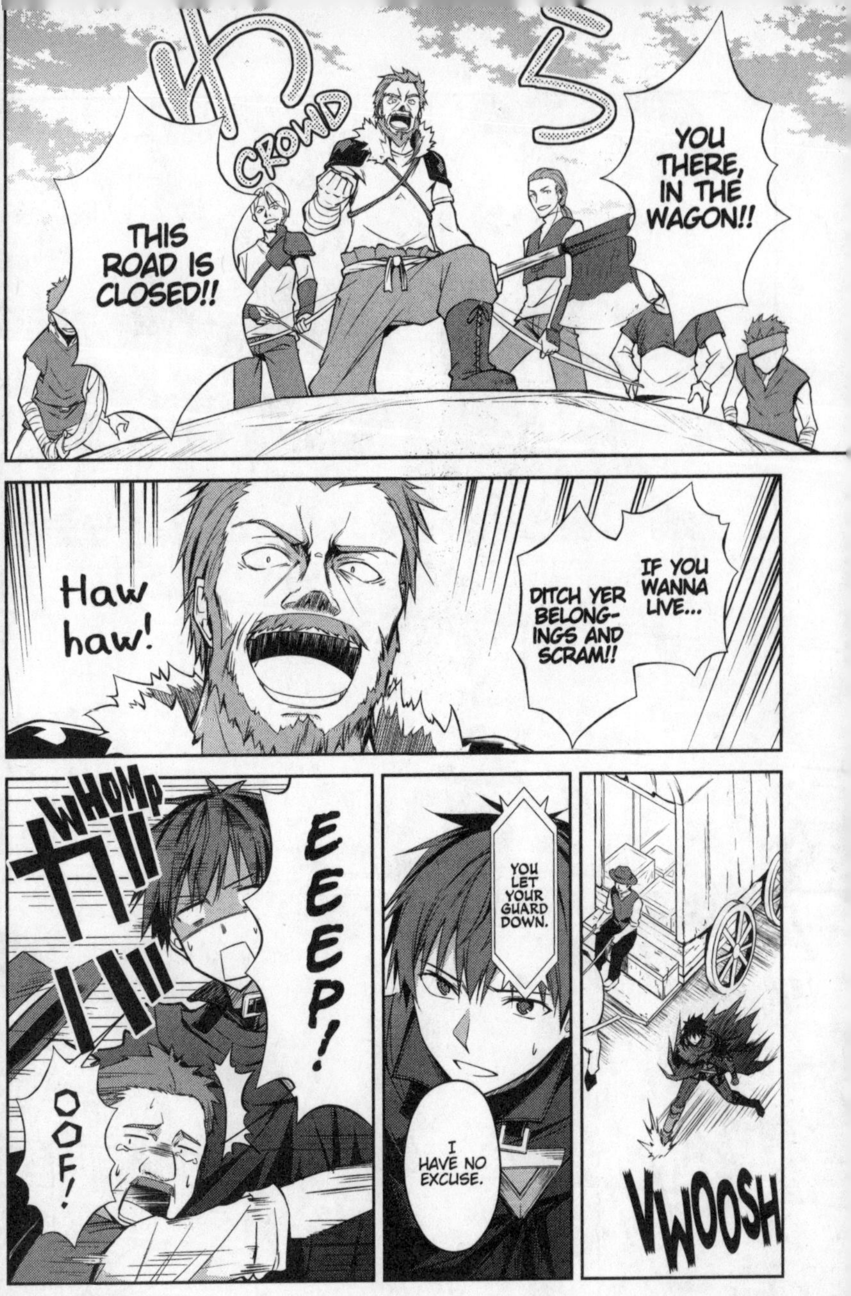
YOU THERE, IN THE WAGON!!
CROWD
THIS ROAD IS CLOSED!!
IF YOU WANNA LIVE...
DITCH YER BELONGINGS AND SCRAM!!
Haw haw!
VWOOSH
YOU LET YOUR GUARD DOWN.
I HAVE NO EXCUSE.
WHOMP
EEEP!
OOF!

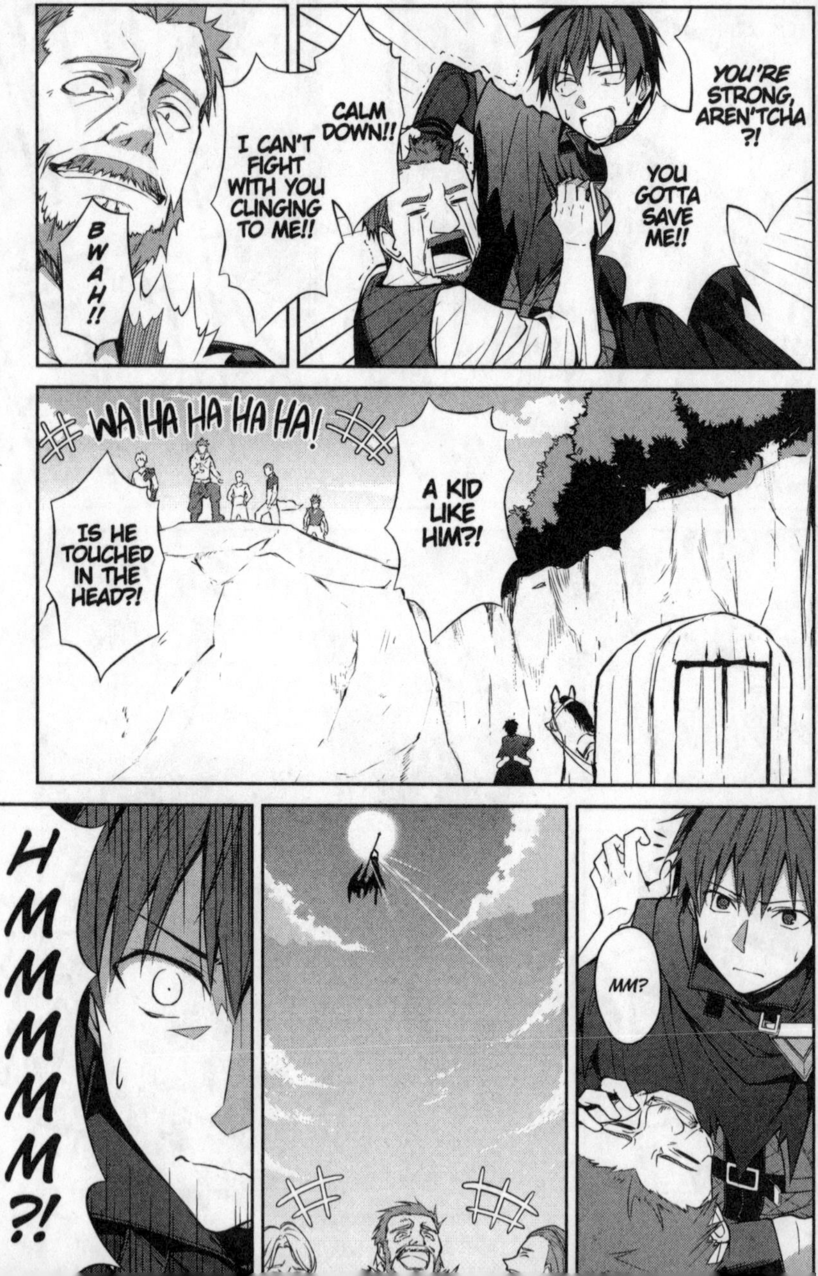
YOU'RE STRONG, AREN'TCHA?!
YOU GOTTA SAVE ME!!
CALM DOWN!!
I CAN'T FIGHT WITH YOU CLINGING TO ME!!
BWAH!!
WA HA HA HA HA!
A KID LIKE HIM?!
IS HE TOUCHED IN THE HEAD?!
MM?
HMMMMM?!

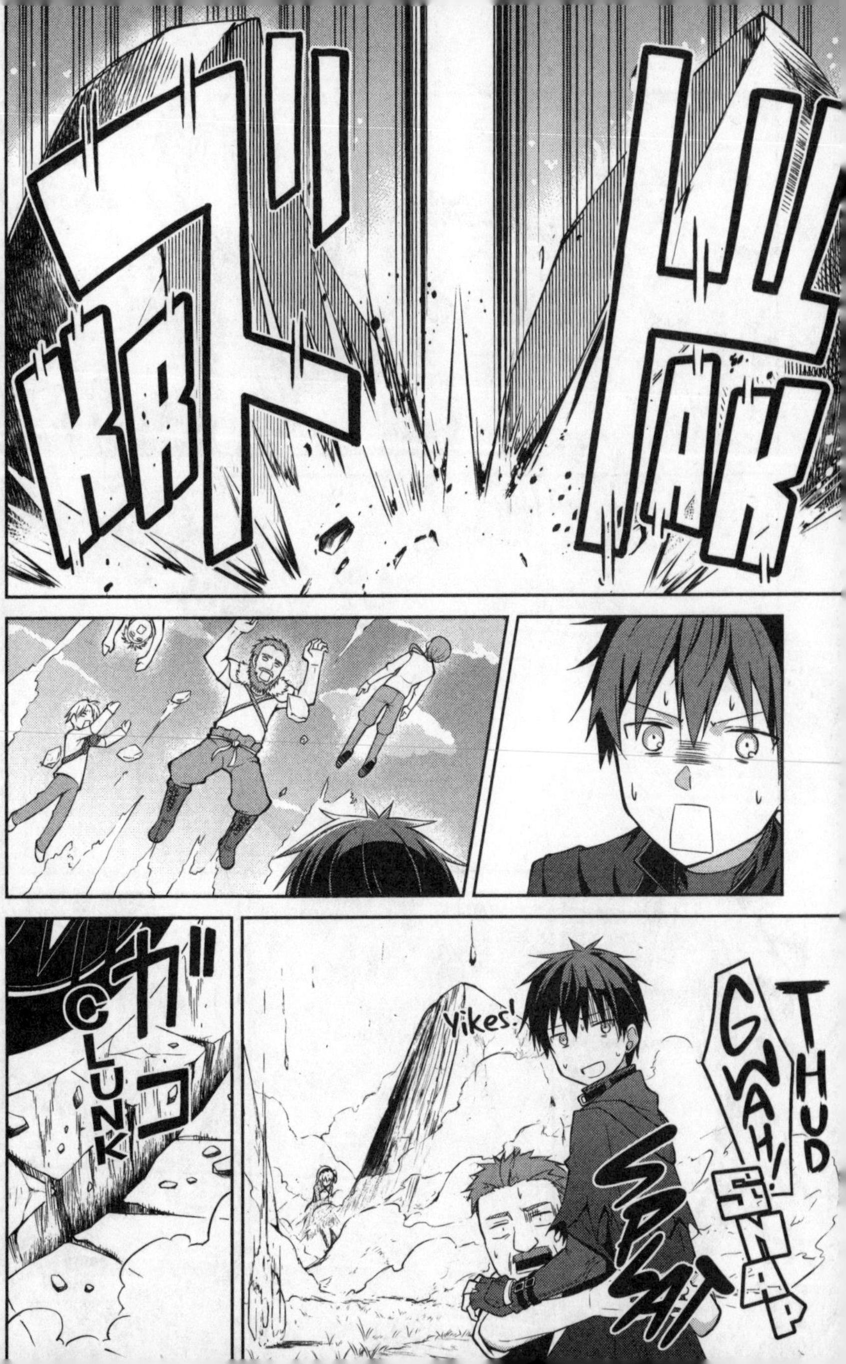
Yikes!
THUD
GWAH!
SNAP
CLUNK

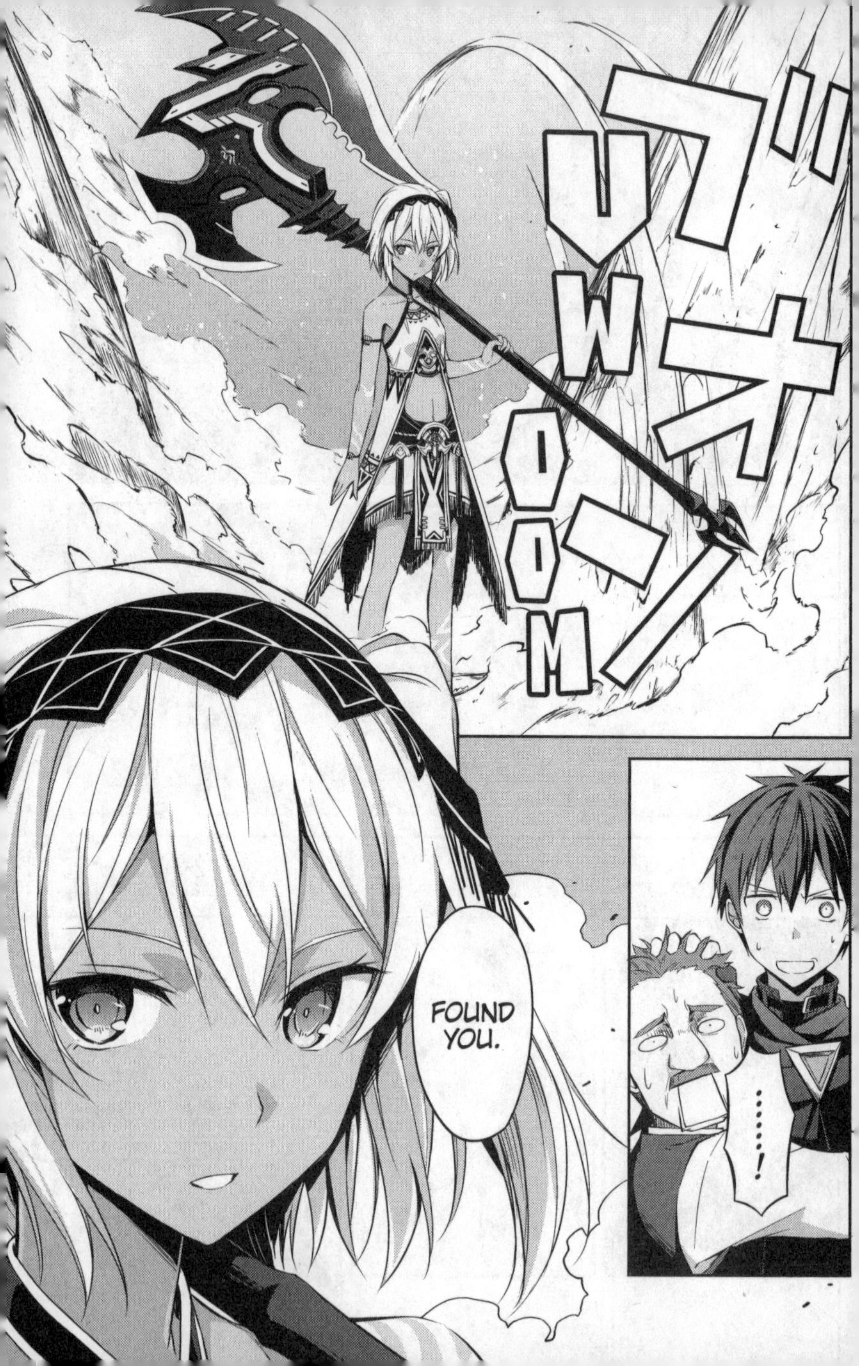
ブオーン
VWOOM
......!
FOUND YOU.

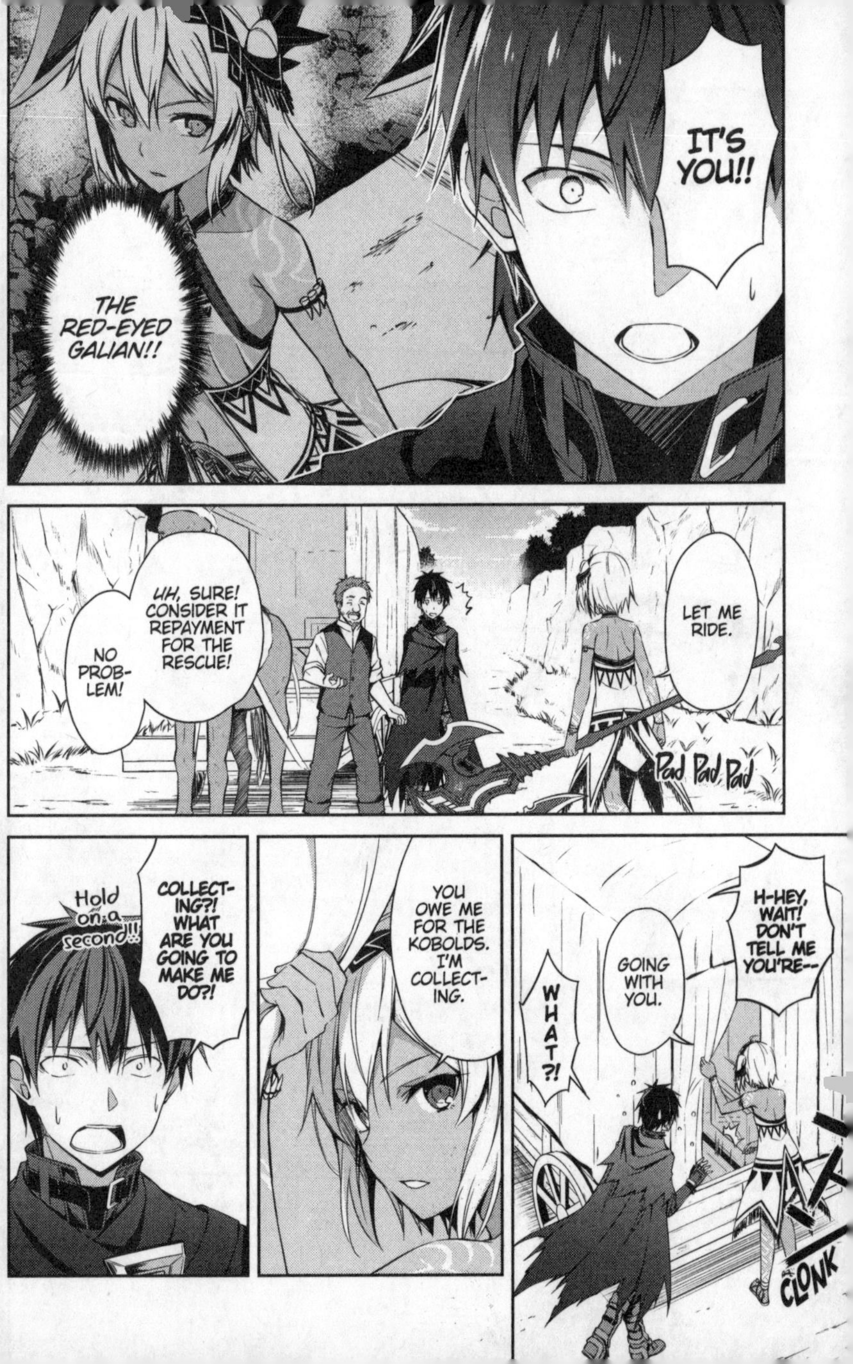
IT'S YOU!!
THE RED-EYED GALIAN!!
LET ME RIDE.
UH, SURE! CONSIDER IT REPAYMENT FOR THE RESCUE!
NO PROB-LEM!
Pad Pad Pad
H-HEY, WAIT! DON'T TELL ME YOU'RE--
GOING WITH YOU.
WHAT?!
CLONK
YOU OWE ME FOR THE KOBOLDS. I'M COLLECT-ING.
COLLECT-ING?! WHAT ARE YOU GOING TO MAKE ME DO?!
Hold on a second!!

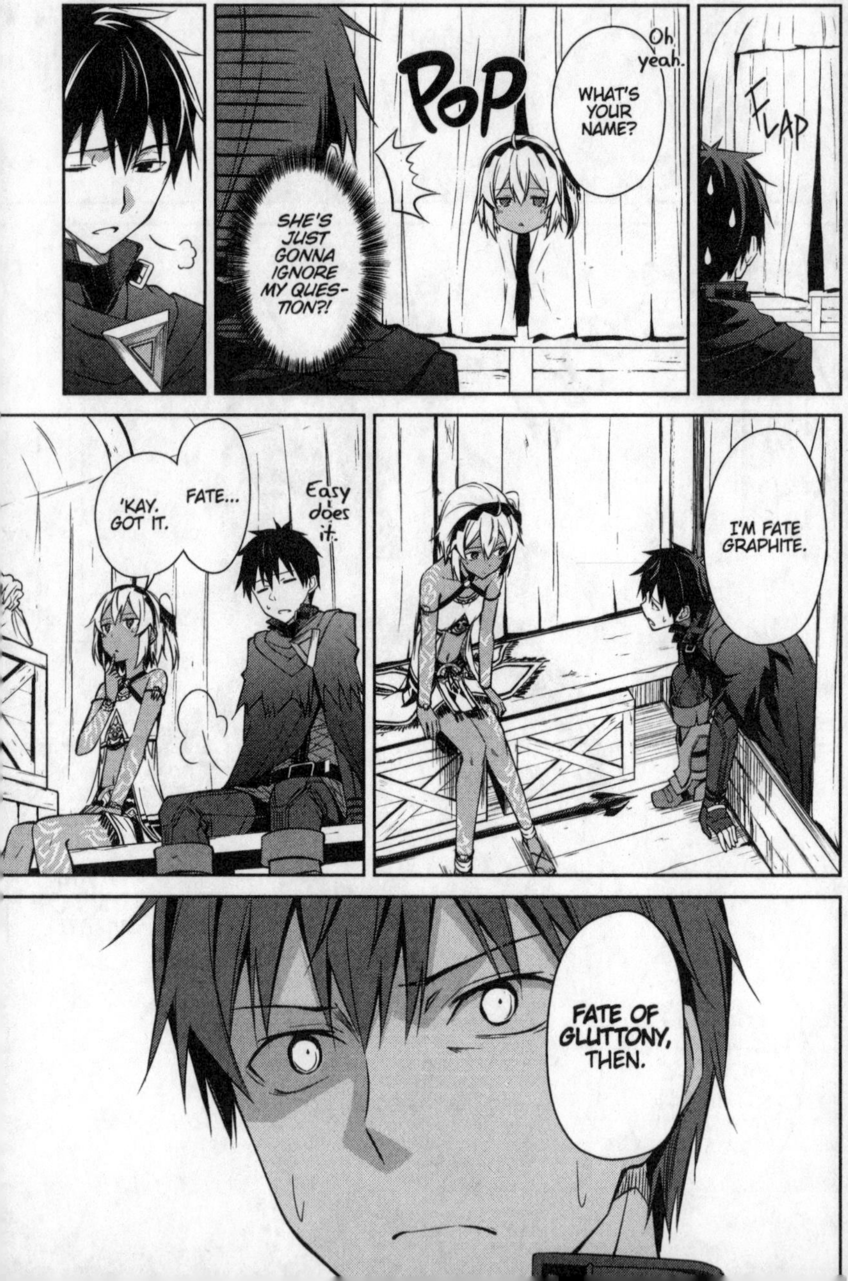
FLAP
Oh yeah.
WHAT'S YOUR NAME?
POP
SHE'S JUST GONNA IGNORE MY QUES-TION?!
I'M FATE GRAPHITE.
Easy does it.
FATE...
'KAY. GOT IT.
FATE OF GLUTTONY, THEN.

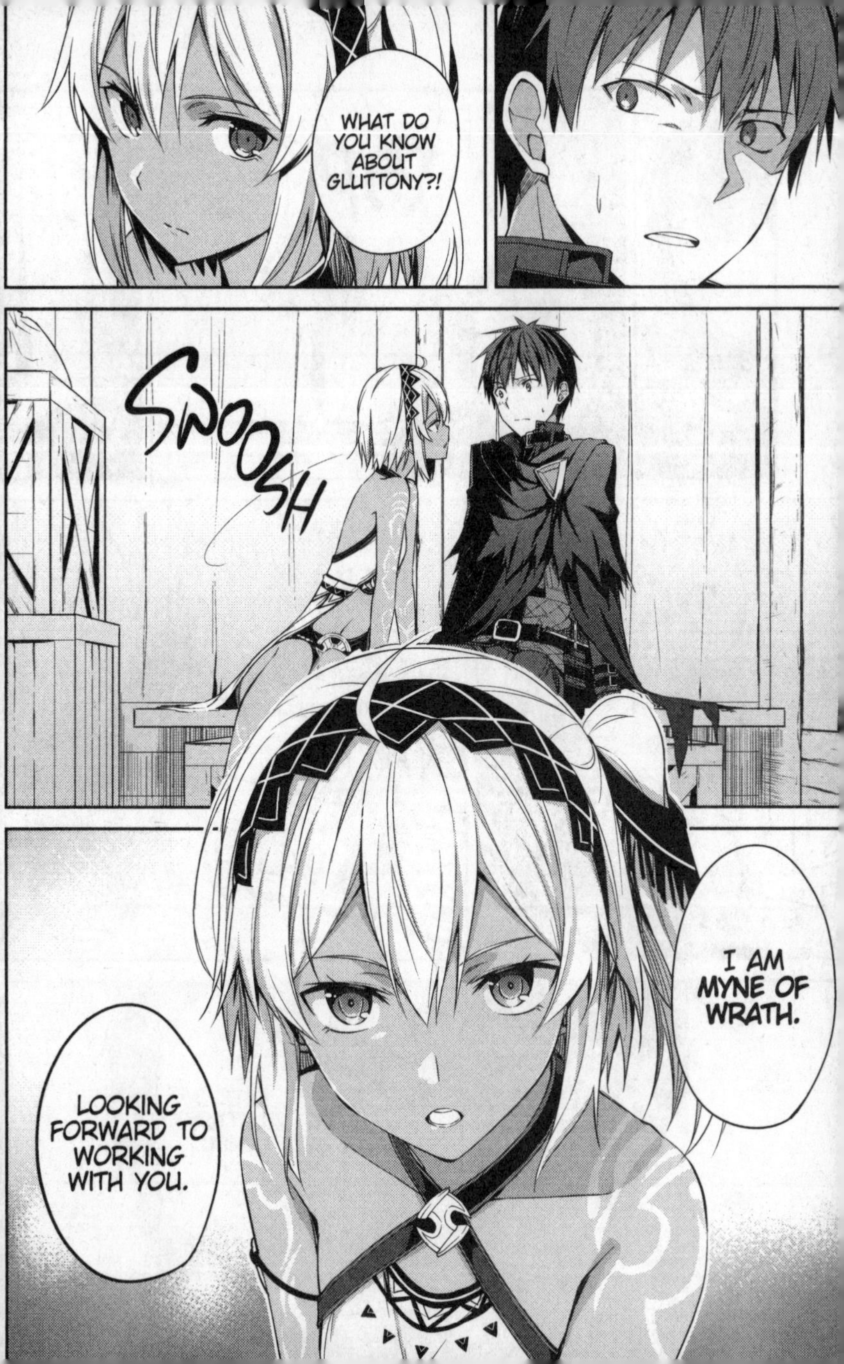
WHAT DO YOU KNOW ABOUT GLUTTONY?!
SWOOSH
I AM MYNE OF WRATH.
LOOKING FORWARD TO WORKING WITH YOU.

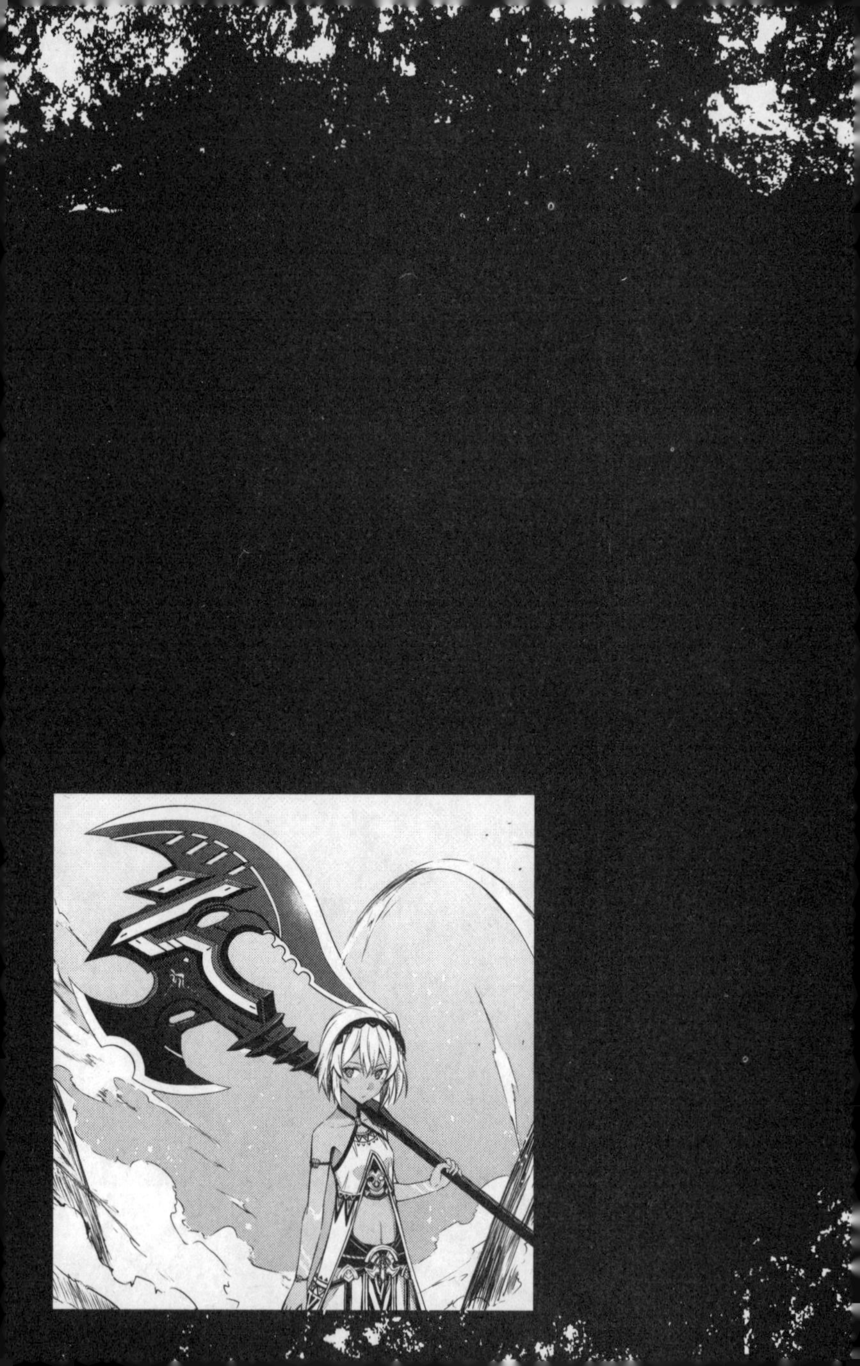

BERSERK OF GLUTTONY

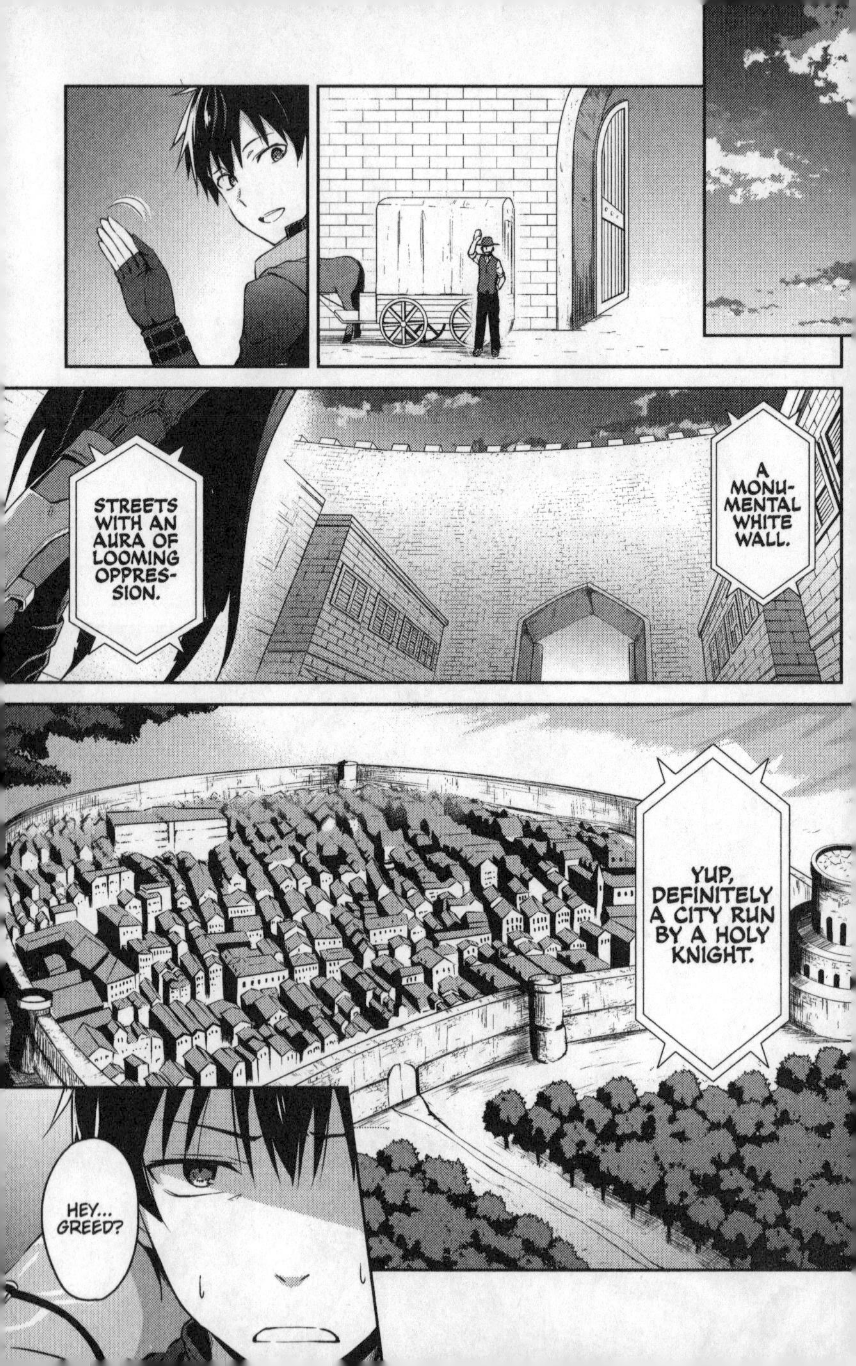
A MONUMENTAL WHITE WALL.
STREETS WITH AN AURA OF LOOMING OPPRESSION.
YUP, DEFINITELY A CITY RUN BY A HOLY KNIGHT.
HEY... GREED?

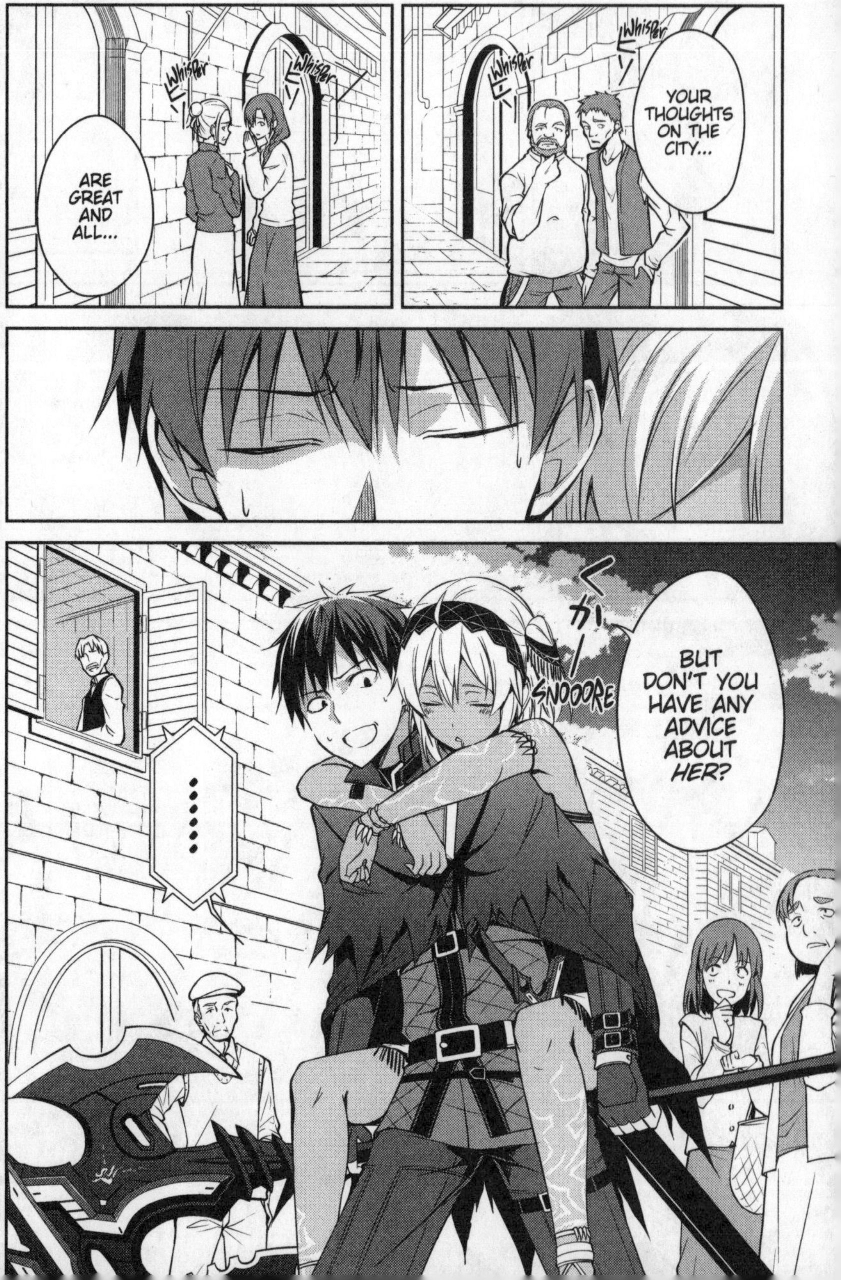
Whisper
YOUR THOUGHTS ON THE CITY...
Whisper
Whisper
ARE GREAT AND ALL...
BUT DON'T YOU HAVE ANY ADVICE ABOUT *HER*?
SNOOORE
......

Chapter 14 ✣ The Desert of Extinction

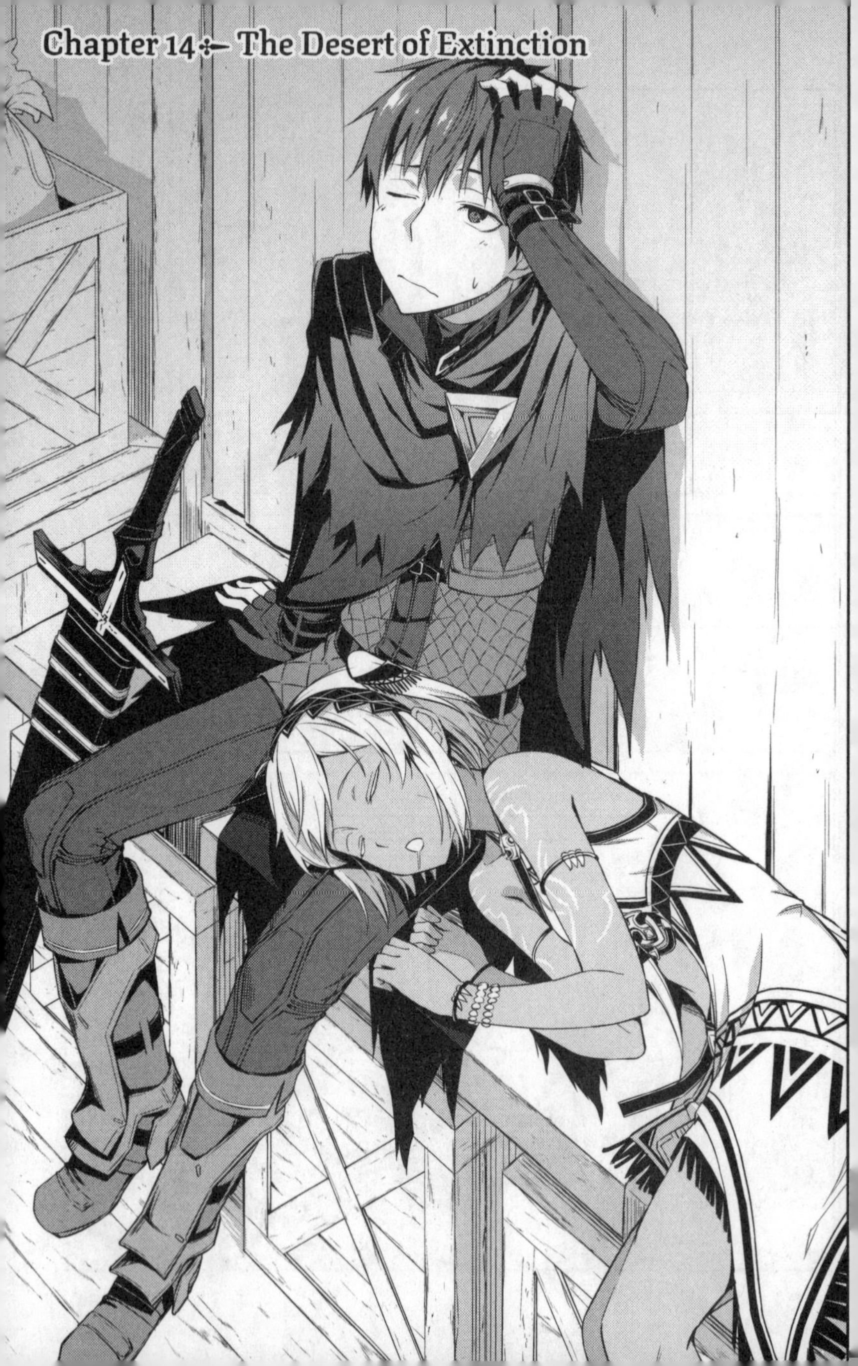

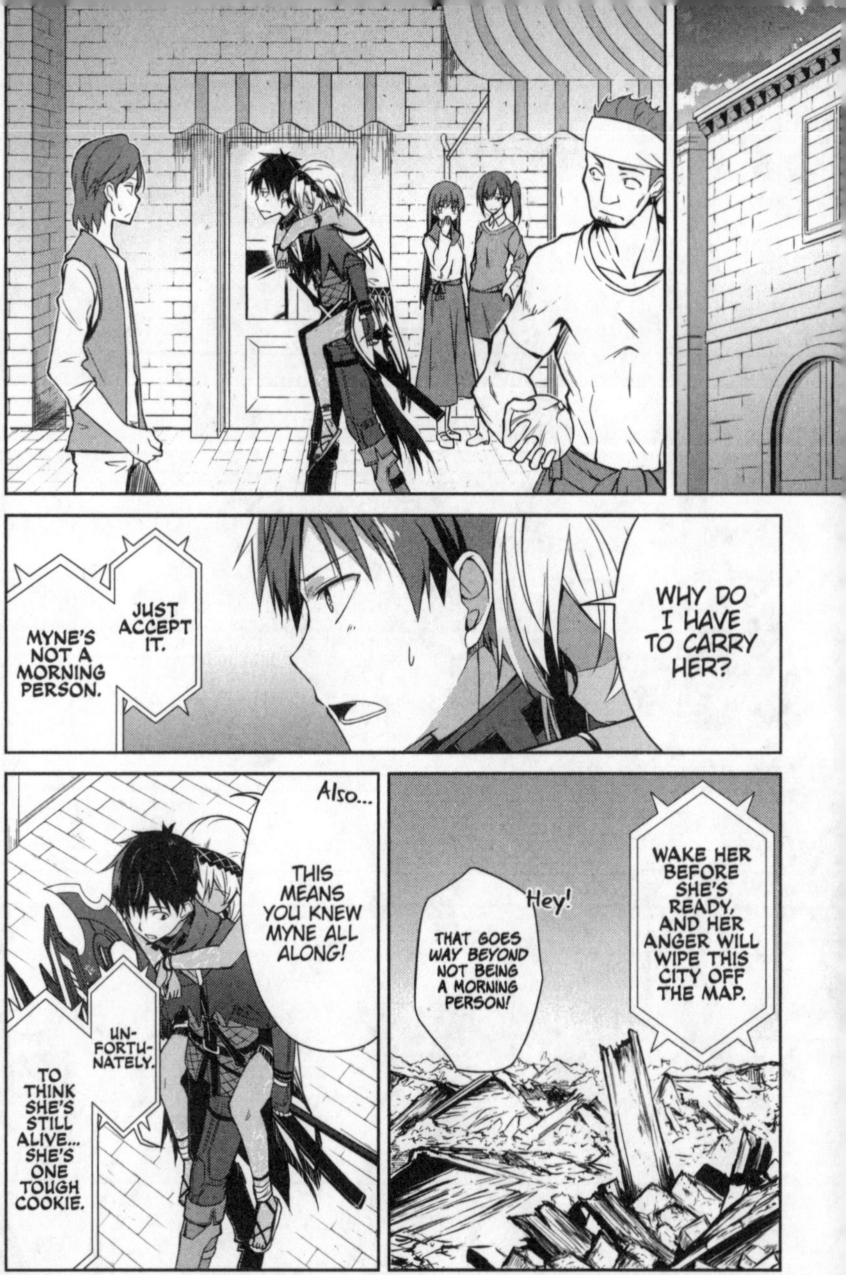
WHY DO I HAVE TO CARRY HER?
JUST ACCEPT IT.
MYNE'S NOT A MORNING PERSON.
WAKE HER BEFORE SHE'S READY, AND HER ANGER WILL WIPE THIS CITY OFF THE MAP.
Hey!
THAT GOES WAY BEYOND NOT BEING A MORNING PERSON!
Also...
THIS MEANS YOU KNEW MYNE ALL ALONG!
UN-FORTU-NATELY.
TO THINK SHE'S STILL ALIVE... SHE'S ONE TOUGH COOKIE.

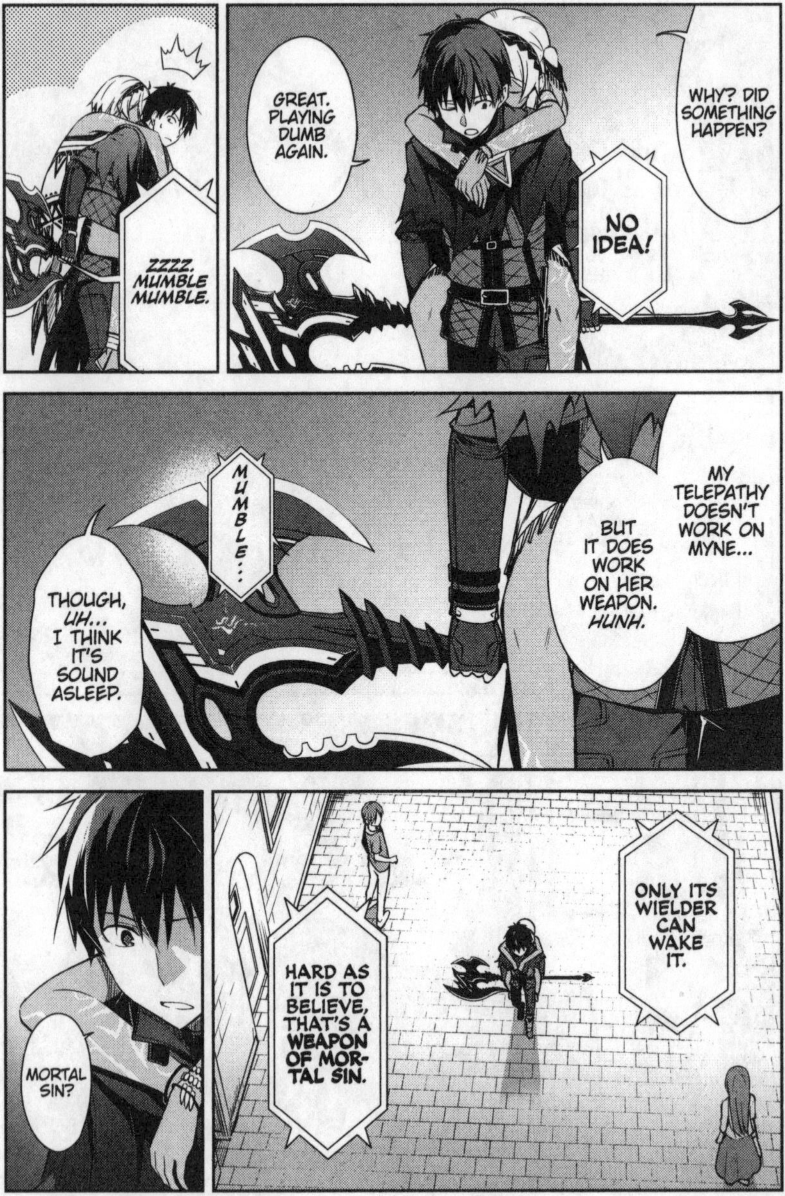
WHY? DID SOMETHING HAPPEN?
NO IDEA!
GREAT. PLAYING DUMB AGAIN.
ZZZZ. MUMBLE MUMBLE.
MY TELEPATHY DOESN'T WORK ON MYNE...
BUT IT DOES WORK ON HER WEAPON. HUNH.
MUMBLE...
THOUGH, UH... I THINK IT'S SOUND ASLEEP.
ONLY ITS WIELDER CAN WAKE IT.
HARD AS IT IS TO BELIEVE, THAT'S A WEAPON OF MORTAL SIN.
MORTAL SIN?

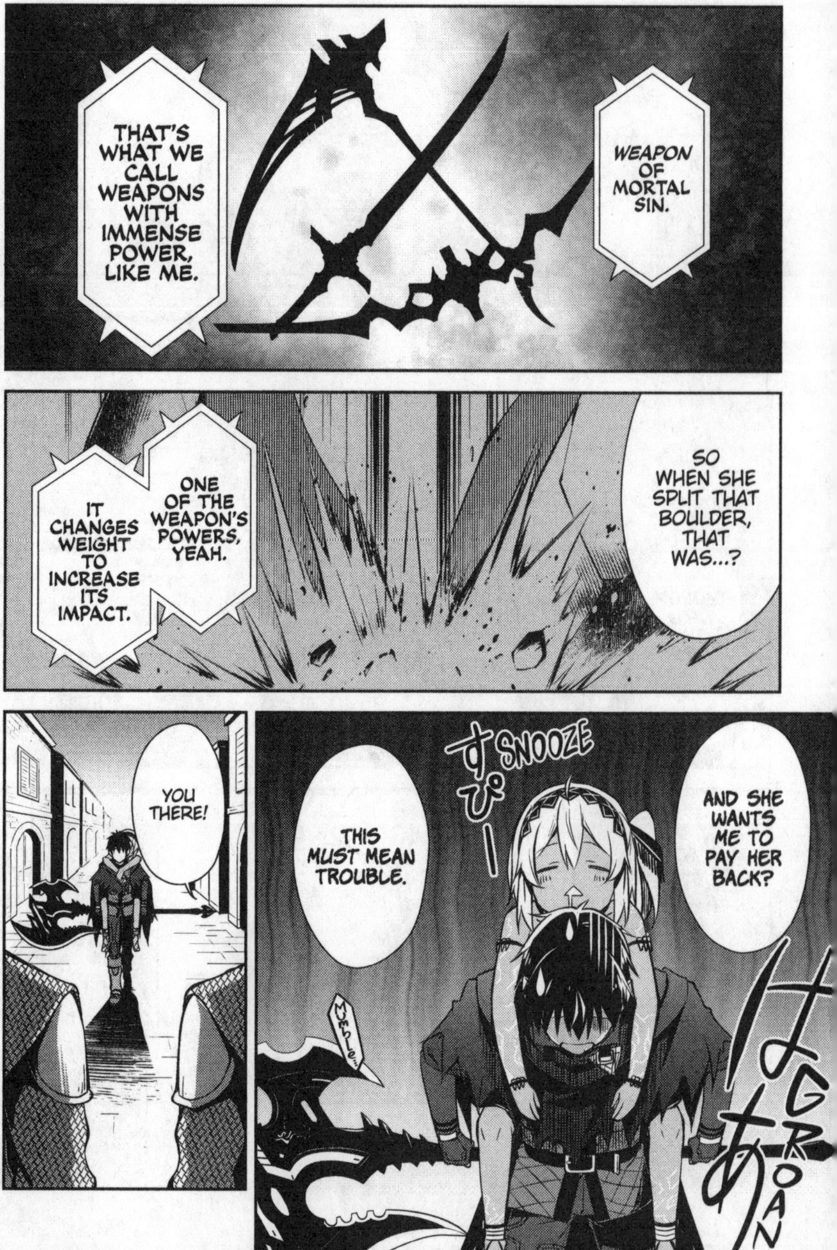
WEAPON OF MORTAL SIN.
THAT'S WHAT WE CALL WEAPONS WITH IMMENSE POWER, LIKE ME.
SO WHEN SHE SPLIT THAT BOULDER, THAT WAS...?
ONE OF THE WEAPON'S POWERS, YEAH.
IT CHANGES WEIGHT TO INCREASE ITS IMPACT.
AND SHE WANTS ME TO PAY HER BACK?
GROAN
すぴー
SNOOZE
THIS MUST MEAN TROUBLE.
MUMBLE...
YOU THERE!

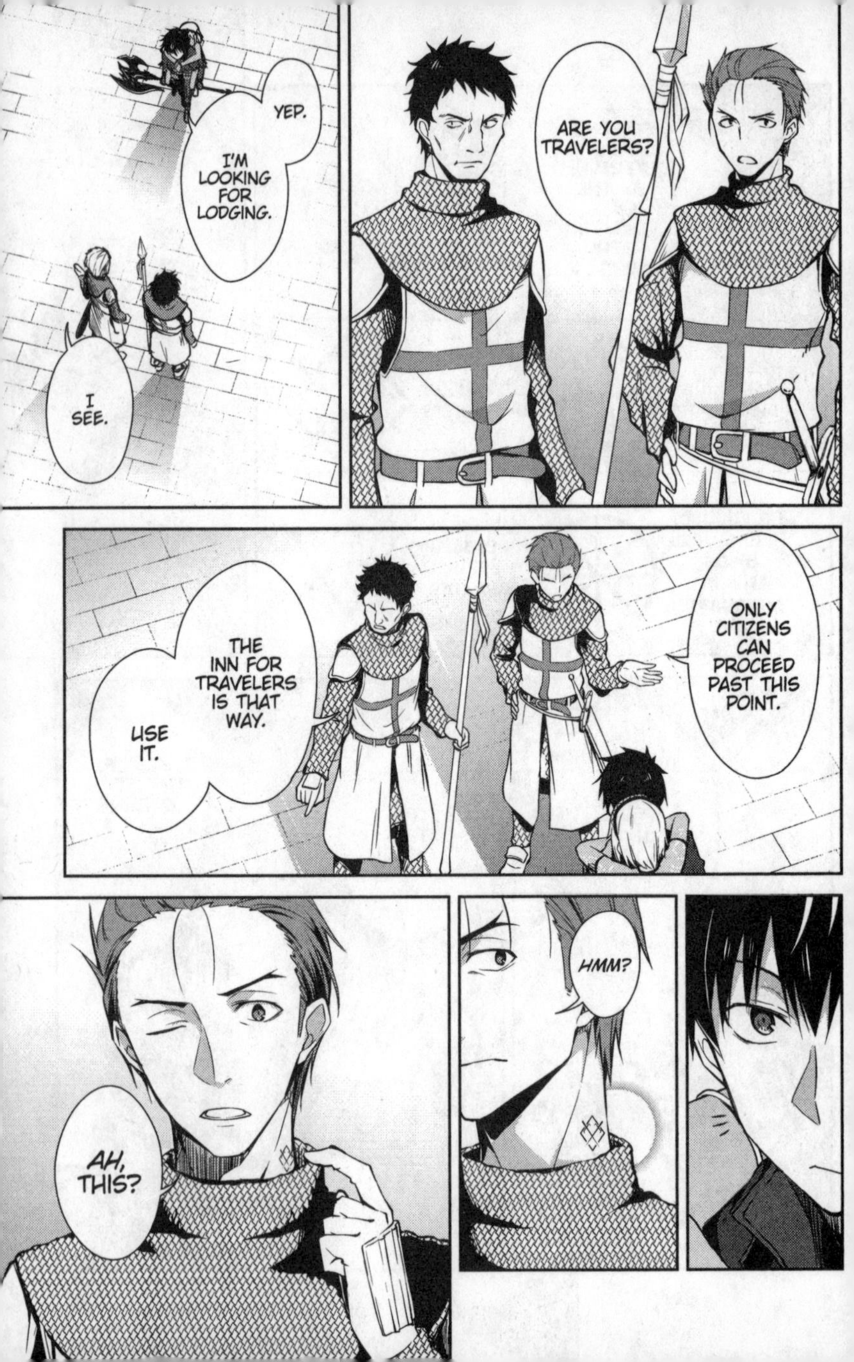
ARE YOU TRAVELERS?
YEP.
I'M LOOKING FOR LODGING.
I SEE.
ONLY CITIZENS CAN PROCEED PAST THIS POINT.
THE INN FOR TRAVELERS IS THAT WAY.
USE IT.
HMM?
AH, THIS?

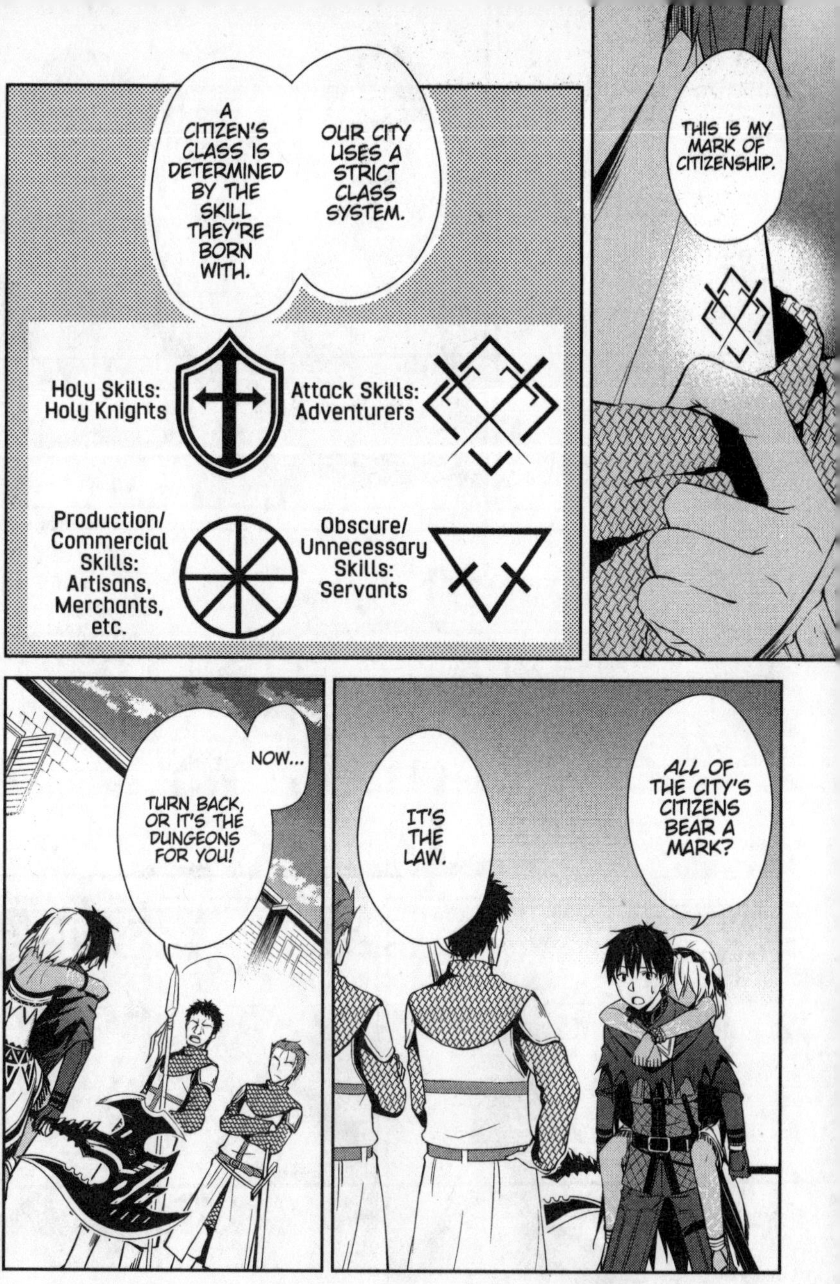
THIS IS MY MARK OF CITIZENSHIP.
OUR CITY USES A STRICT CLASS SYSTEM.
A CITIZEN'S CLASS IS DETERMINED BY THE SKILL THEY'RE BORN WITH.
Holy Skills: Holy Knights
Attack Skills: Adventurers
Production/ Commercial Skills: Artisans, Merchants, etc.
Obscure/ Unnecessary Skills: Servants
ALL OF THE CITY'S CITIZENS BEAR A MARK?
IT'S THE LAW.
NOW...
TURN BACK, OR IT'S THE DUNGEONS FOR YOU!

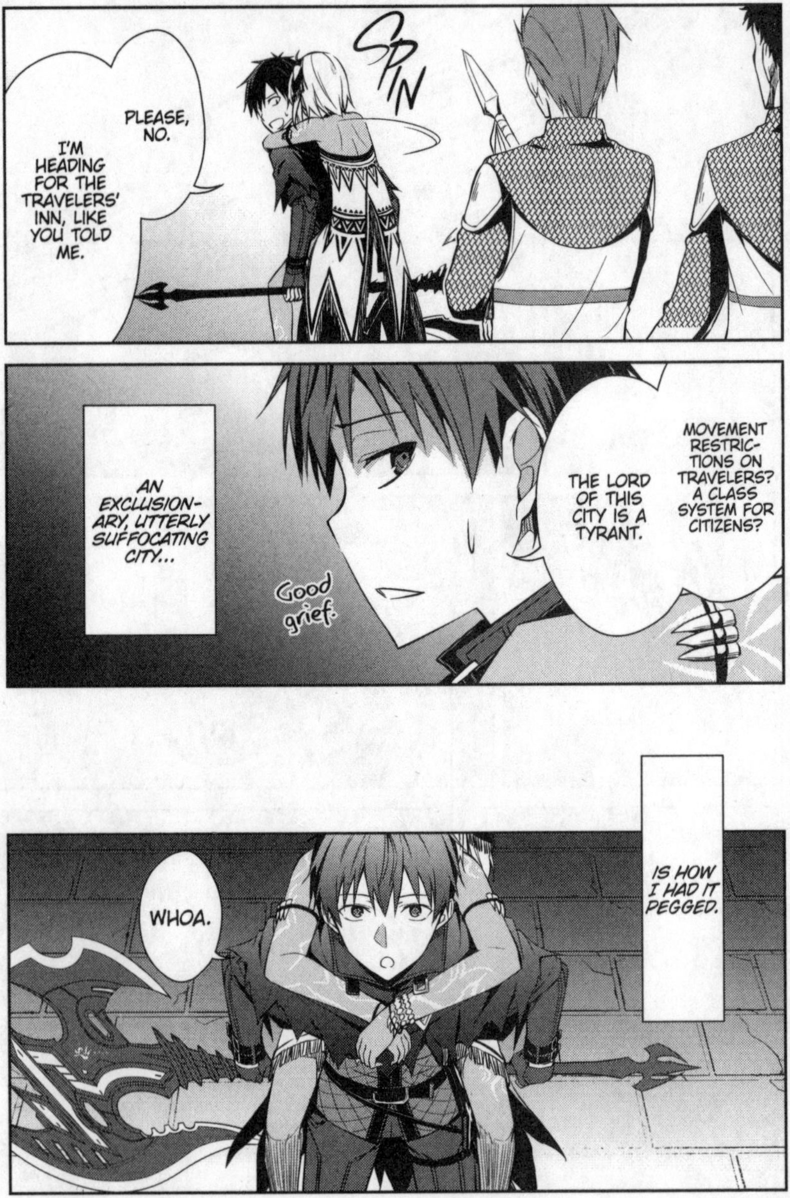
SPIN
PLEASE, NO.
I'M HEADING FOR THE TRAVELERS' INN, LIKE YOU TOLD ME.
MOVEMENT RESTRICTIONS ON TRAVELERS? A CLASS SYSTEM FOR CITIZENS?
THE LORD OF THIS CITY IS A TYRANT.
Good grief.
AN EXCLUSIONARY, UTTERLY SUFFOCATING CITY...
IS HOW I HAD IT PEGGED.
WHOA.

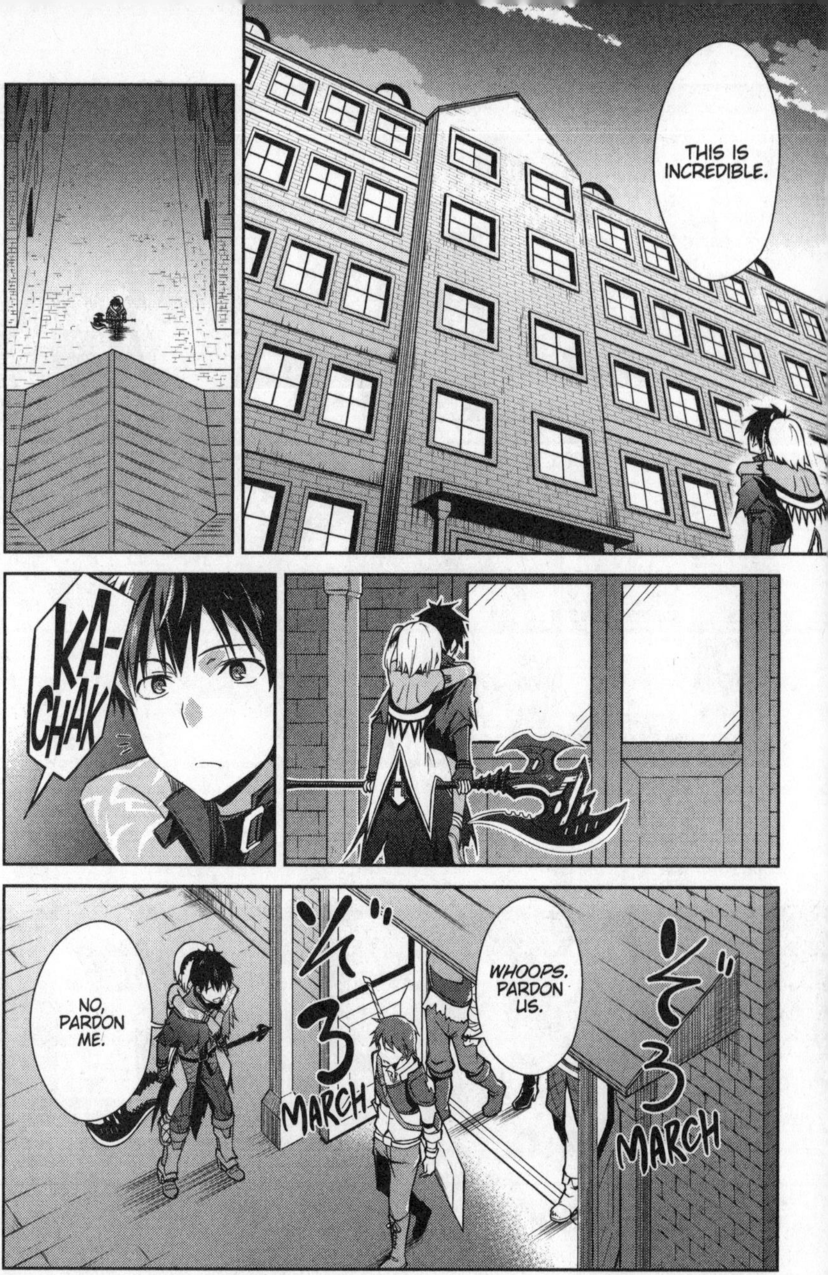
THIS IS INCREDIBLE.
KA-CHAK
WHOOPS. PARDON US.
MARCH
MARCH
NO, PARDON ME.

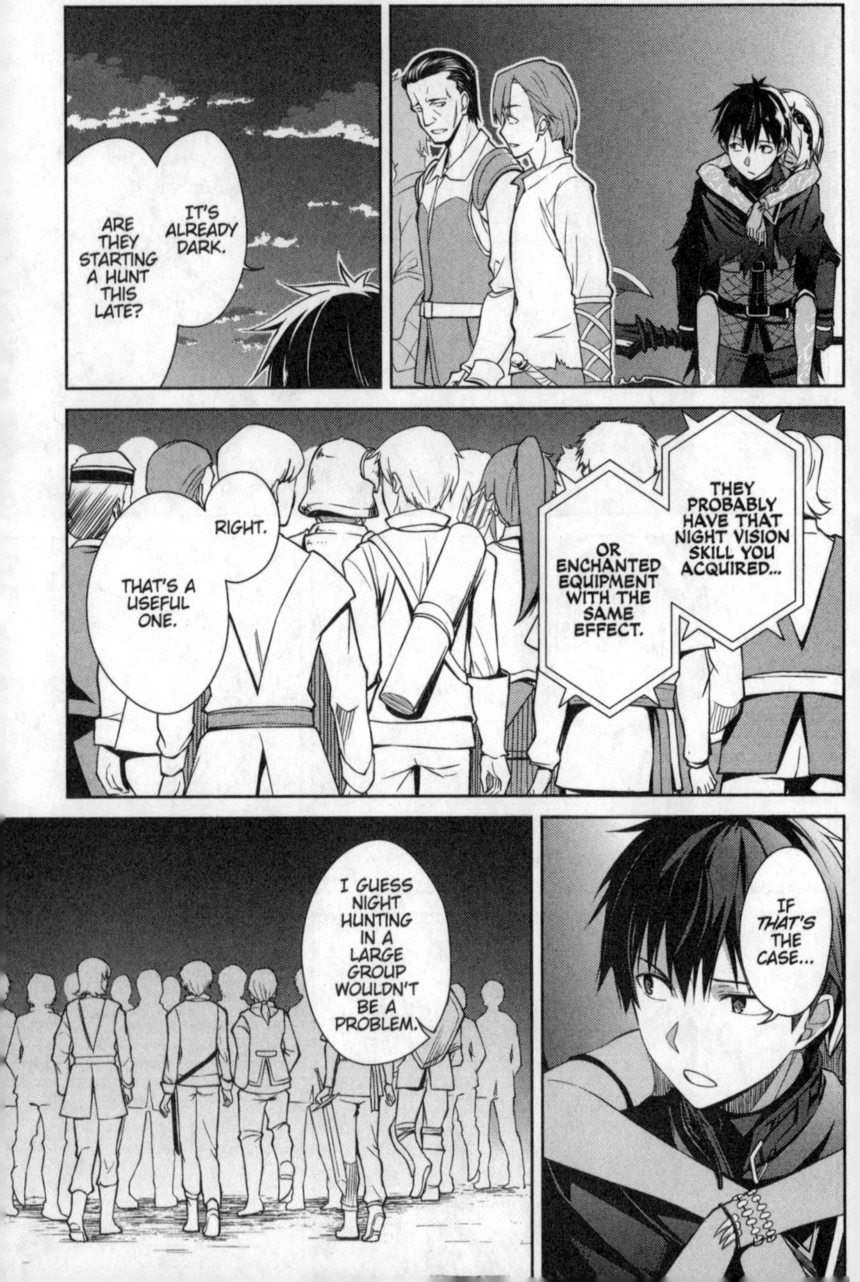
IT'S ALREADY DARK.
ARE THEY STARTING A HUNT THIS LATE?
THEY PROBABLY HAVE THAT NIGHT VISION SKILL YOU ACQUIRED...
OR ENCHANTED EQUIPMENT WITH THE SAME EFFECT.
RIGHT.
THAT'S A USEFUL ONE.
IF *THAT'S* THE CASE...
I GUESS NIGHT HUNTING IN A LARGE GROUP WOULDN'T BE A PROBLEM.

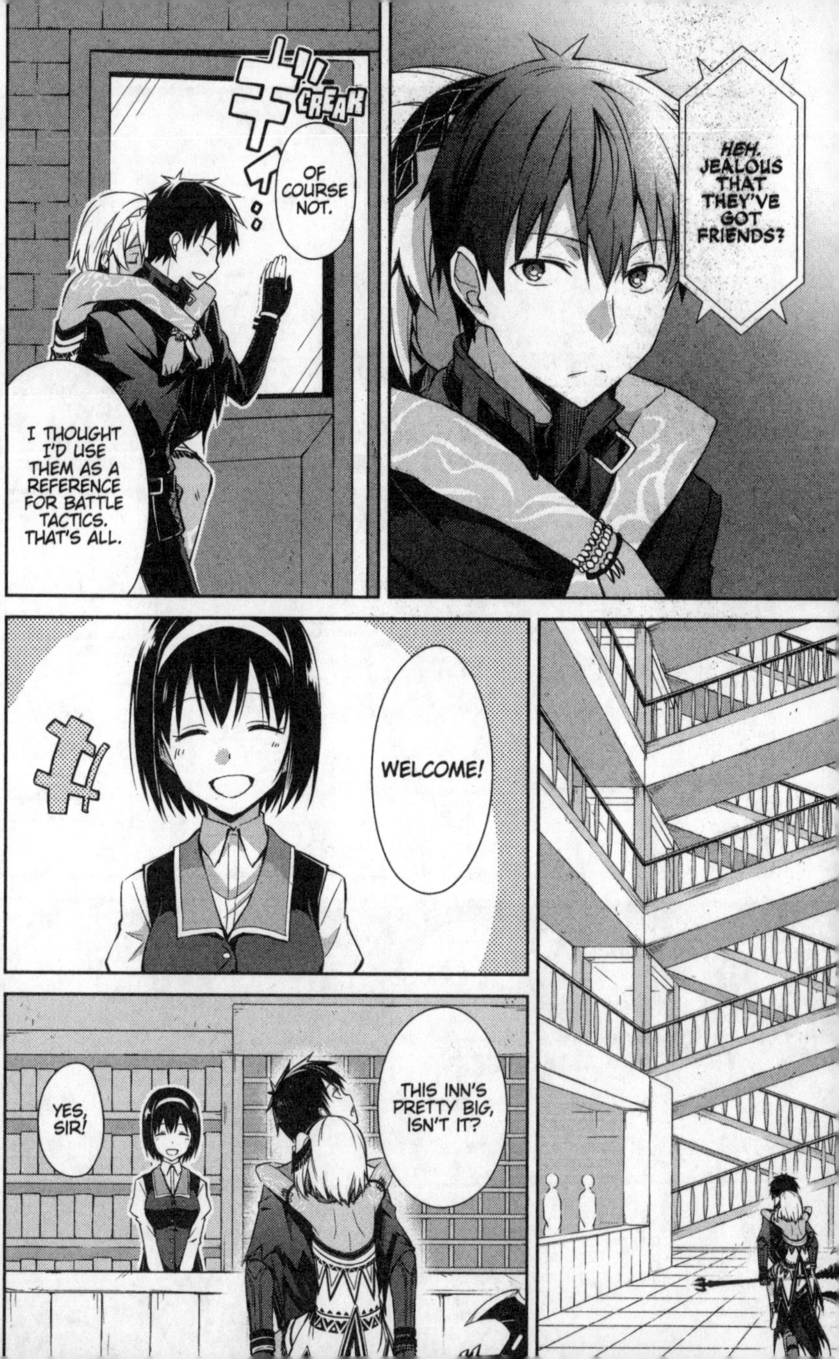
HEH. JEALOUS THAT THEY'VE GOT FRIENDS?
CREAK
OF COURSE NOT.
I THOUGHT I'D USE THEM AS A REFERENCE FOR BATTLE TACTICS. THAT'S ALL.
WELCOME!
THIS INN'S PRETTY BIG, ISN'T IT?
YES, SIR!

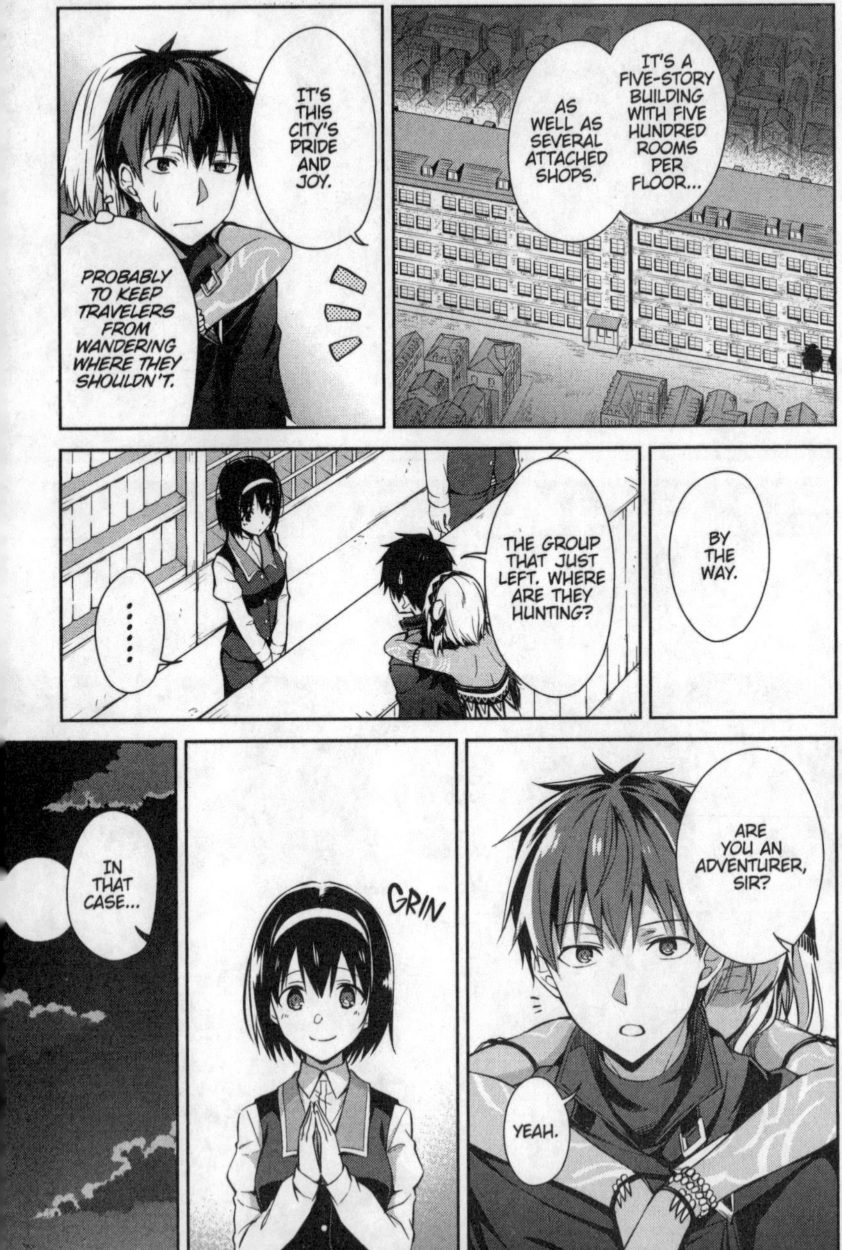
IT'S A FIVE-STORY BUILDING WITH FIVE HUNDRED ROOMS PER FLOOR...
AS WELL AS SEVERAL ATTACHED SHOPS.
IT'S THIS CITY'S PRIDE AND JOY.
PROBABLY TO KEEP TRAVELERS FROM WANDERING WHERE THEY SHOULDN'T.
BY THE WAY.
THE GROUP THAT JUST LEFT. WHERE ARE THEY HUNTING?
......
ARE YOU AN ADVENTURER, SIR?
YEAH.
GRIN
IN THAT CASE...

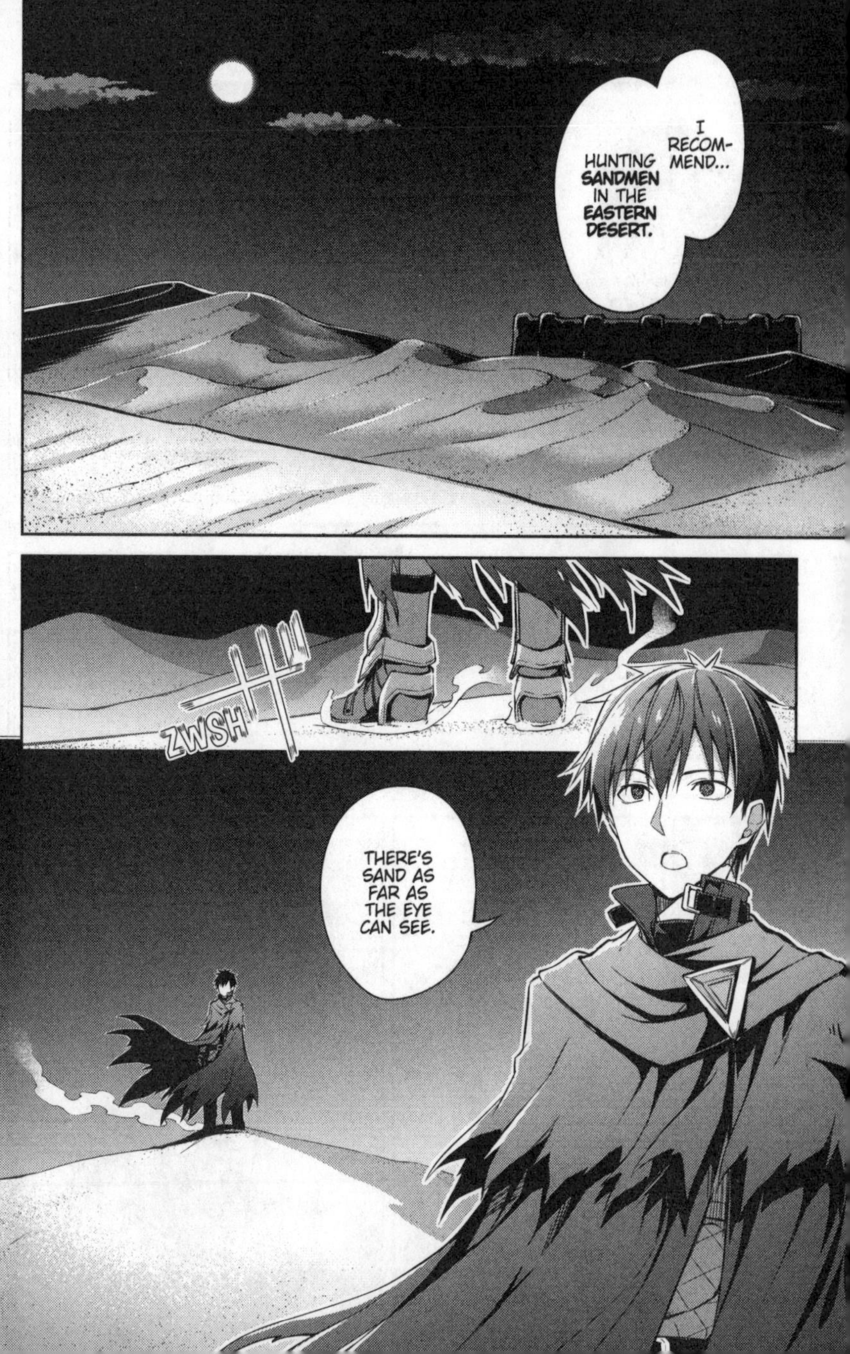
I RECOMMEND... HUNTING SANDMEN IN THE EASTERN DESERT.
ZWSH
THERE'S SAND AS FAR AS THE EYE CAN SEE.

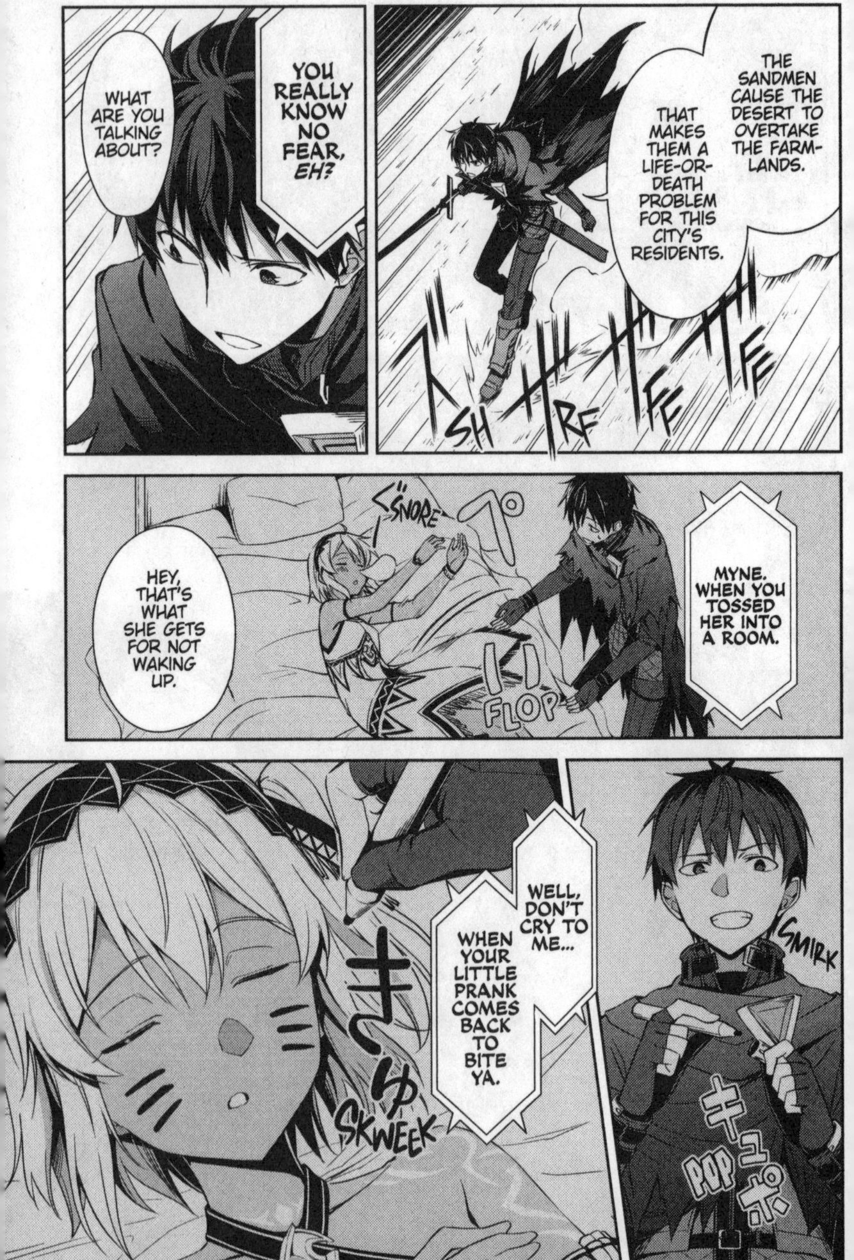
THE SANDMEN CAUSE THE DESERT TO OVERTAKE THE FARMLANDS.
THAT MAKES THEM A LIFE-OR-DEATH PROBLEM FOR THIS CITY'S RESIDENTS.
SH RF F F
YOU REALLY KNOW NO FEAR, EH?
WHAT ARE YOU TALKING ABOUT?
MYNE. WHEN YOU TOSSED HER INTO A ROOM.
SNORE
HEY, THAT'S WHAT SHE GETS FOR NOT WAKING UP.
FLOP
SMIRK
キュポ
POP
WELL, DON'T CRY TO ME...
WHEN YOUR LITTLE PRANK COMES BACK TO BITE YA.
きゅ
SKWEEK

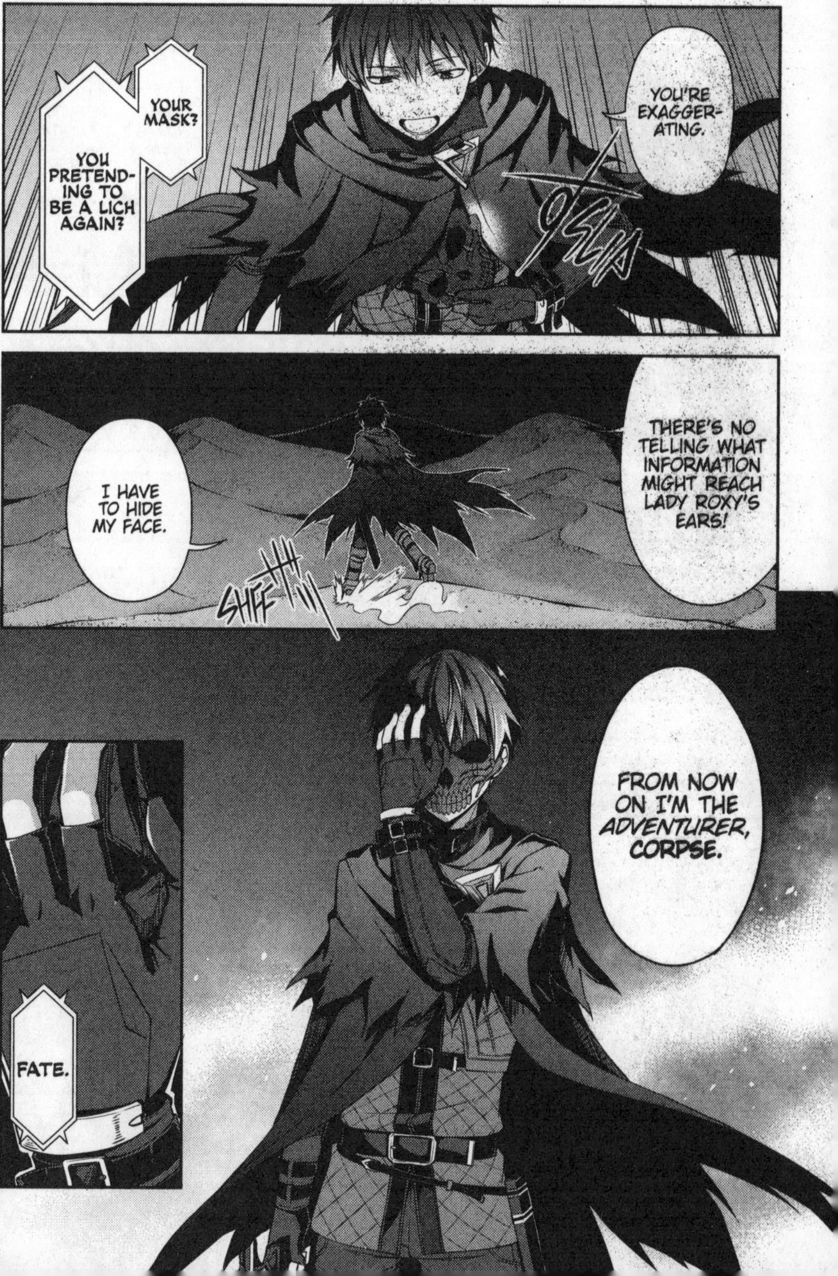
YOU'RE EXAGGERATING.
YOUR MASK?
YOU PRETENDING TO BE A LICH AGAIN?
THERE'S NO TELLING WHAT INFORMATION MIGHT REACH LADY ROXY'S EARS!
I HAVE TO HIDE MY FACE.
SHFF
FROM NOW ON I'M THE *ADVENTURER*, CORPSE.
FATE.

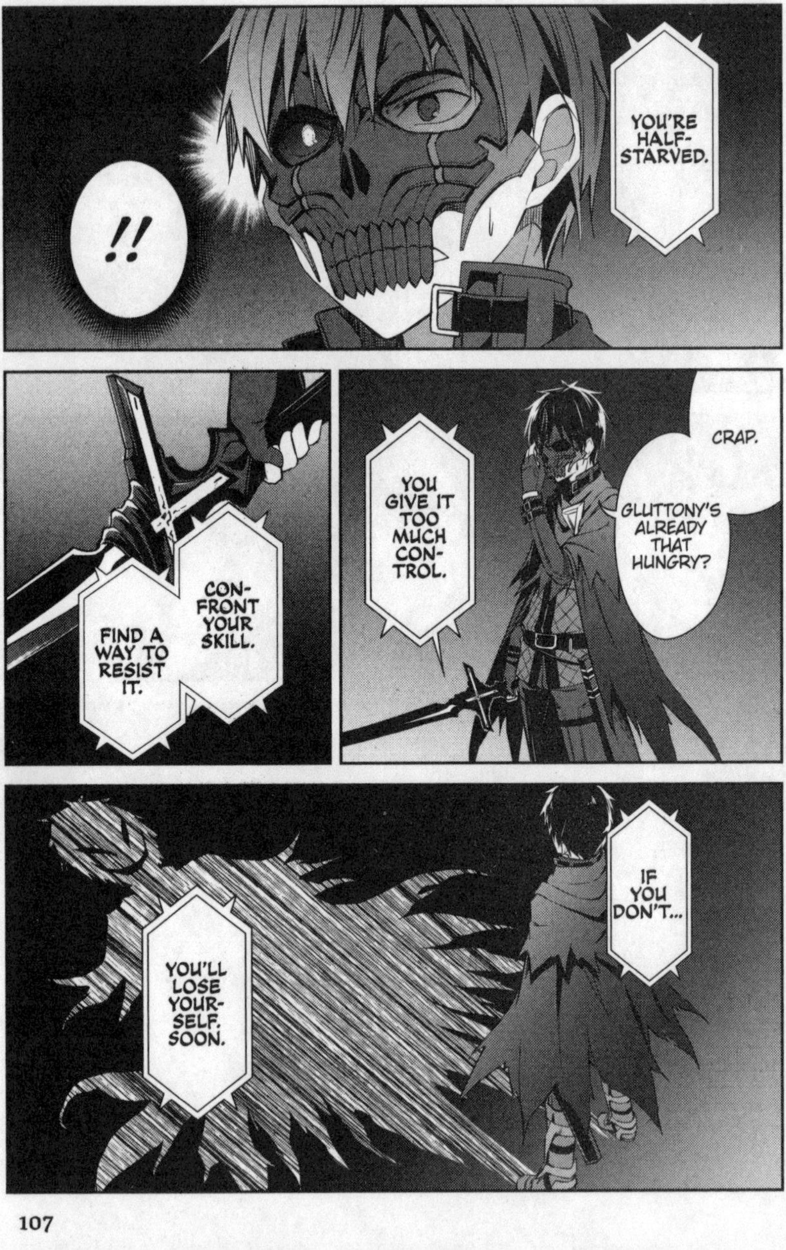
YOU'RE HALF-STARVED.
!!
CRAP.
GLUTTONY'S ALREADY THAT HUNGRY?
YOU GIVE IT TOO MUCH CONTROL.
CONFRONT YOUR SKILL.
FIND A WAY TO RESIST IT.
IF YOU DON'T...
YOU'LL LOSE YOURSELF. SOON.

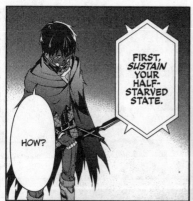

FIRST, *SUSTAIN* YOUR HALF-STARVED STATE.

HOW?

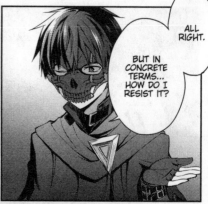

ALL RIGHT.

BUT IN CONCRETE TERMS... HOW DO I RESIST IT?

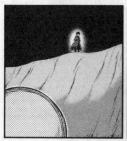

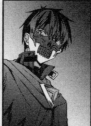

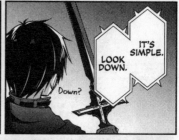

IT'S SIMPLE.

LOOK DOWN.

Down?

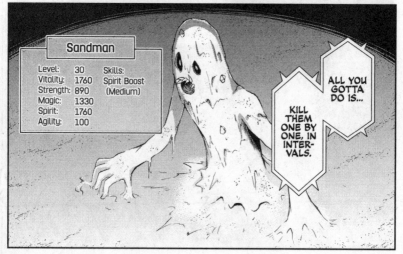

Sandman

Level:	30	Skills:
Vitality:	1760	Spirit Boost
Strength:	890	(Medium)
Magic:	1330	
Spirit:	1760	
Agility:	100	

ALL YOU GOTTA DO IS...

KILL THEM ONE BY ONE, IN INTERVALS.

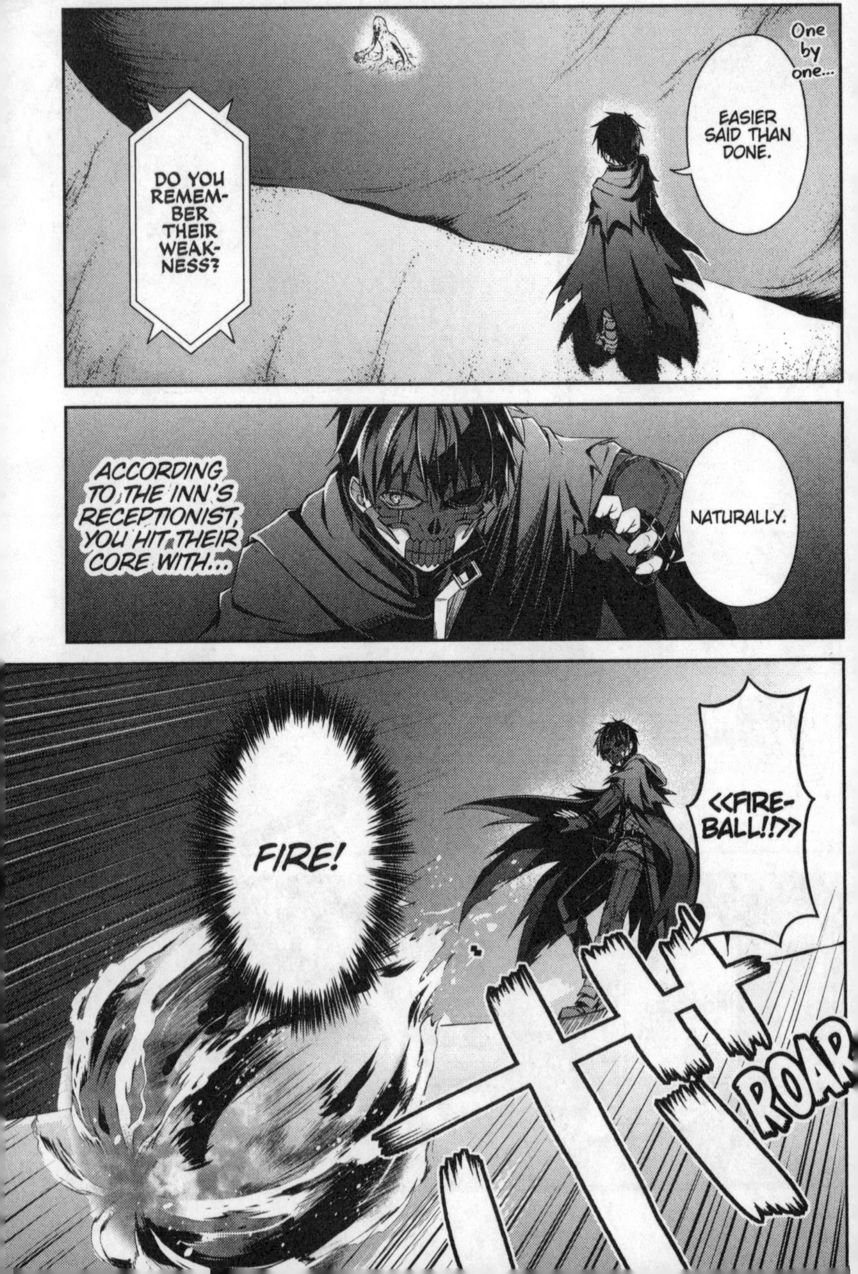
One by one...
EASIER SAID THAN DONE.
DO YOU REMEMBER THEIR WEAKNESS?
NATURALLY.
ACCORDING TO THE INN'S RECEPTIONIST, YOU HIT THEIR CORE WITH...
<<FIREBALL!!>>
FIRE!
ROAR

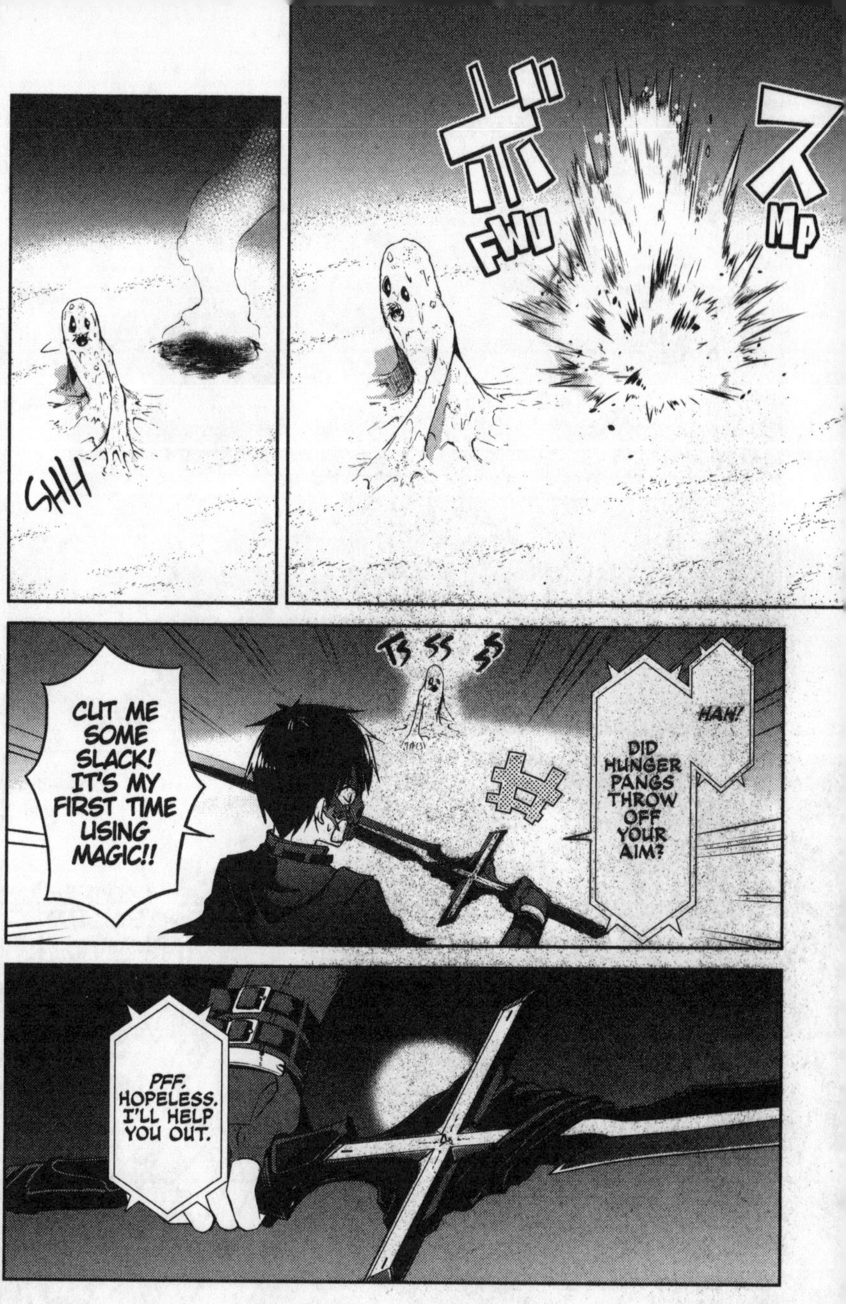
ボス
FWU Mp
SHH
HAH!
DID HUNGER PANGS THROW OFF YOUR AIM?
TS SS S
CUT ME SOME SLACK! IT'S MY FIRST TIME USING MAGIC!!
PFF. HOPELESS. I'LL HELP YOU OUT.

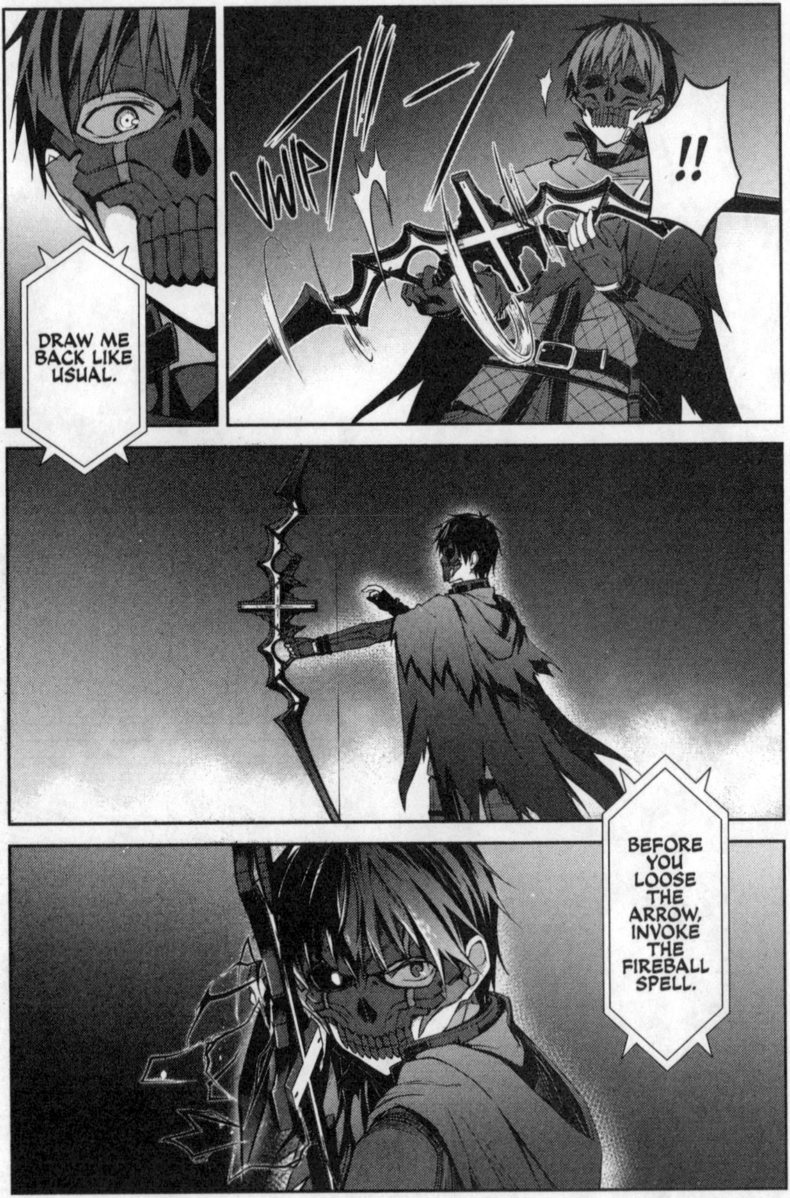
VWIP
!!
DRAW ME BACK LIKE USUAL.
BEFORE YOU LOOSE THE ARROW, INVOKE THE FIREBALL SPELL.

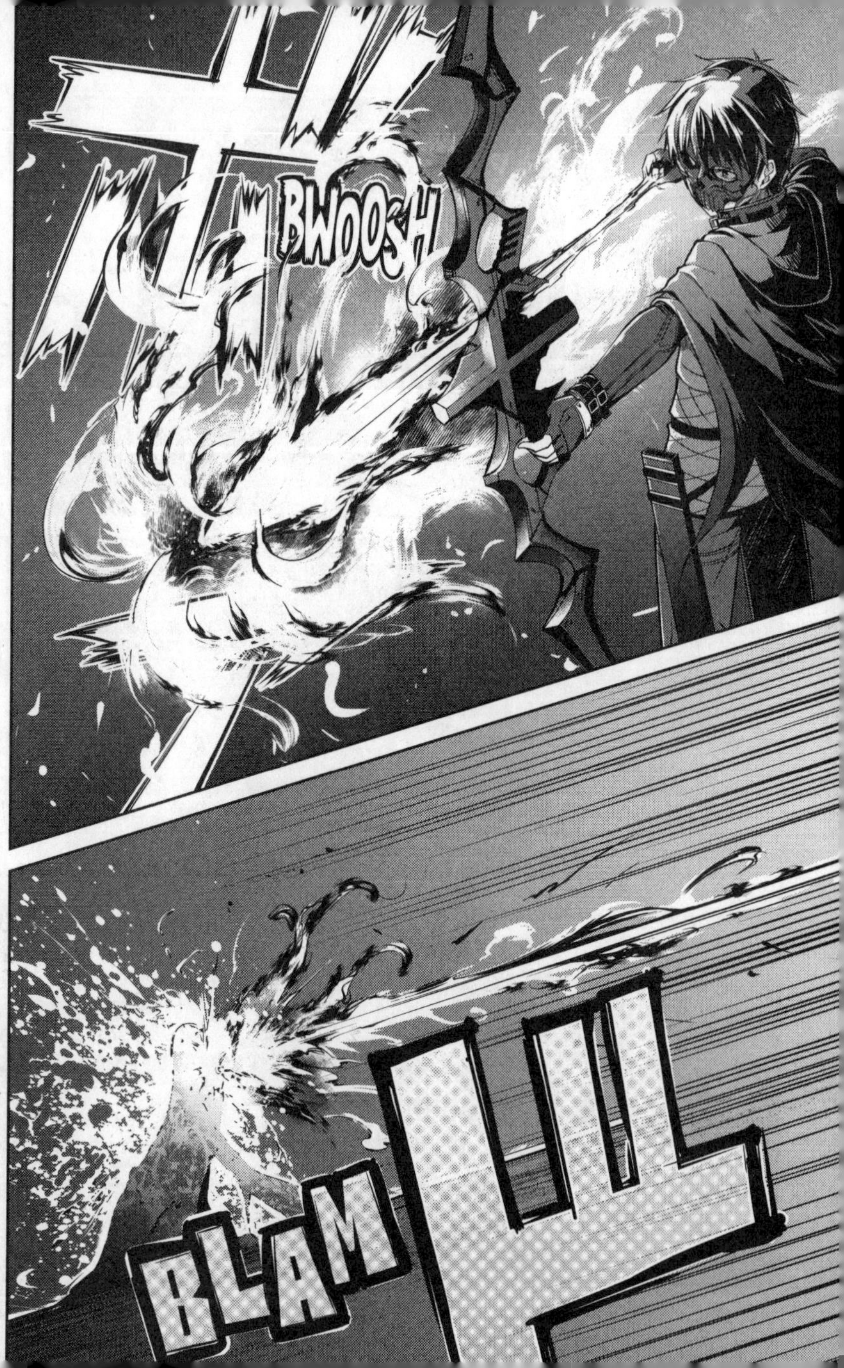
BWOOSH
BLAM

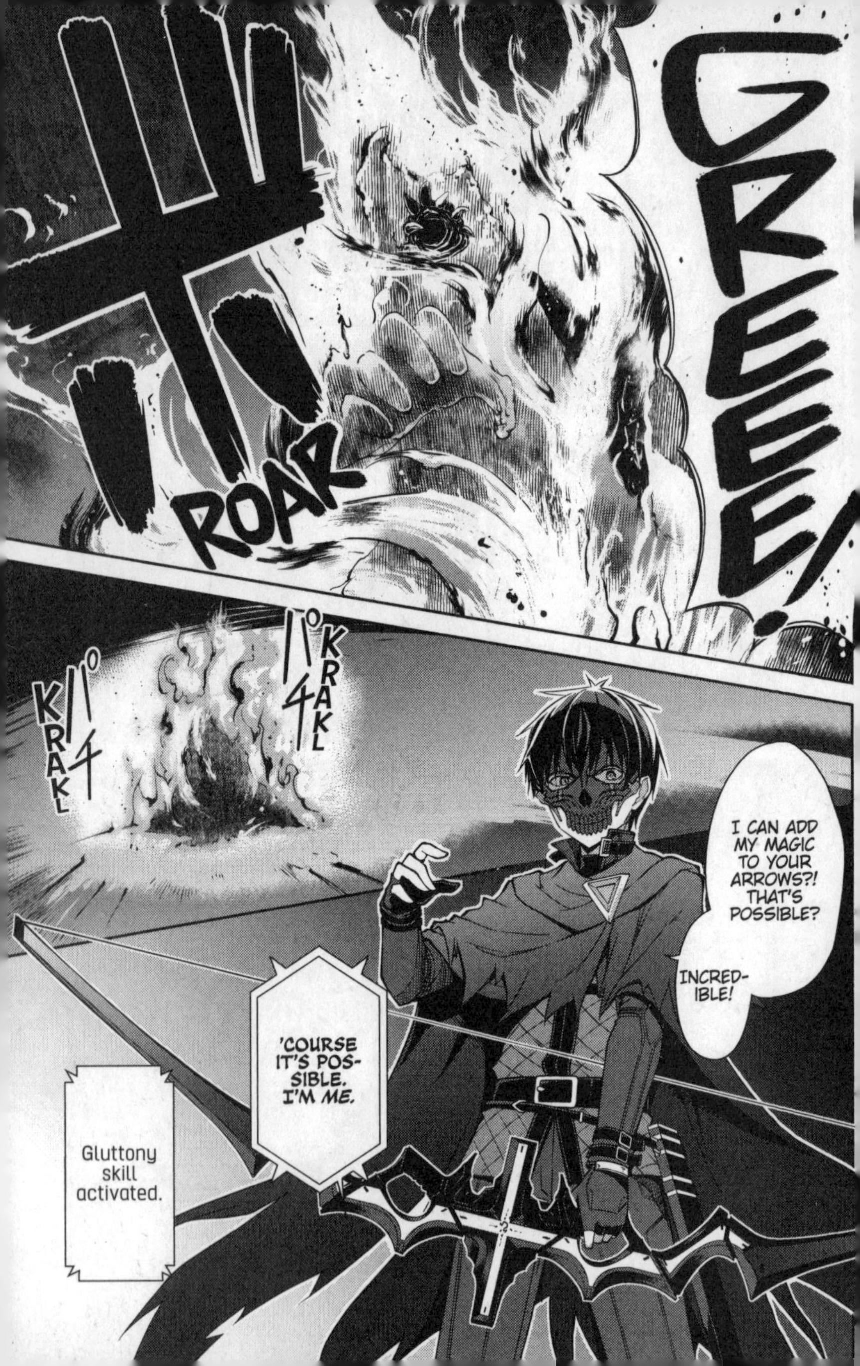
GREEE!
ROAR
パチ KRAKL
パチ KRAKL
I CAN ADD MY MAGIC TO YOUR ARROWS?! THAT'S POSSIBLE?
INCRED-IBLE!
'COURSE IT'S POS-SIBLE. I'M *ME.*
Gluttony skill activated.

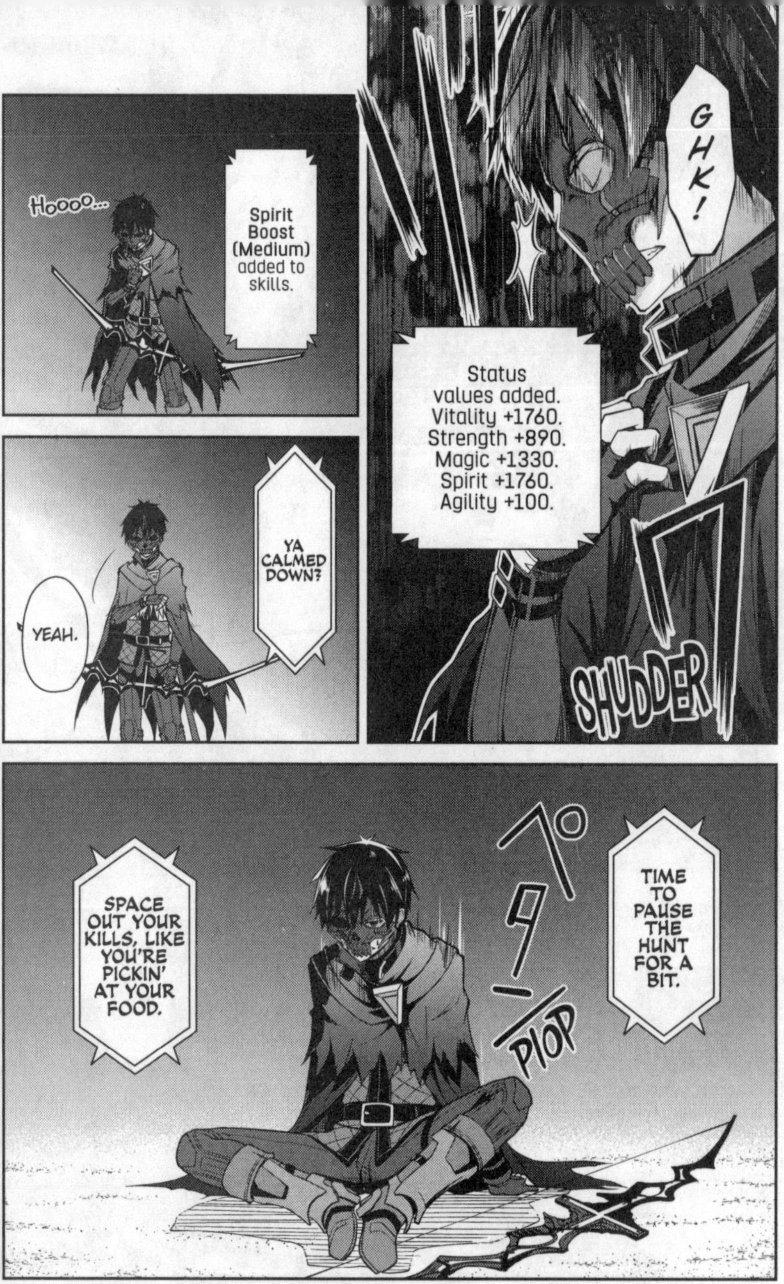
GHK!
Status values added. Vitality +1760. Strength +890. Magic +1330. Spirit +1760. Agility +100.
SHUDDER
Hoooo...
Spirit Boost (Medium) added to skills.
YA CALMED DOWN?
YEAH.
TIME TO PAUSE THE HUNT FOR A BIT.
PLOP
SPACE OUT YOUR KILLS, LIKE YOU'RE PICKIN' AT YOUR FOOD.

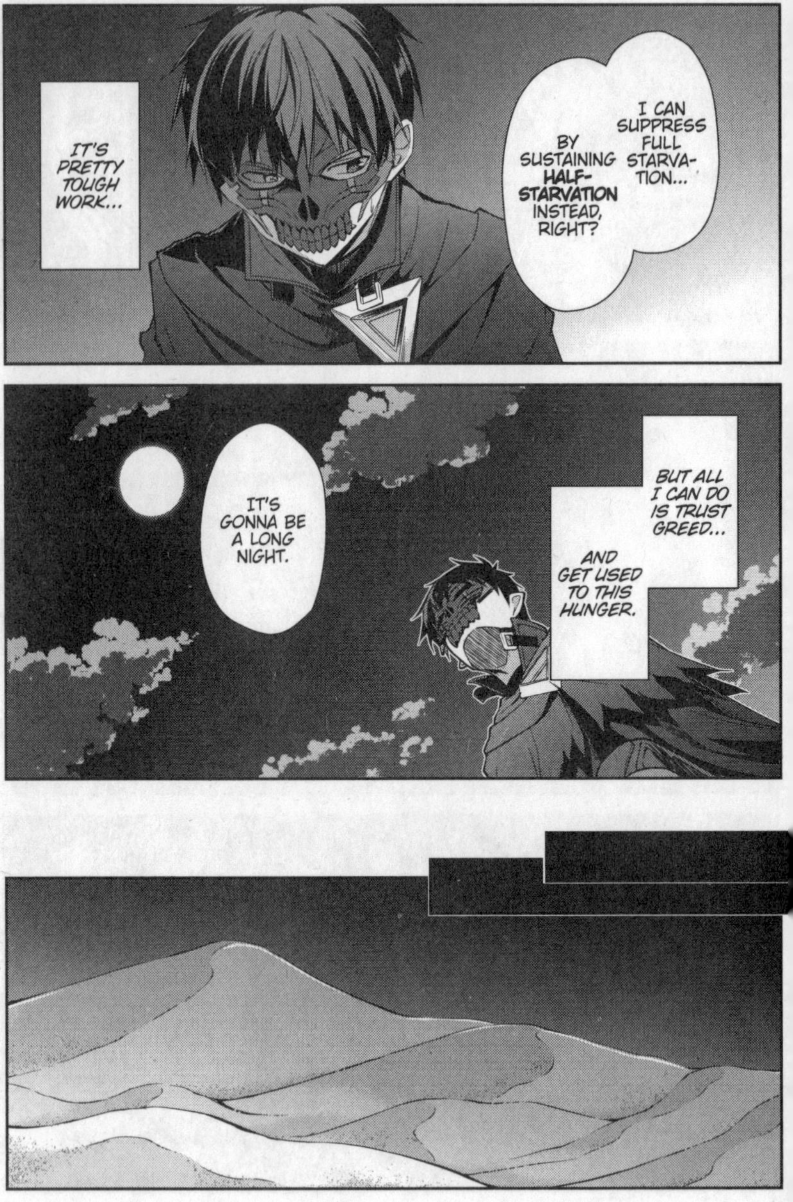
I CAN SUPPRESS FULL STARVATION...
BY SUSTAINING HALF-STARVATION INSTEAD, RIGHT?
IT'S PRETTY TOUGH WORK...
BUT ALL I CAN DO IS TRUST GREED...
AND GET USED TO THIS HUNGER.
IT'S GONNA BE A LONG NIGHT.

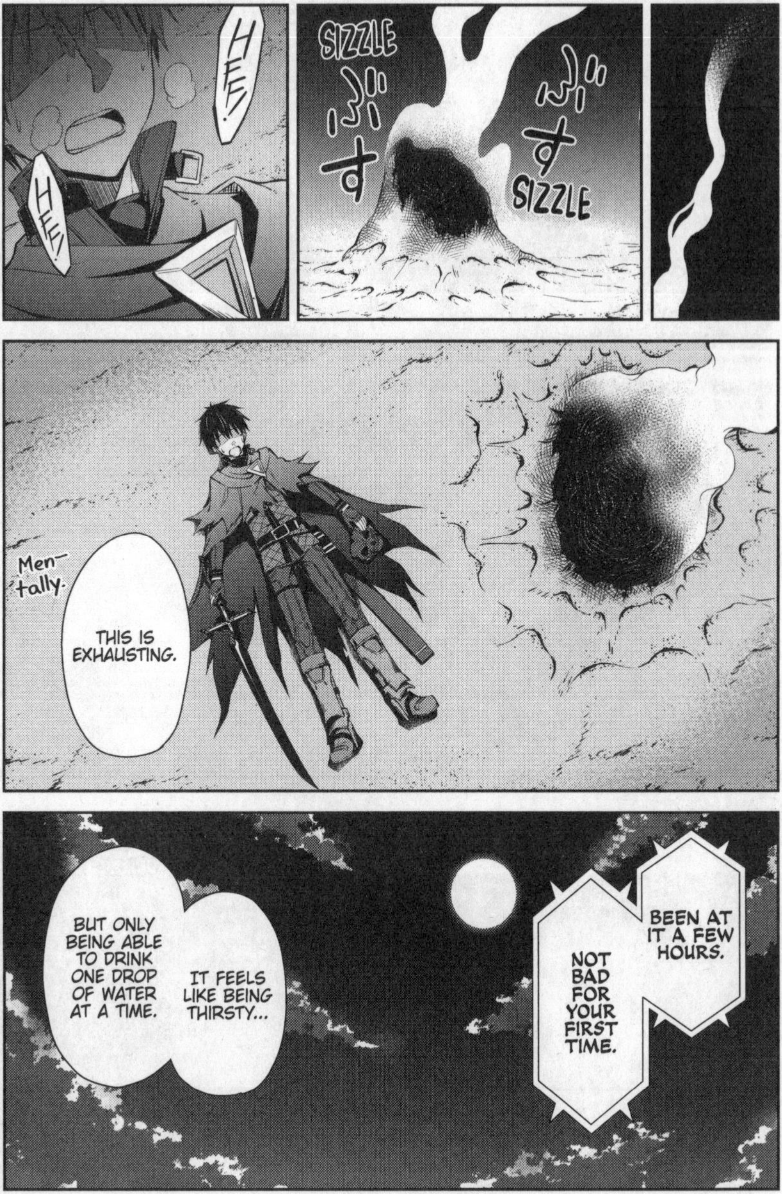
ぶす
SIZZLE
SIZZLE
ぶす
HEH!
HEH!
THIS IS EXHAUSTING.
Men-tally.
BEEN AT IT A FEW HOURS.
NOT BAD FOR YOUR FIRST TIME.
IT FEELS LIKE BEING THIRSTY...
BUT ONLY BEING ABLE TO DRINK ONE DROP OF WATER AT A TIME.

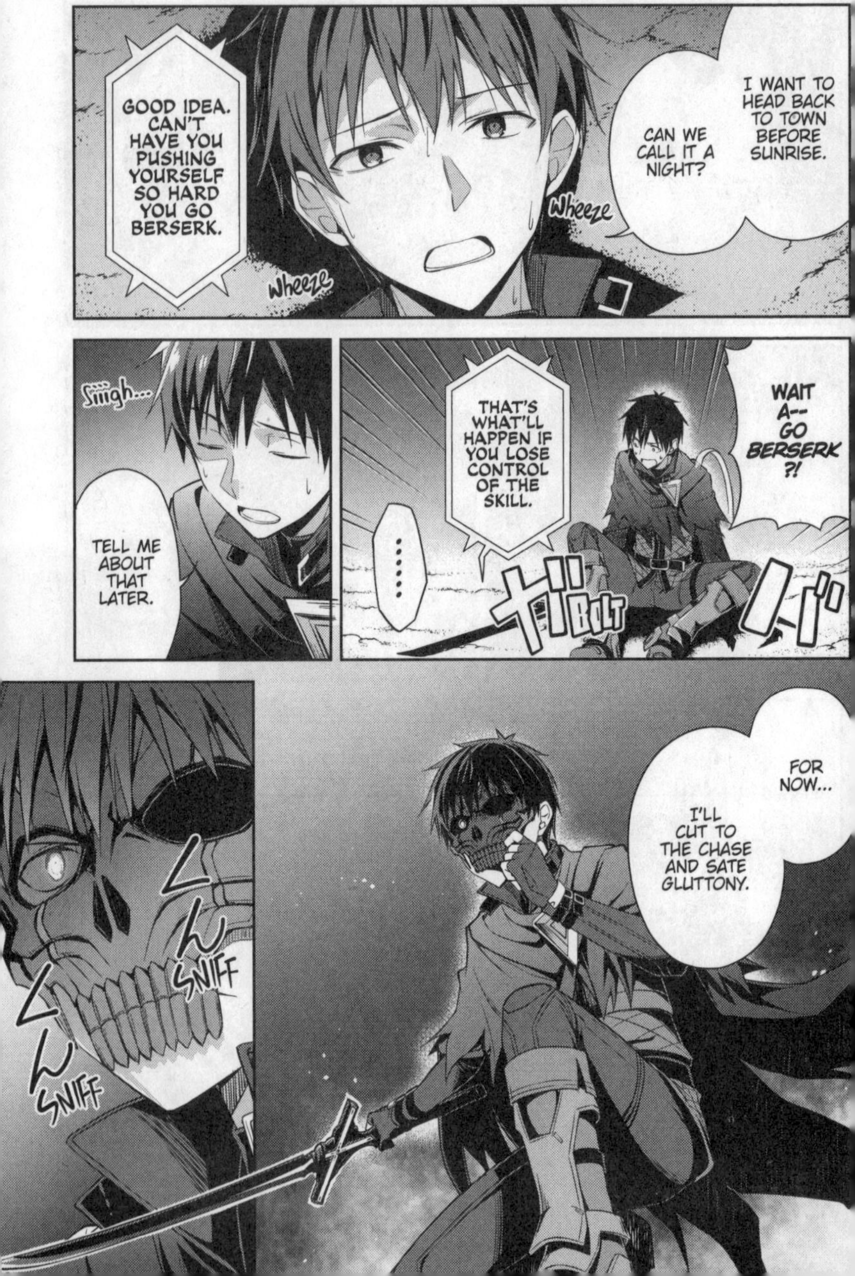
I WANT TO HEAD BACK TO TOWN BEFORE SUNRISE.
CAN WE CALL IT A NIGHT?
Wheeze
GOOD IDEA. CAN'T HAVE YOU PUSHING YOURSELF SO HARD YOU GO BERSERK.
Wheeze
WAIT A-- GO BERSERK?!
THAT'S WHAT'LL HAPPEN IF YOU LOSE CONTROL OF THE SKILL.
......
BOLT
Siiigh...
TELL ME ABOUT THAT LATER.
FOR NOW...
I'LL CUT TO THE CHASE AND SATE GLUTTONY.
SNIFF
SNIFF

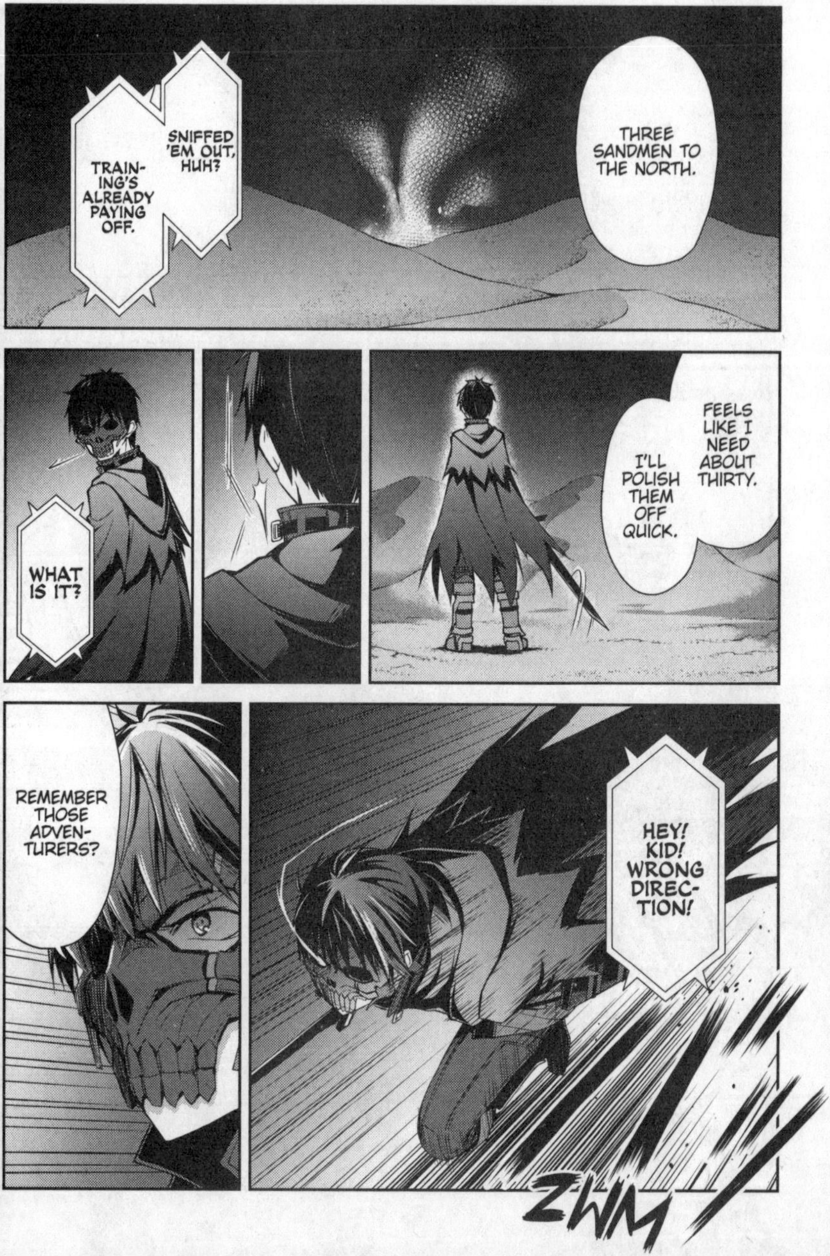
THREE SANDMEN TO THE NORTH.
SNIFFED 'EM OUT, HUH?
TRAIN-ING'S ALREADY PAYING OFF.
FEELS LIKE I NEED ABOUT THIRTY.
I'LL POLISH THEM OFF QUICK.
WHAT IS IT?
HEY! KID! WRONG DIREC-TION!
ZWM
REMEMBER THOSE ADVEN-TURERS?

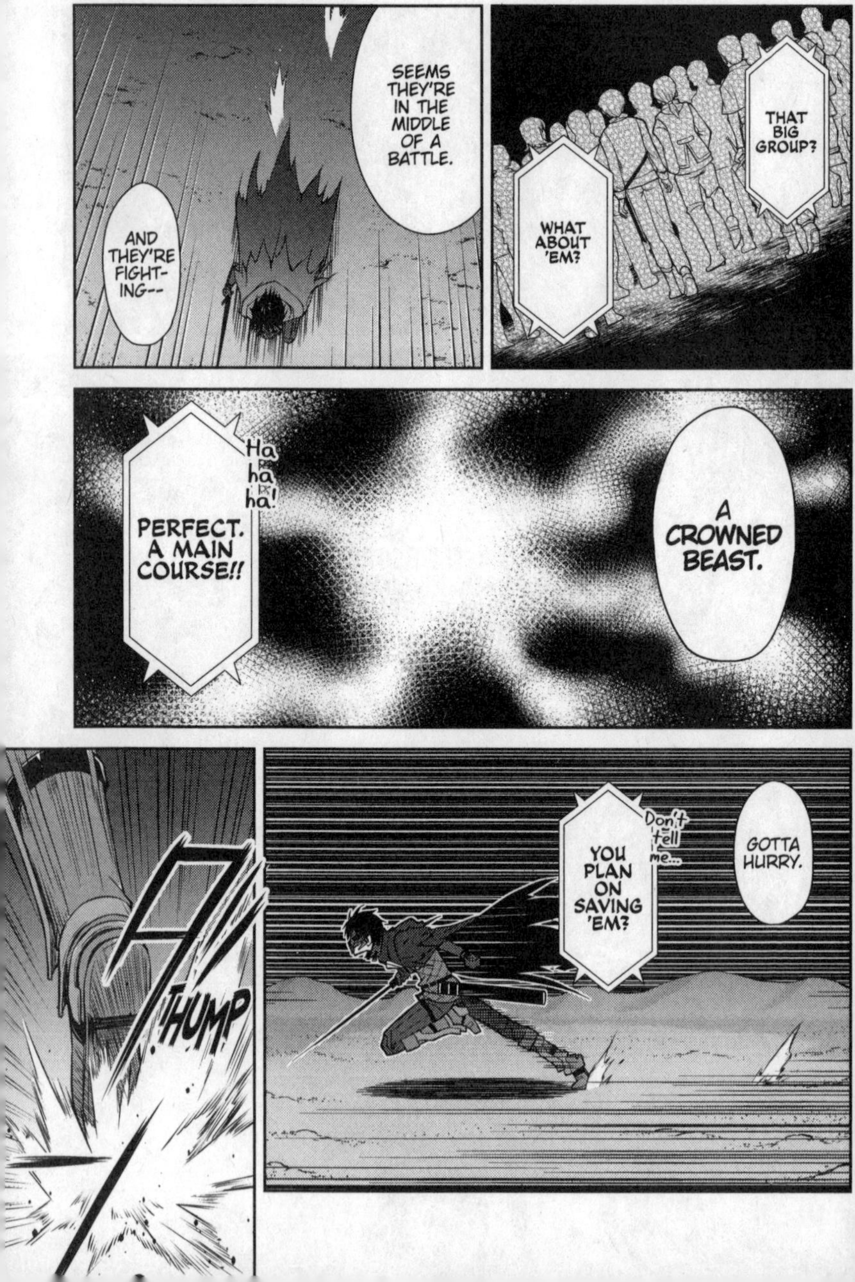
THAT BIG GROUP?
WHAT ABOUT 'EM?
SEEMS THEY'RE IN THE MIDDLE OF A BATTLE.
AND THEY'RE FIGHT- ING--
A CROWNED BEAST.
Ha ha ha!
PERFECT. A MAIN COURSE!!
GOTTA HURRY.
Don't tell me...
YOU PLAN ON SAVING 'EM?
THUMP

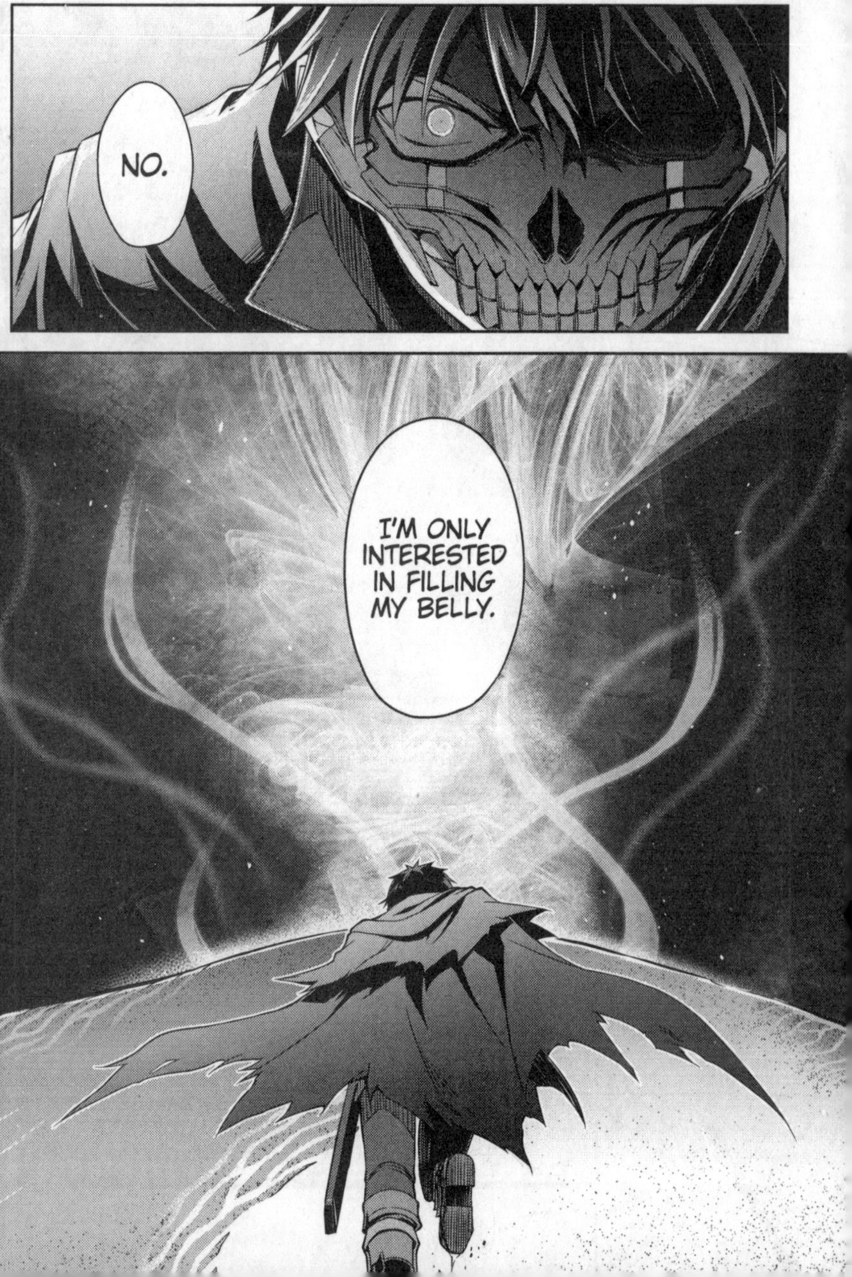
NO.
I'M ONLY INTERESTED IN FILLING MY BELLY.

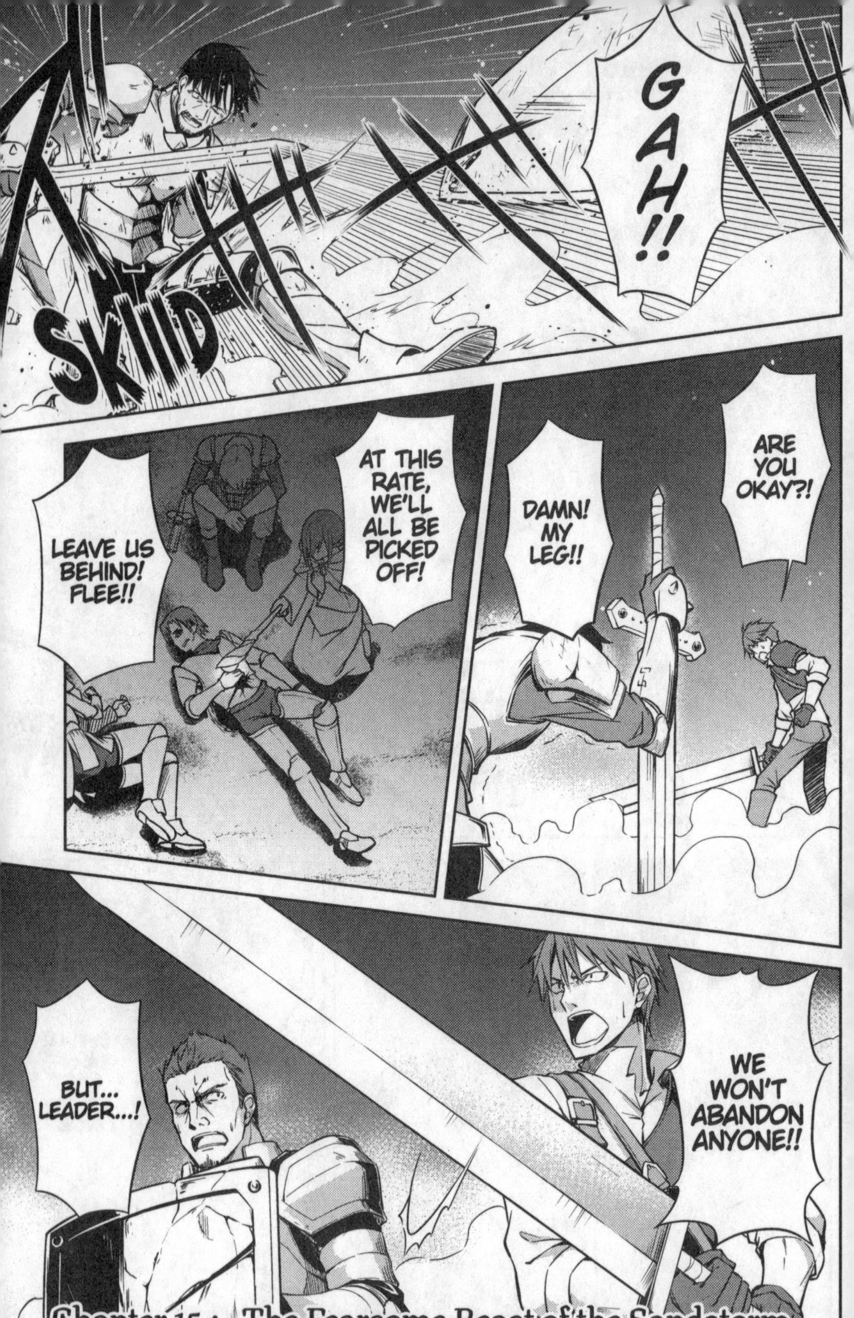
GAH!!
SKIIID
ARE YOU OKAY?!
DAMN! MY LEG!!
AT THIS RATE, WE'LL ALL BE PICKED OFF!
LEAVE US BEHIND! FLEE!!
WE WON'T ABANDON ANYONE!!
BUT... LEADER...!

Chapter 15 ⸭ The Fearsome Beast of the Sandstorm

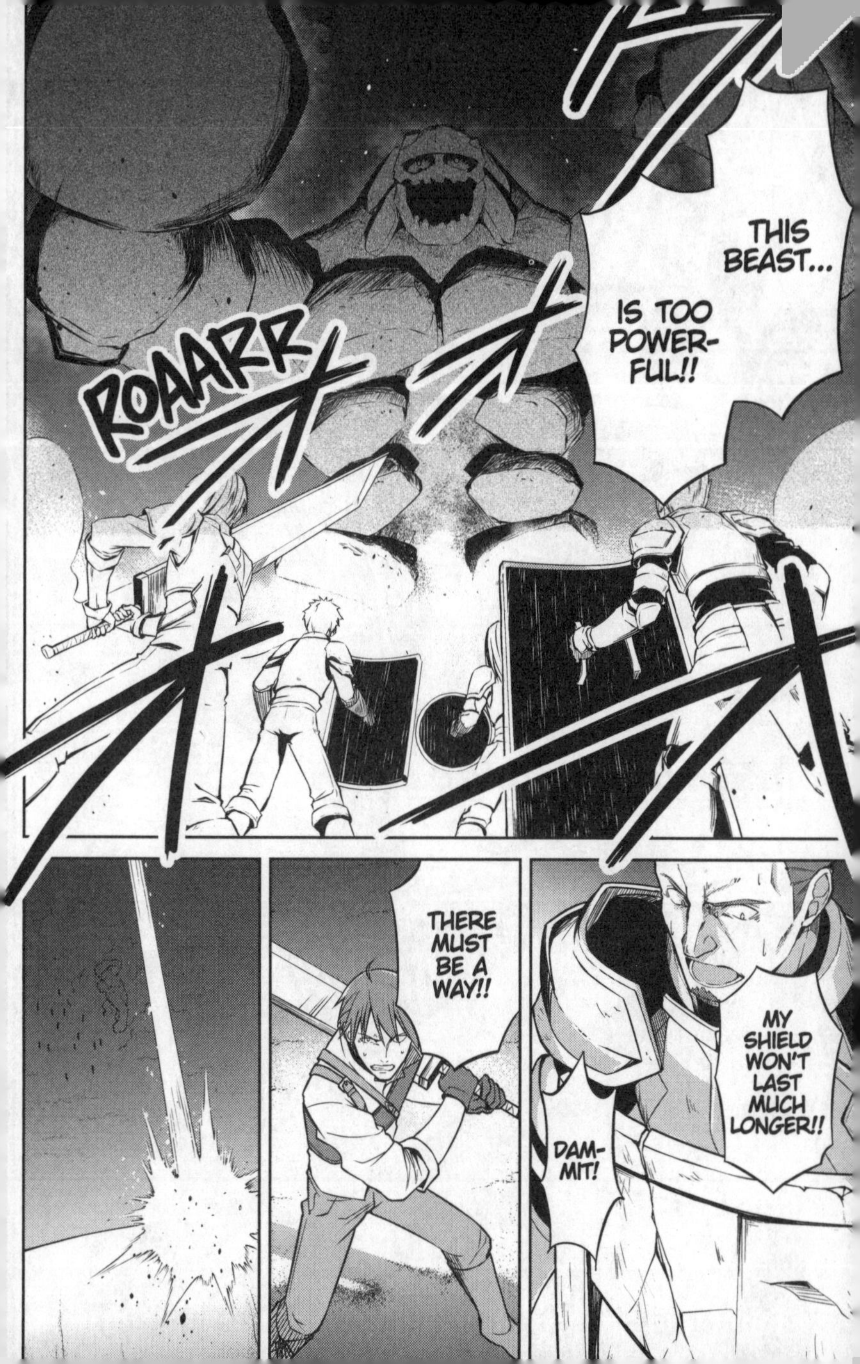
THIS BEAST...
IS TOO POWER-FUL!!
ROAARR
MY SHIELD WON'T LAST MUCH LONGER!!
DAM-MIT!
THERE MUST BE A WAY!!

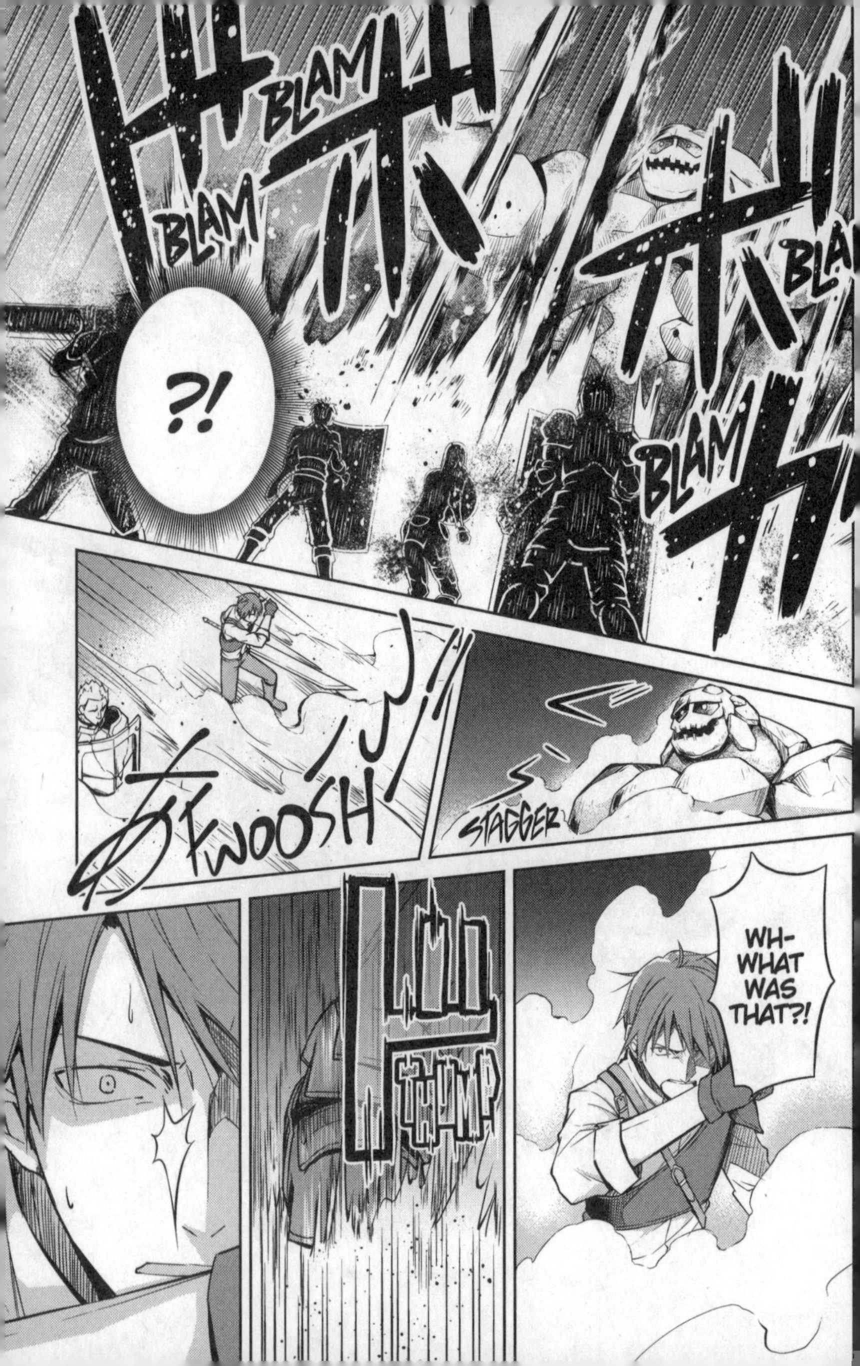

BLAM
BLAM
BLAM BLAM
?!
STAGGER
WOOSH
WH- WHAT WAS THAT?!
THUMP

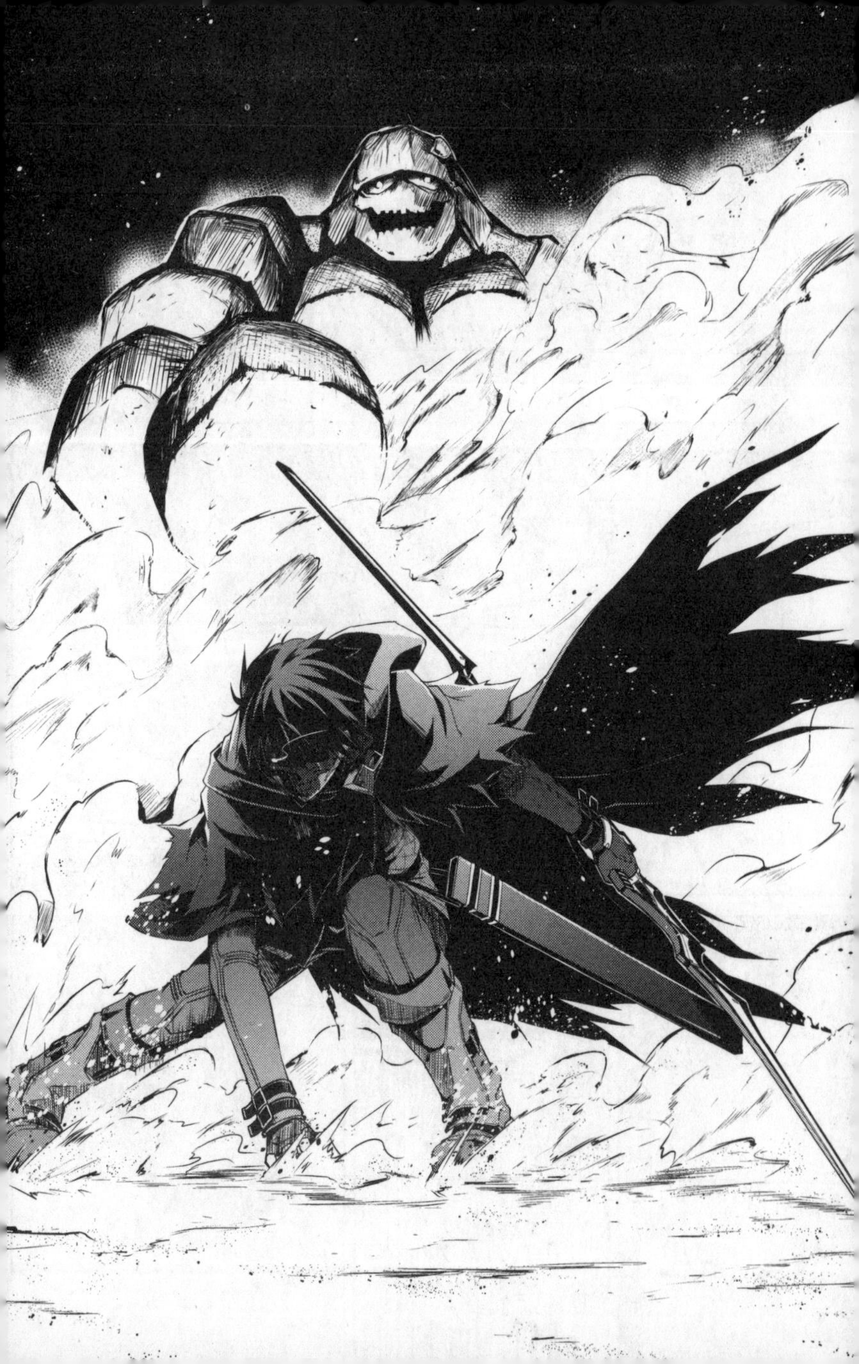

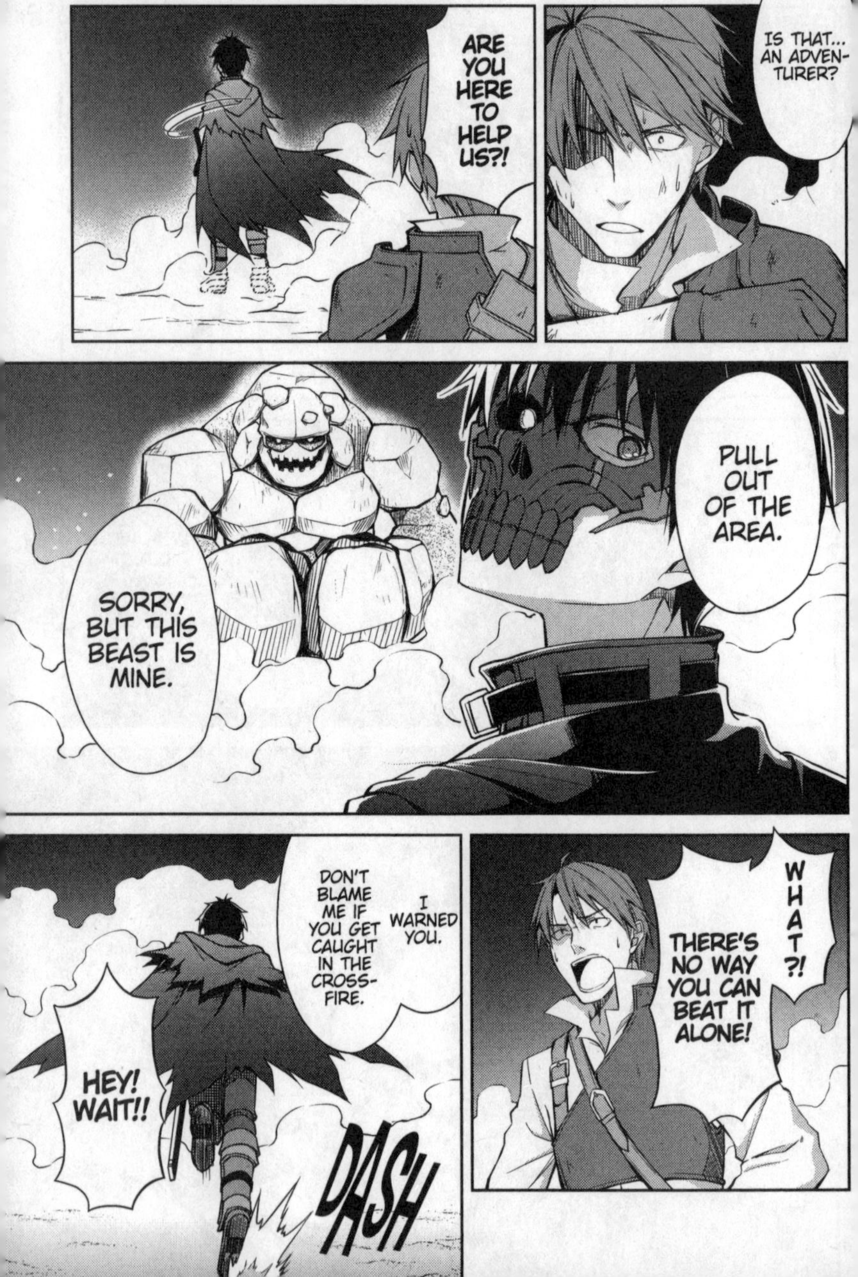
IS THAT... AN ADVENTURER?
ARE YOU HERE TO HELP US?!
PULL OUT OF THE AREA.
SORRY, BUT THIS BEAST IS MINE.
WHAT?!
THERE'S NO WAY YOU CAN BEAT IT ALONE!
I WARNED YOU.
DON'T BLAME ME IF YOU GET CAUGHT IN THE CROSS-FIRE.
HEY! WAIT!!
DASH

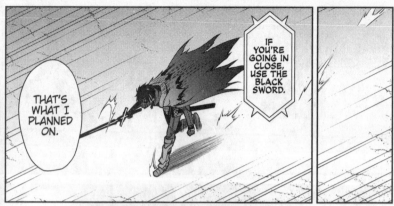

IF YOU'RE GOING IN CLOSE, USE THE BLACK SWORD.

THAT'S WHAT I PLANNED ON.

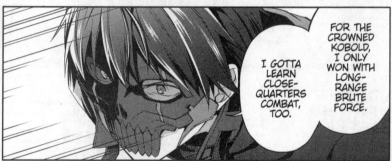

FOR THE CROWNED KOBOLD, I ONLY WON WITH LONG-RANGE BRUTE FORCE.

I GOTTA LEARN CLOSE-QUARTERS COMBAT, TOO.

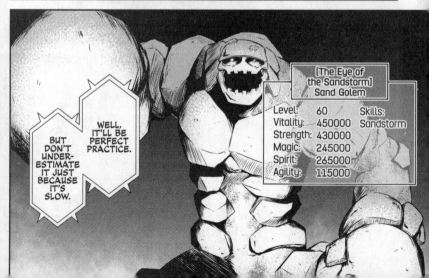

WELL, IT'LL BE PERFECT PRACTICE.

BUT DON'T UNDER-ESTIMATE IT JUST BECAUSE IT'S SLOW.

[The Eye of the Sandstorm] Sand Golem		
Level:	60	Skills:
Vitality:	450000	Sandstorm
Strength:	430000	
Magic:	245000	
Spirit:	265000	
Agility:	115000	

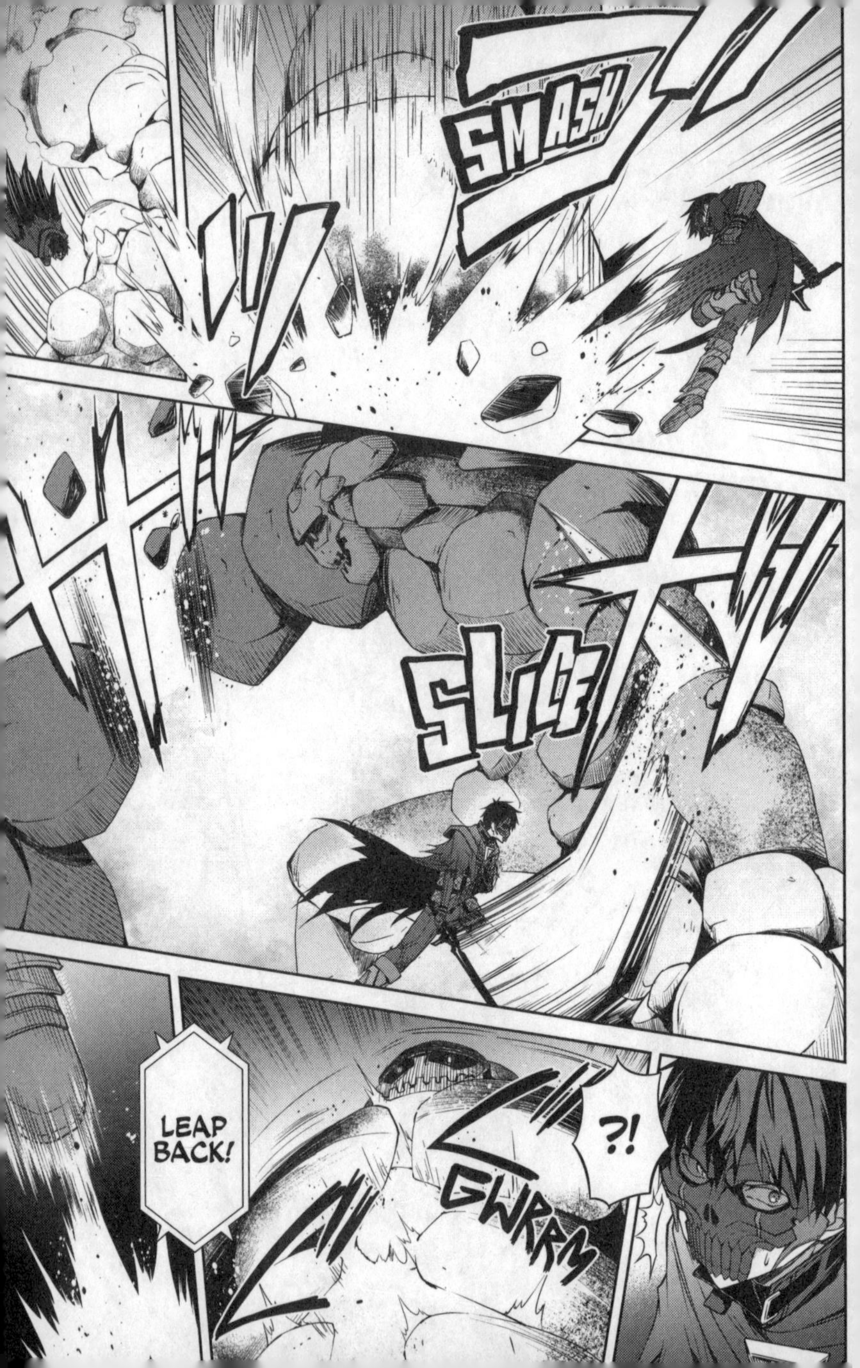
SMASH
SLICE
?!
GWRRM
LEAP BACK!

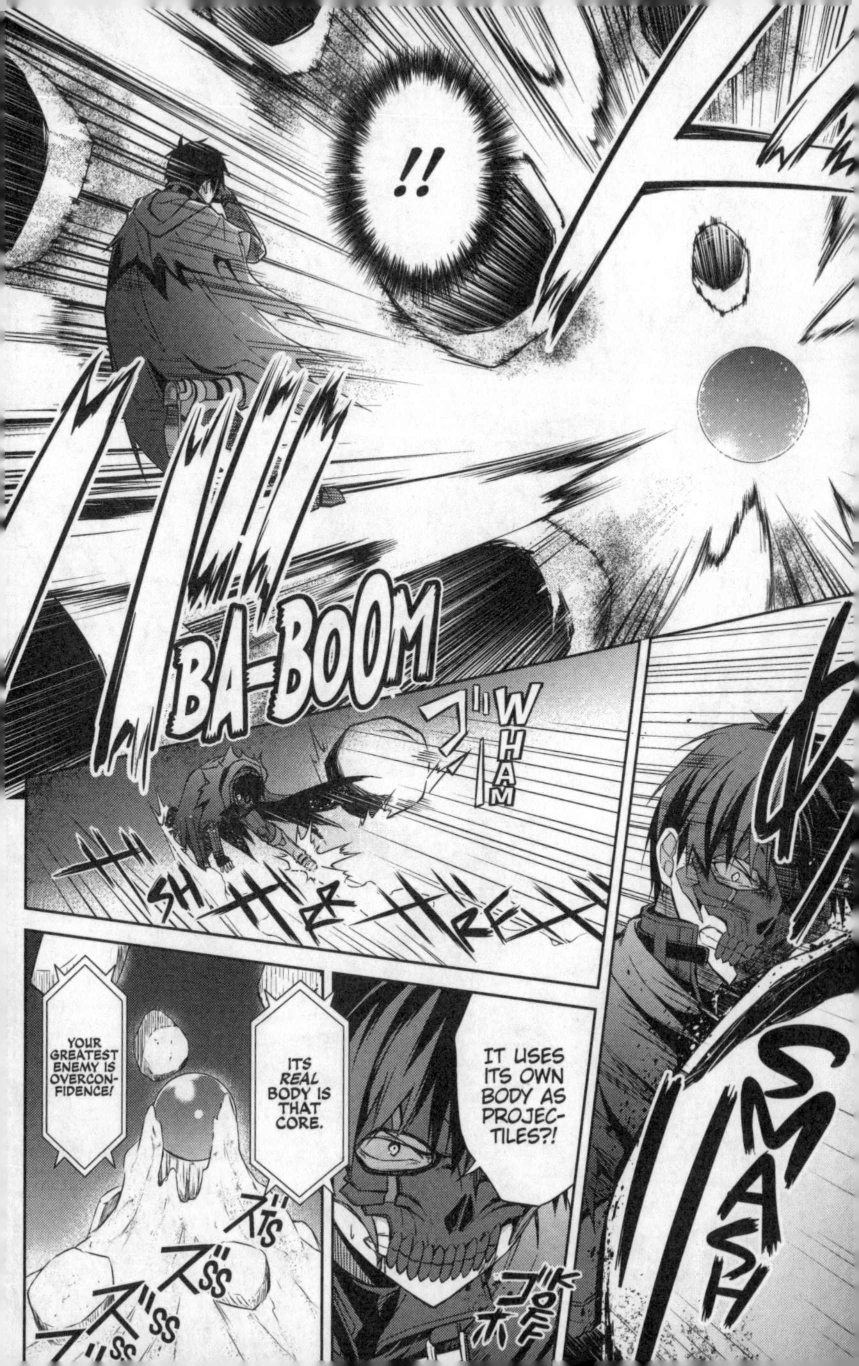
!!
BA-BOOM
WHAM
SMASH
IT USES ITS OWN BODY AS PROJECTILES?!
KOFF
ITS *REAL* BODY IS THAT CORE.
YOUR GREATEST ENEMY IS OVERCONFIDENCE!
TS
SS
SS

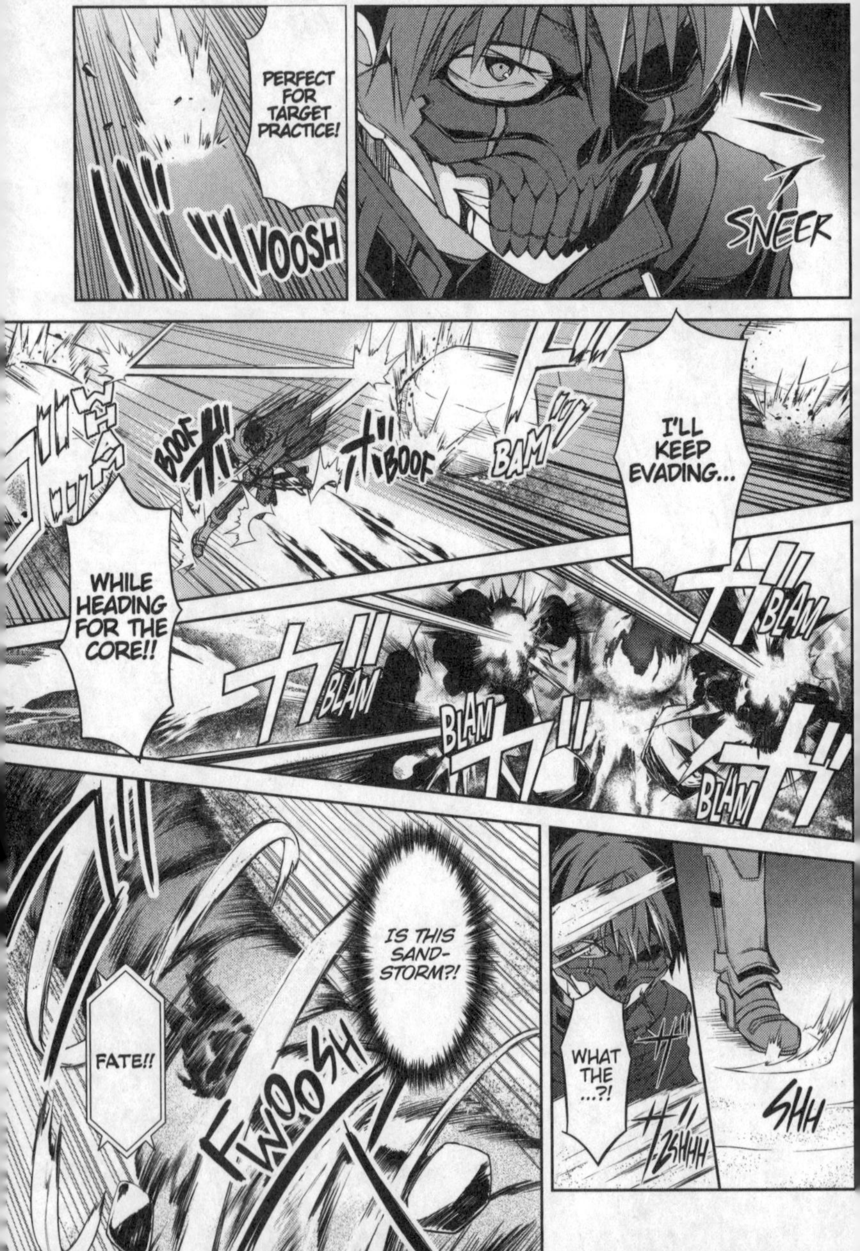
SNEER
PERFECT FOR TARGET PRACTICE!
VOOSH
I'LL KEEP EVADING...
BAM
BOOF
BOOF
BLAM
BLAM
BLAM
BLAM
WHILE HEADING FOR THE CORE!!
SHH
WHAT THE ...?!
ZSHHH
IS THIS SAND-STORM?!
FWOOSH
FATE!!

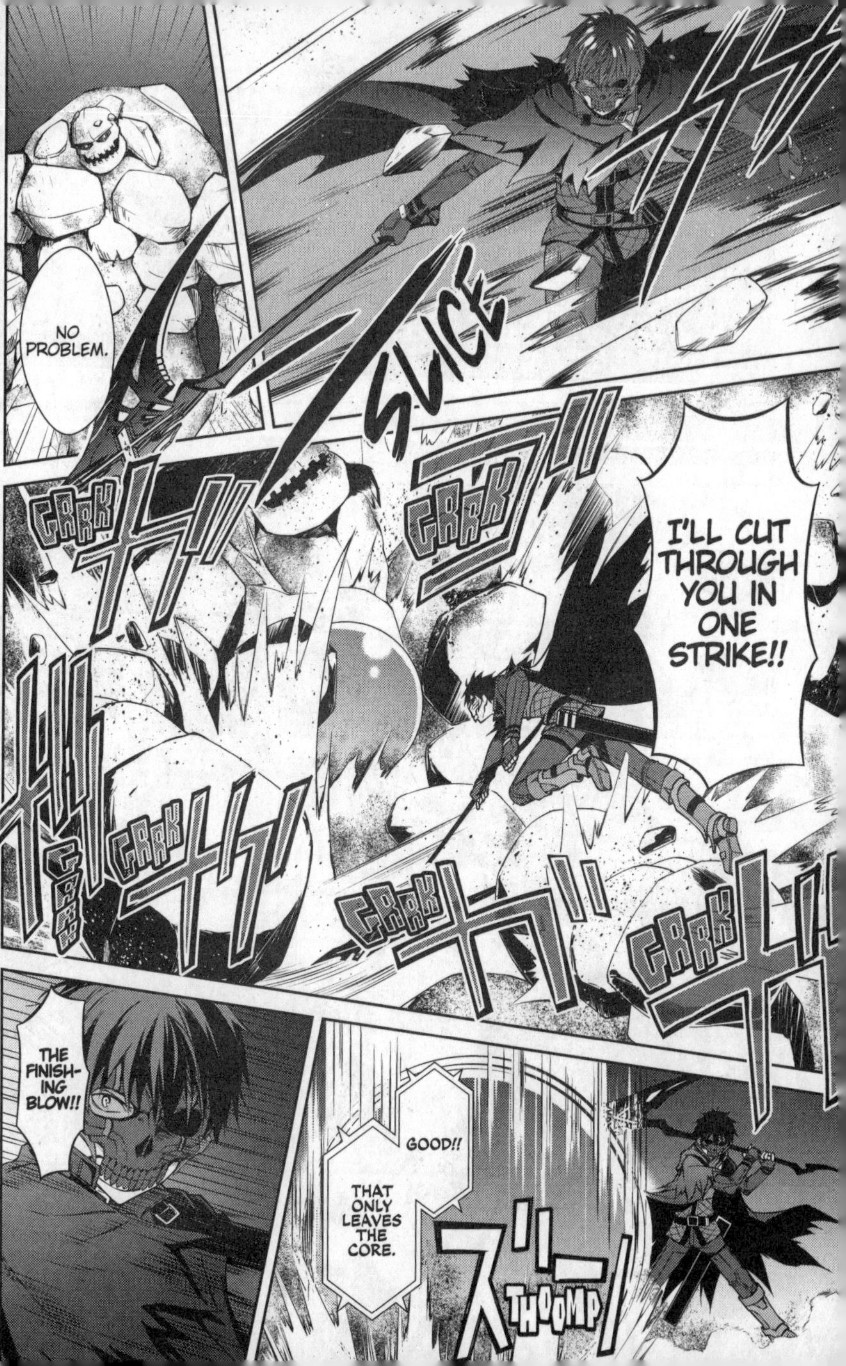
SLICE
NO PROBLEM.
I'LL CUT THROUGH YOU IN ONE STRIKE!!
GRRK
GRRK
GRRK
GRRK
GRRK
GRRK
GOOD!!
THAT ONLY LEAVES THE CORE.
THOOMP
THE FINISHING BLOW!!

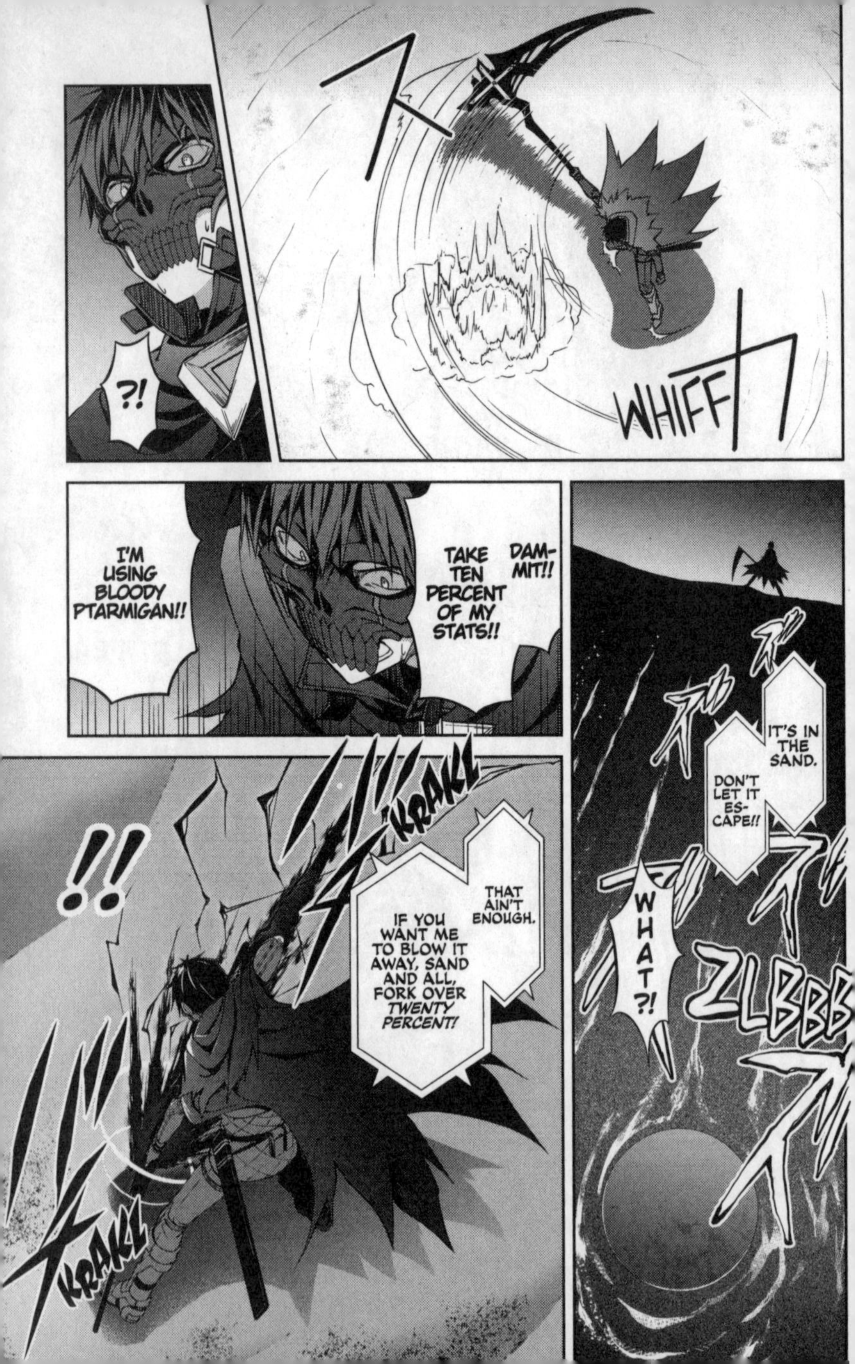
WHIFF
?!
IT'S IN THE SAND.
DON'T LET IT ES-CAPE!!
WHAT?!
ZLBBB
DAM-MIT!!
TAKE TEN PERCENT OF MY STATS!!
I'M USING BLOODY PTARMIGAN!!
KRAK!
THAT AIN'T ENOUGH.
IF YOU WANT ME TO BLOW IT AWAY, SAND AND ALL, FORK OVER *TWENTY PERCENT!*
!!
KRAK!

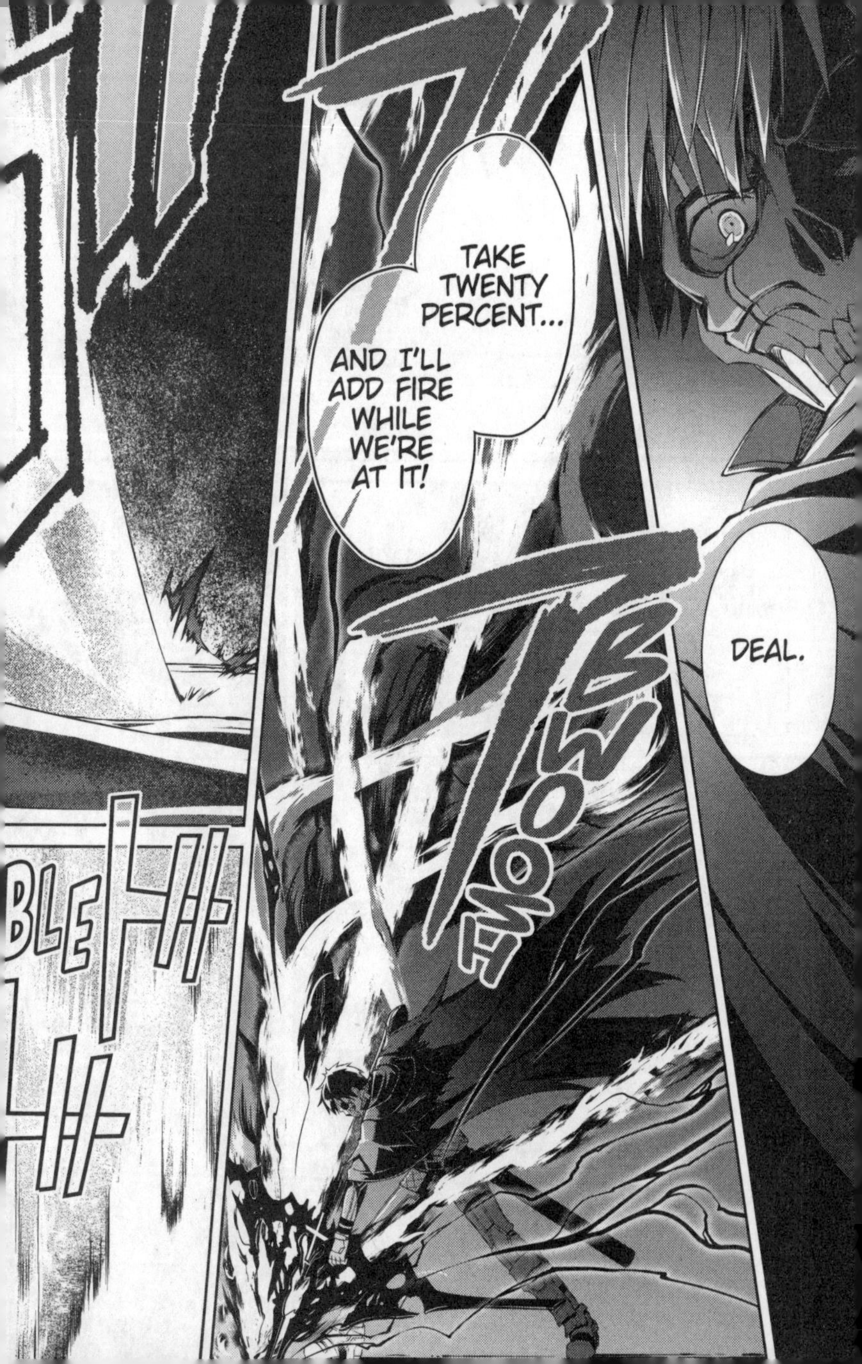
TAKE TWENTY PERCENT...
AND I'LL ADD FIRE WHILE WE'RE AT IT!
DEAL.
WHOOSH

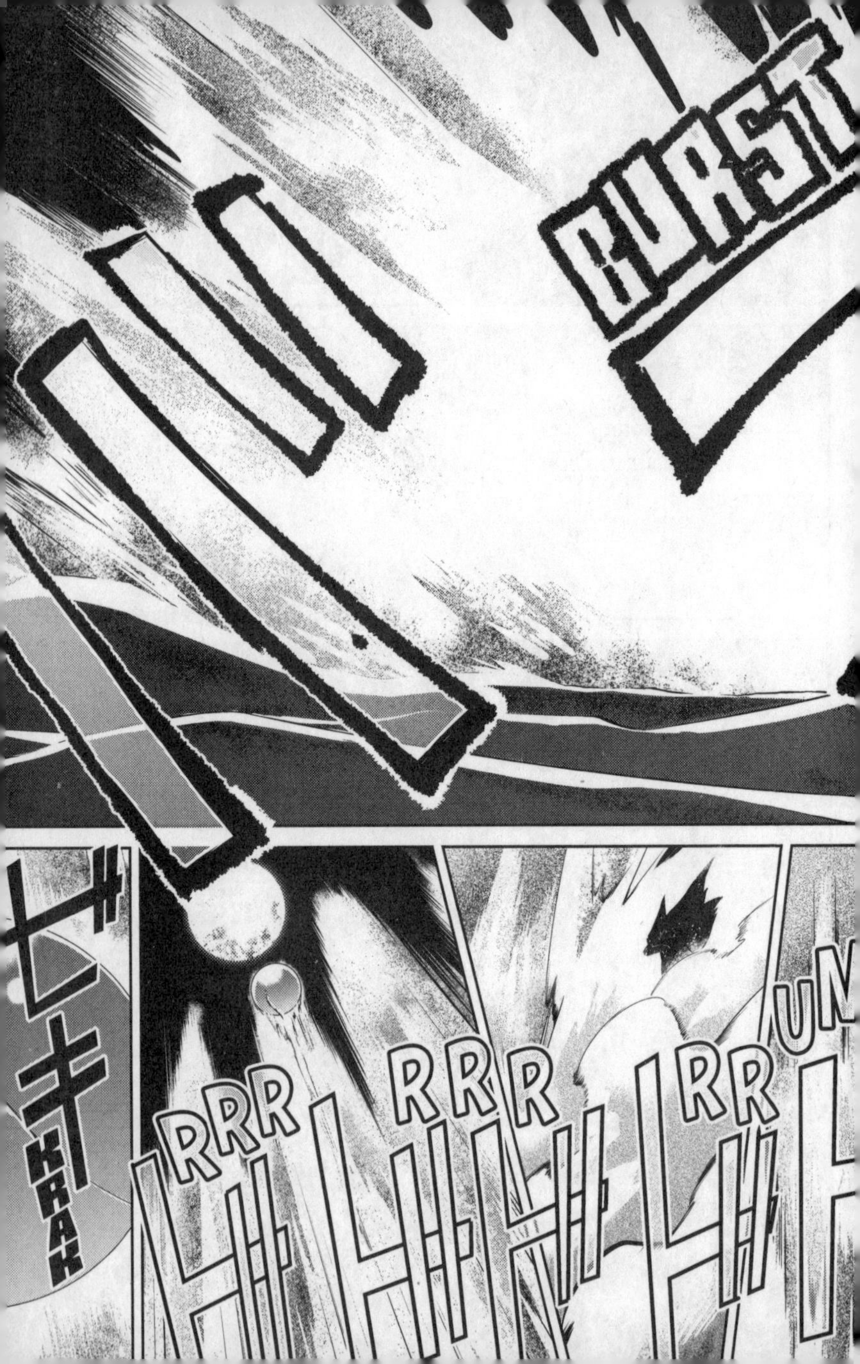
BURST
RRRRRRRRUM
KRAK

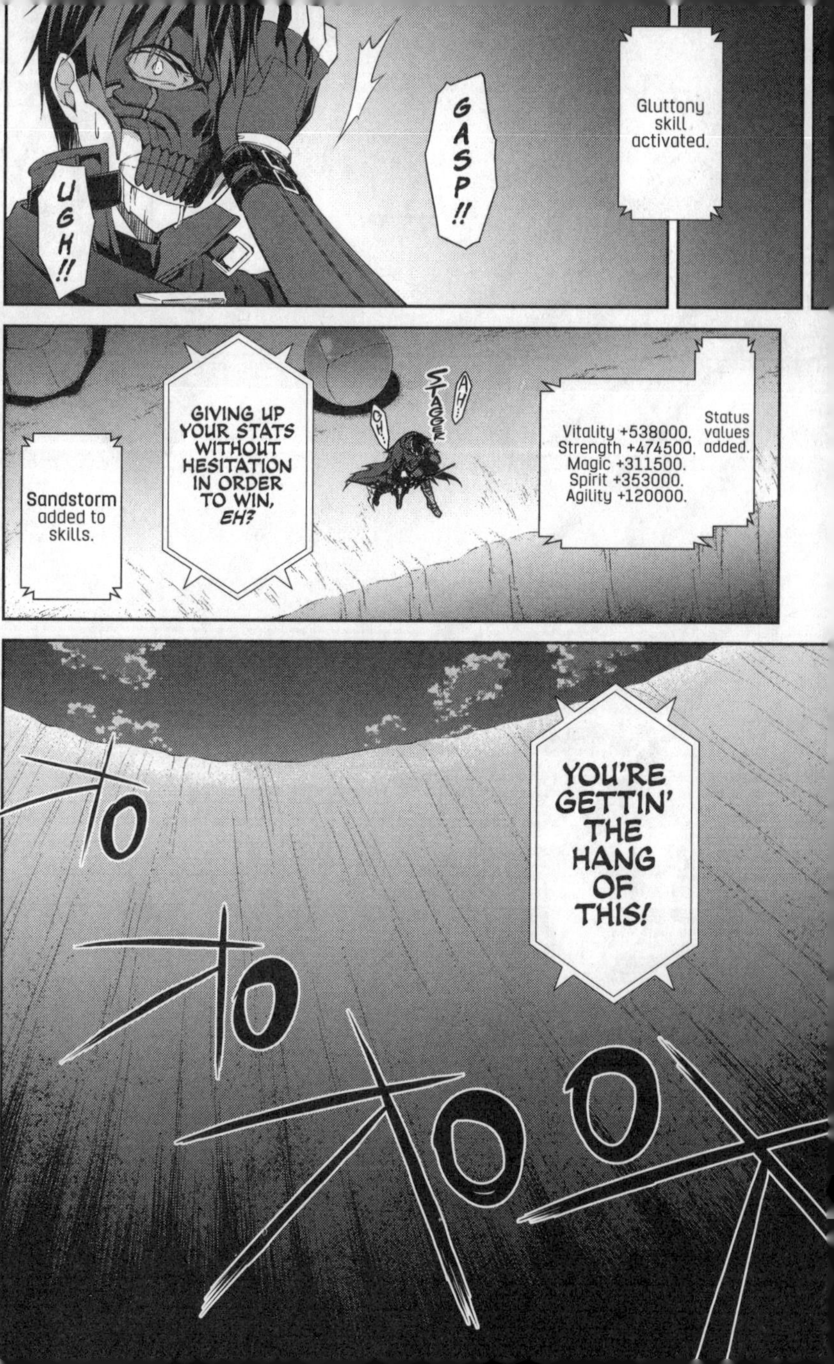
Gluttony skill activated.
GASP!!
UGH!!
Status values added.
Vitality +538000.
Strength +474500.
Magic +311500.
Spirit +353000.
Agility +120000.
AH...
STAGGER
OH...
GIVING UP YOUR STATS WITHOUT HESITATION IN ORDER TO WIN, EH?
Sandstorm added to skills.
YOU'RE GETTIN' THE HANG OF THIS!

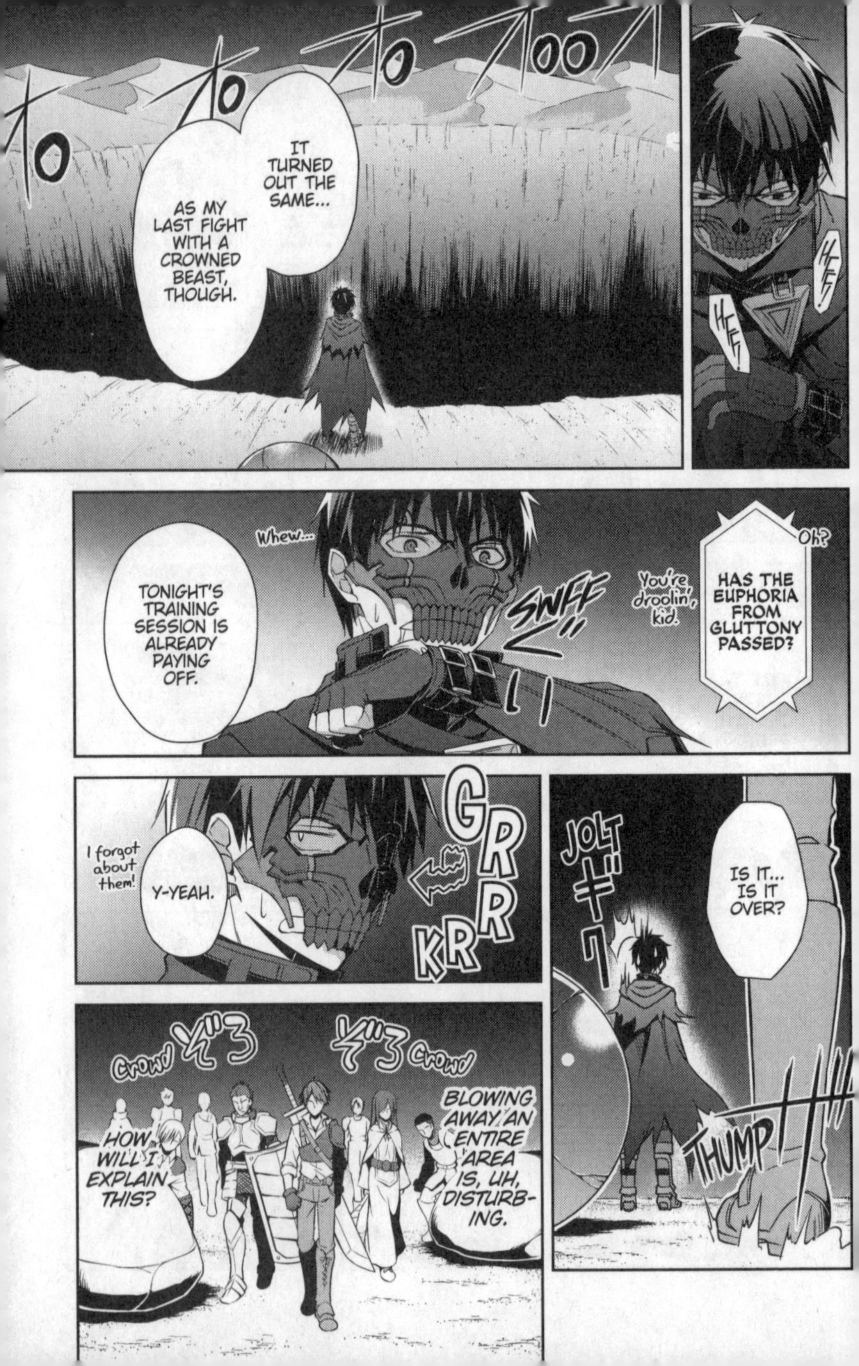
HFF!
HFF!
IT TURNED OUT THE SAME...
AS MY LAST FIGHT WITH A CROWNED BEAST, THOUGH.
Oh?
HAS THE EUPHORIA FROM GLUTTONY PASSED?
You're droolin', kid.
SWFF
Whew...
TONIGHT'S TRAINING SESSION IS ALREADY PAYING OFF.
IS IT... IS IT OVER?
JOLT
THUMP
GRR
KRR
Y-YEAH.
I forgot about them!
Crowd
Crowd
BLOWING AWAY AN ENTIRE AREA IS, UH, DISTURBING.
HOW WILL I EXPLAIN THIS?

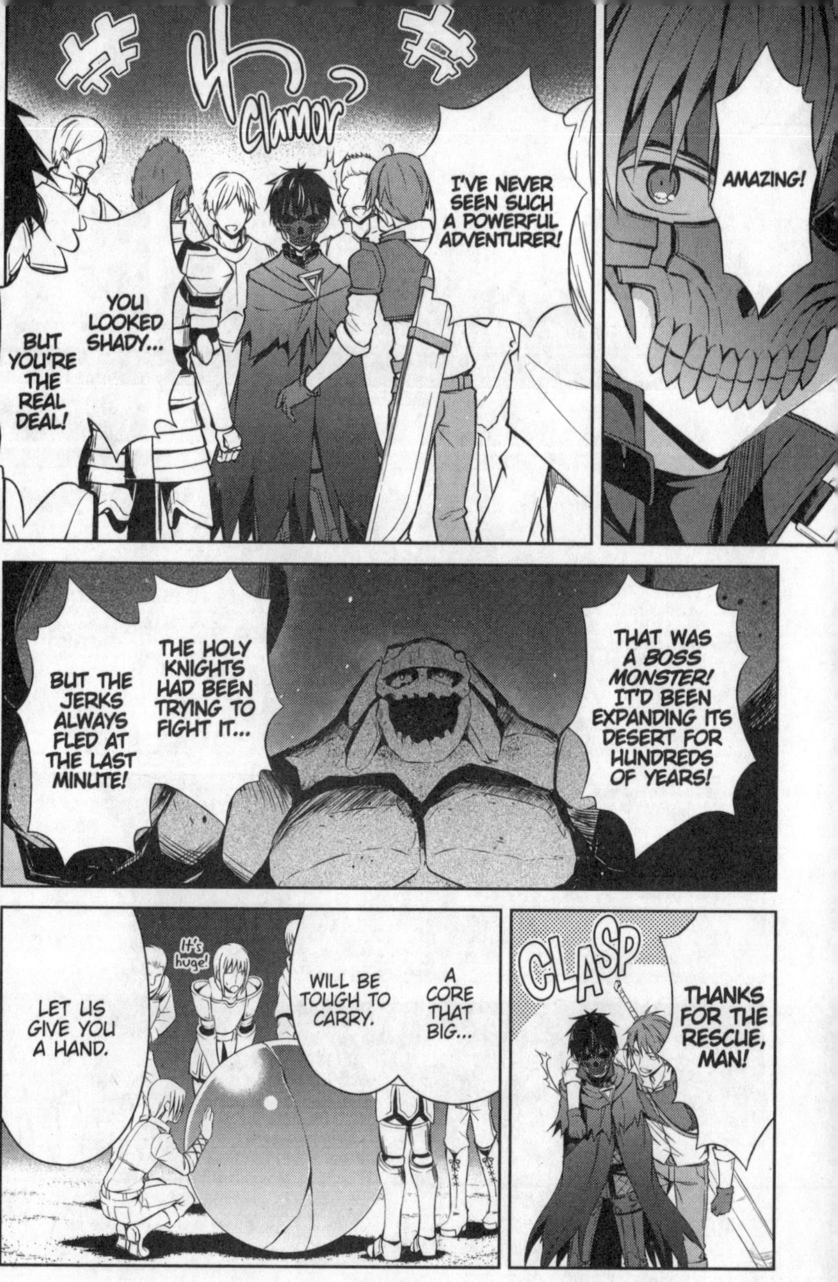
AMAZING!
Clamor
I'VE NEVER SEEN SUCH A POWERFUL ADVENTURER!
YOU LOOKED SHADY...
BUT YOU'RE THE REAL DEAL!
THAT WAS A *BOSS MONSTER!* IT'D BEEN EXPANDING ITS DESERT FOR HUNDREDS OF YEARS!
THE HOLY KNIGHTS HAD BEEN TRYING TO FIGHT IT...
BUT THE JERKS ALWAYS FLED AT THE LAST MINUTE!
CLASP
THANKS FOR THE RESCUE, MAN!
A CORE THAT BIG...
WILL BE TOUGH TO CARRY.
It's huge!
LET US GIVE YOU A HAND.

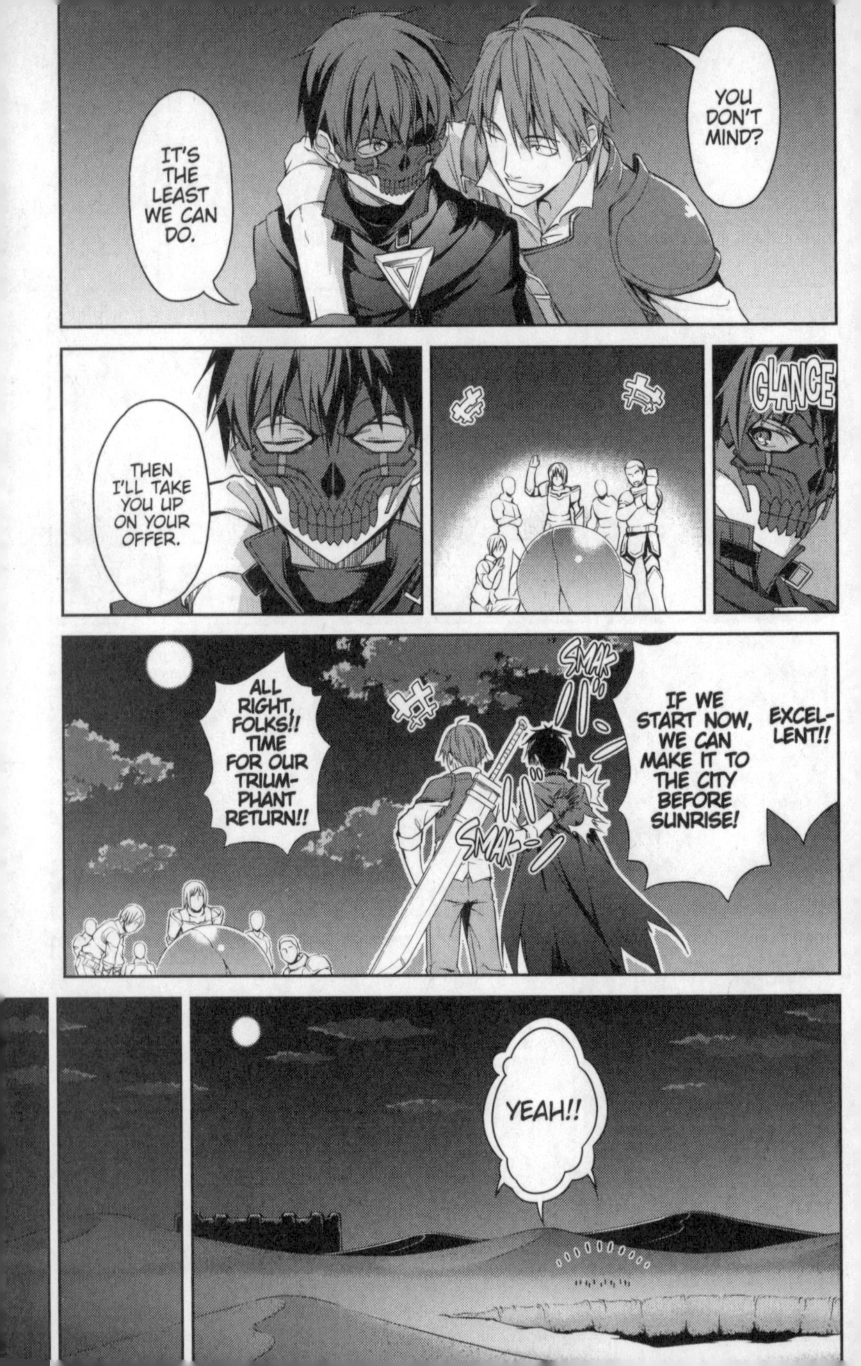
YOU DON'T MIND?
IT'S THE LEAST WE CAN DO.
GLANCE
THEN I'LL TAKE YOU UP ON YOUR OFFER.
EXCEL-LENT!!
IF WE START NOW, WE CAN MAKE IT TO THE CITY BEFORE SUNRISE!
SMAK
ALL RIGHT, FOLKS!! TIME FOR OUR TRIUM-PHANT RETURN!!
SMAK
YEAH!!

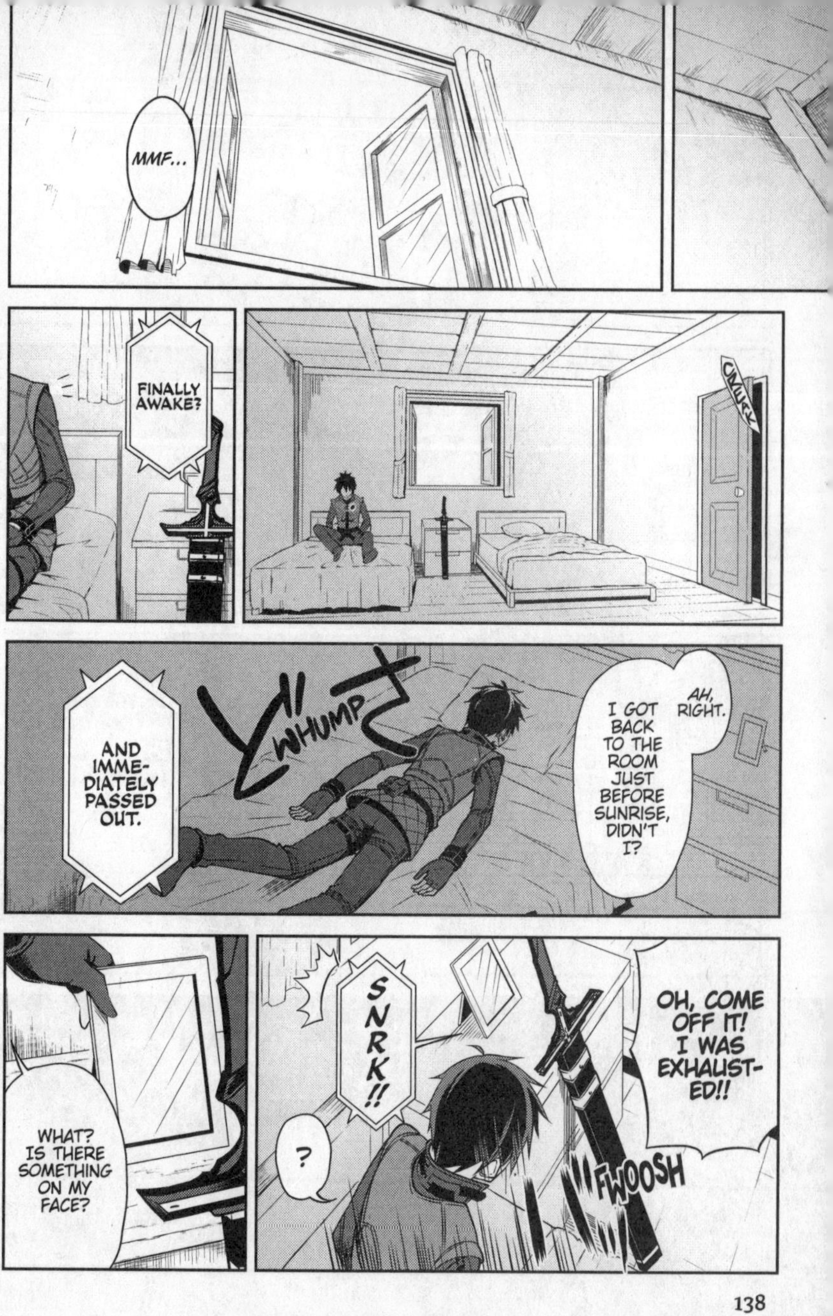
MMF...
CREAK
FINALLY AWAKE?
AH, RIGHT.
I GOT BACK TO THE ROOM JUST BEFORE SUNRISE, DIDN'T I?
WHUMP
AND IMME-DIATELY PASSED OUT.
OH, COME OFF IT! I WAS EXHAUST-ED!!
FWOOSH
SNRK!!
?
WHAT? IS THERE SOMETHING ON MY FACE?

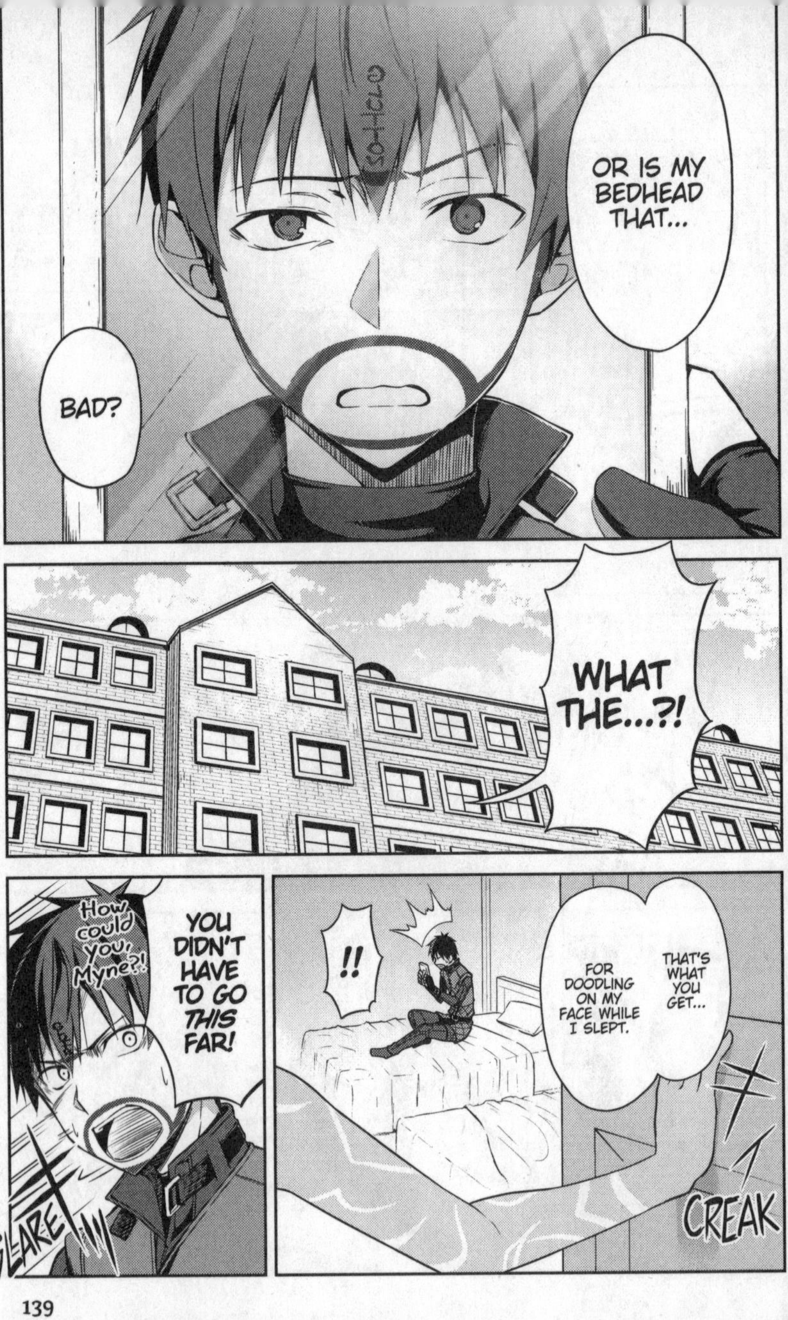
OR IS MY BEDHEAD THAT...
BAD?
WHAT THE...?!
THAT'S WHAT YOU GET...
FOR DOODLING ON MY FACE WHILE I SLEPT.
!!
CREAK
YOU DIDN'T HAVE TO GO *THIS* FAR!
How could you, Myne?!
GLARE

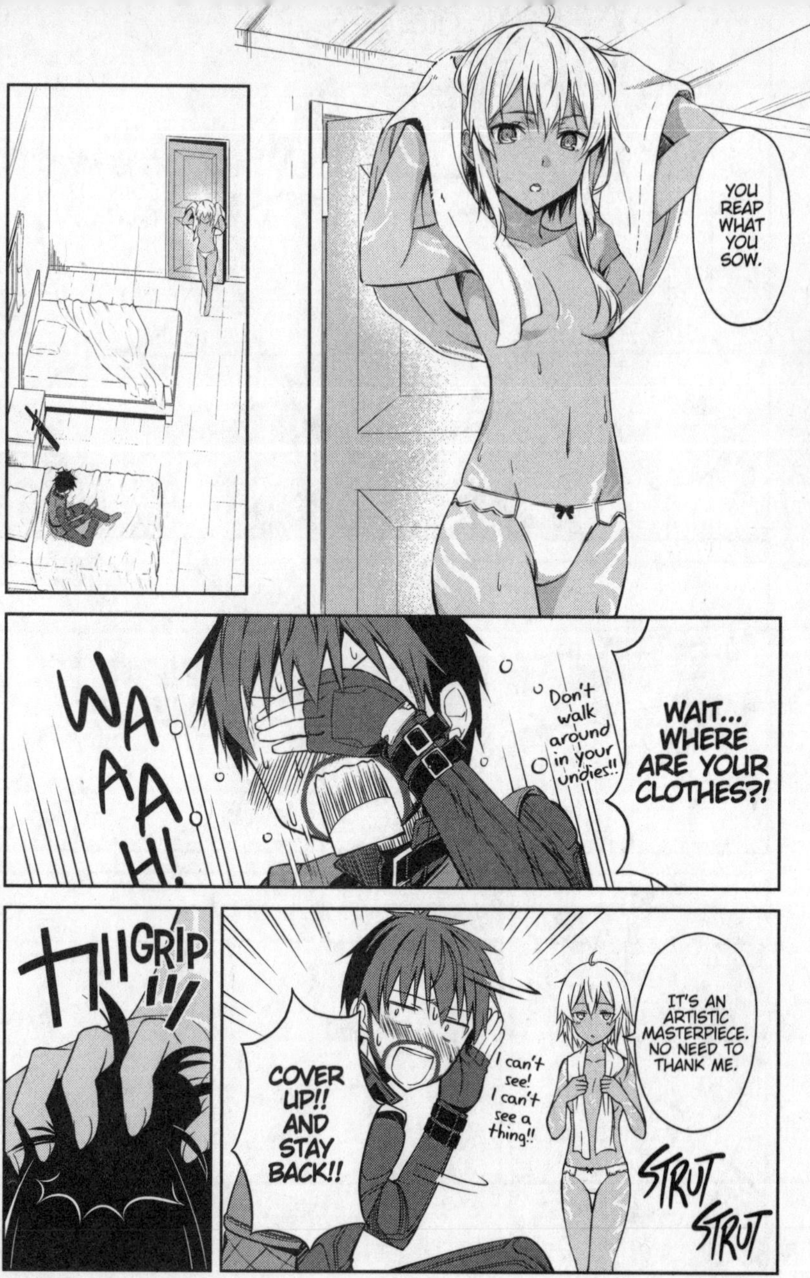
YOU REAP WHAT YOU SOW.
WAIT... WHERE ARE YOUR CLOTHES?!
Don't walk around in your undies!!
WAAAH!
IT'S AN ARTISTIC MASTERPIECE. NO NEED TO THANK ME.
STRUT STRUT
I can't see! I can't see a thing!!
COVER UP!! AND STAY BACK!!
GRIP

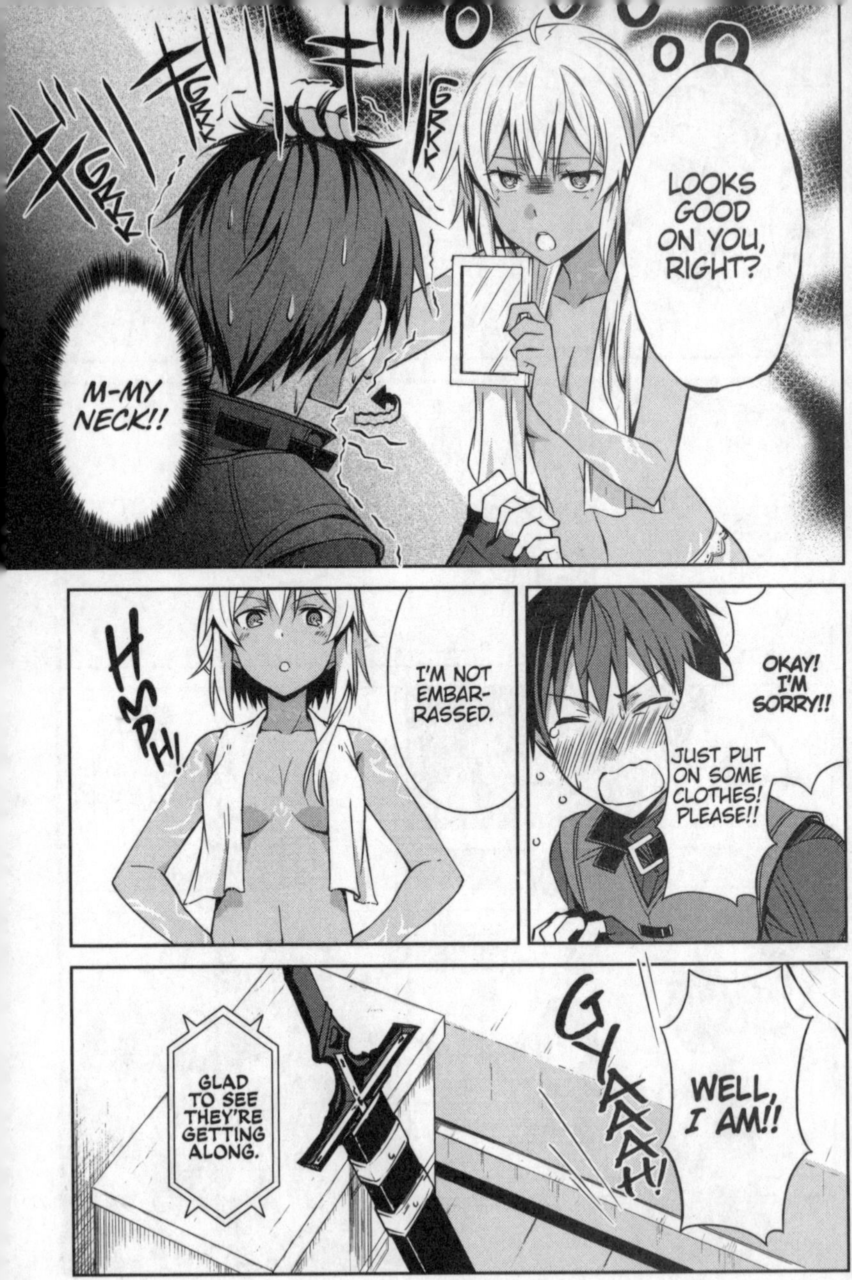
LOOKS GOOD ON YOU, RIGHT?
GRKK GRKK GRKK
M-MY NECK!!
OKAY! I'M SORRY!!
JUST PUT ON SOME CLOTHES! PLEASE!!
I'M NOT EMBARRASSED.
HMPH!
WELL, I AM!!
GYAAAH!
GLAD TO SEE THEY'RE GETTING ALONG.

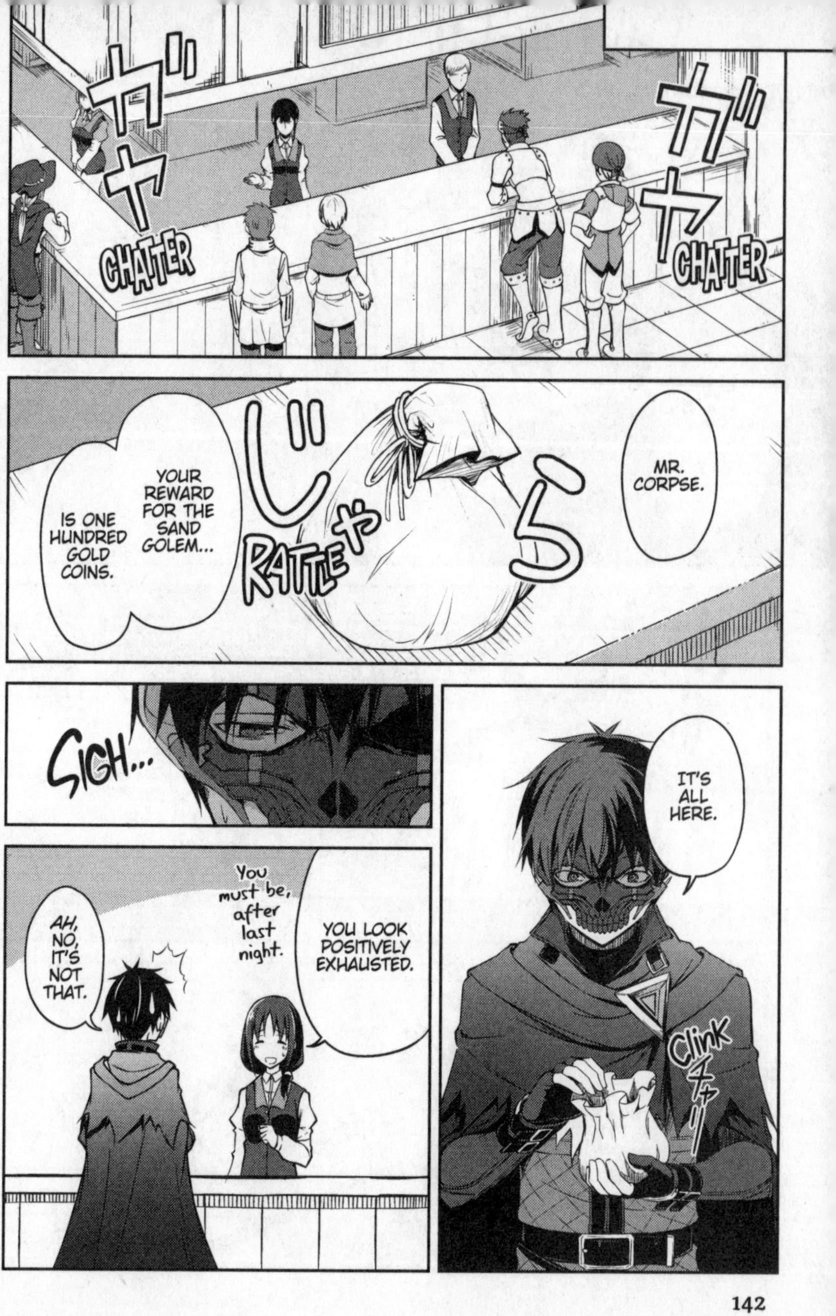
ガヤ
CHATTER
ガヤ
CHATTER
MR. CORPSE.
じゃら
RATTLE
YOUR REWARD FOR THE SAND GOLEM...
IS ONE HUNDRED GOLD COINS.
IT'S ALL HERE.
Clink
チャリ
SIGH...
YOU LOOK POSITIVELY EXHAUSTED.
You must be, after last night.
AH, NO, IT'S NOT THAT.

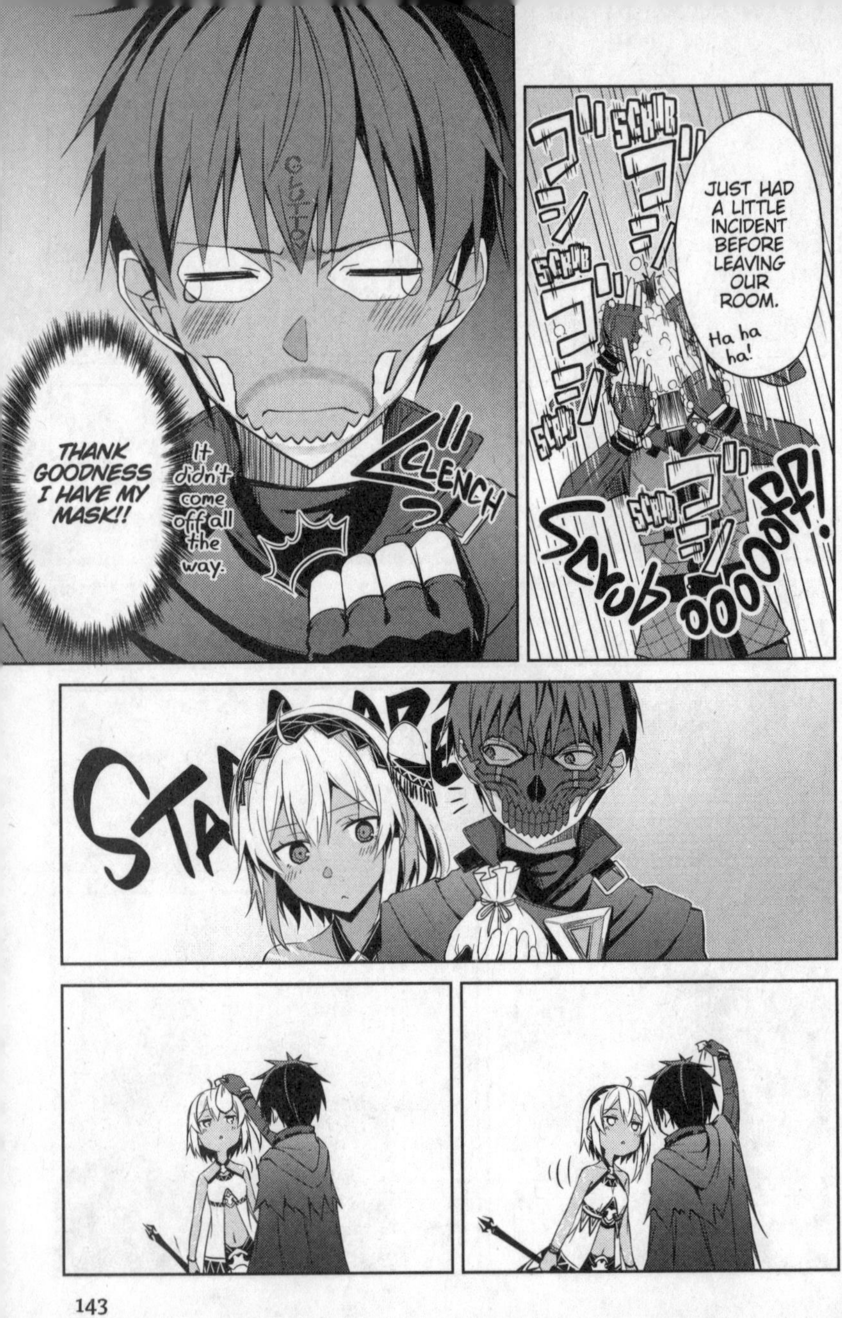
SCRUB
JUST HAD A LITTLE INCIDENT BEFORE LEAVING OUR ROOM.
Ha ha ha!
SCRUB
SCRUB
SCRUB
Scrub ooooooff!
THANK GOODNESS I HAVE MY MASK!!
It didn't come off all the way.
CLENCH

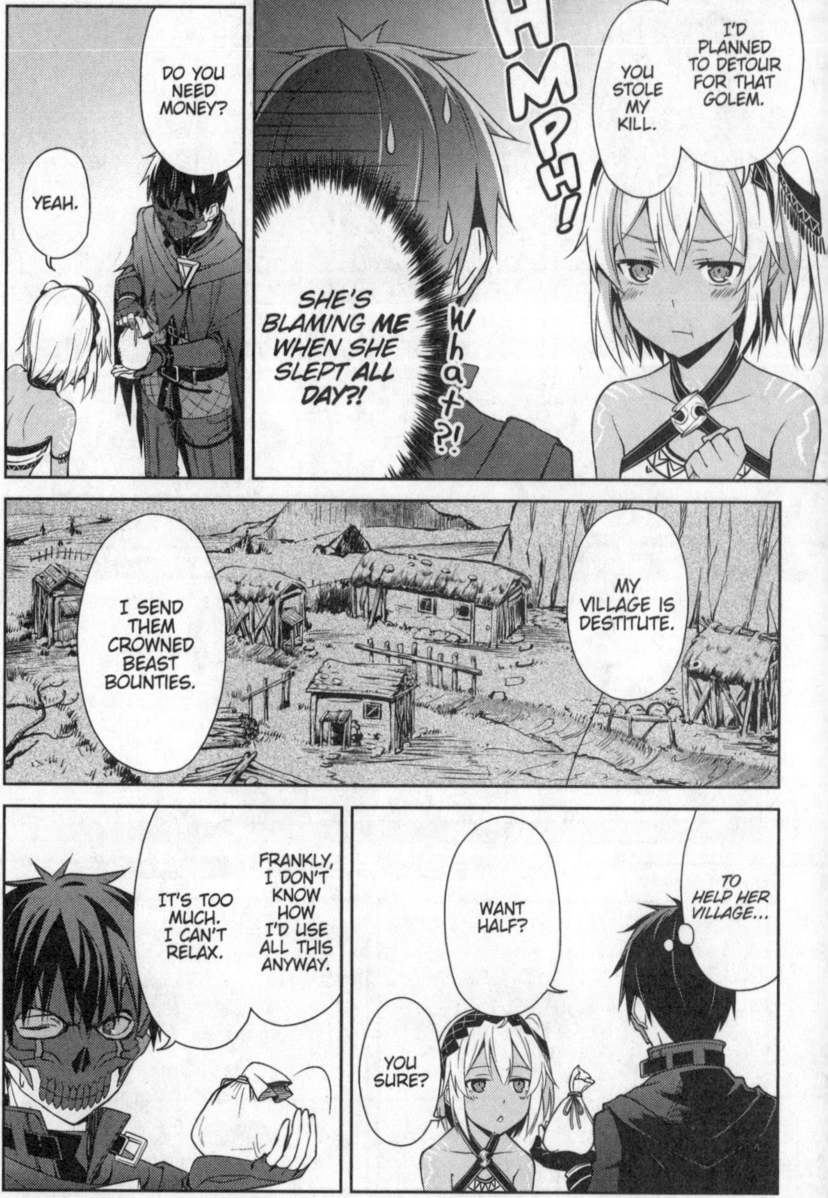
I'D PLANNED TO DETOUR FOR THAT GOLEM.
YOU STOLE MY KILL.
HMPH!
What?!
SHE'S BLAMING ME WHEN SHE SLEPT ALL DAY?!
DO YOU NEED MONEY?
YEAH.
MY VILLAGE IS DESTITUTE.
I SEND THEM CROWNED BEAST BOUNTIES.
TO HELP HER VILLAGE...
WANT HALF?
YOU SURE?
FRANKLY, I DON'T KNOW HOW I'D USE ALL THIS ANYWAY.
IT'S TOO MUCH. I CAN'T RELAX.

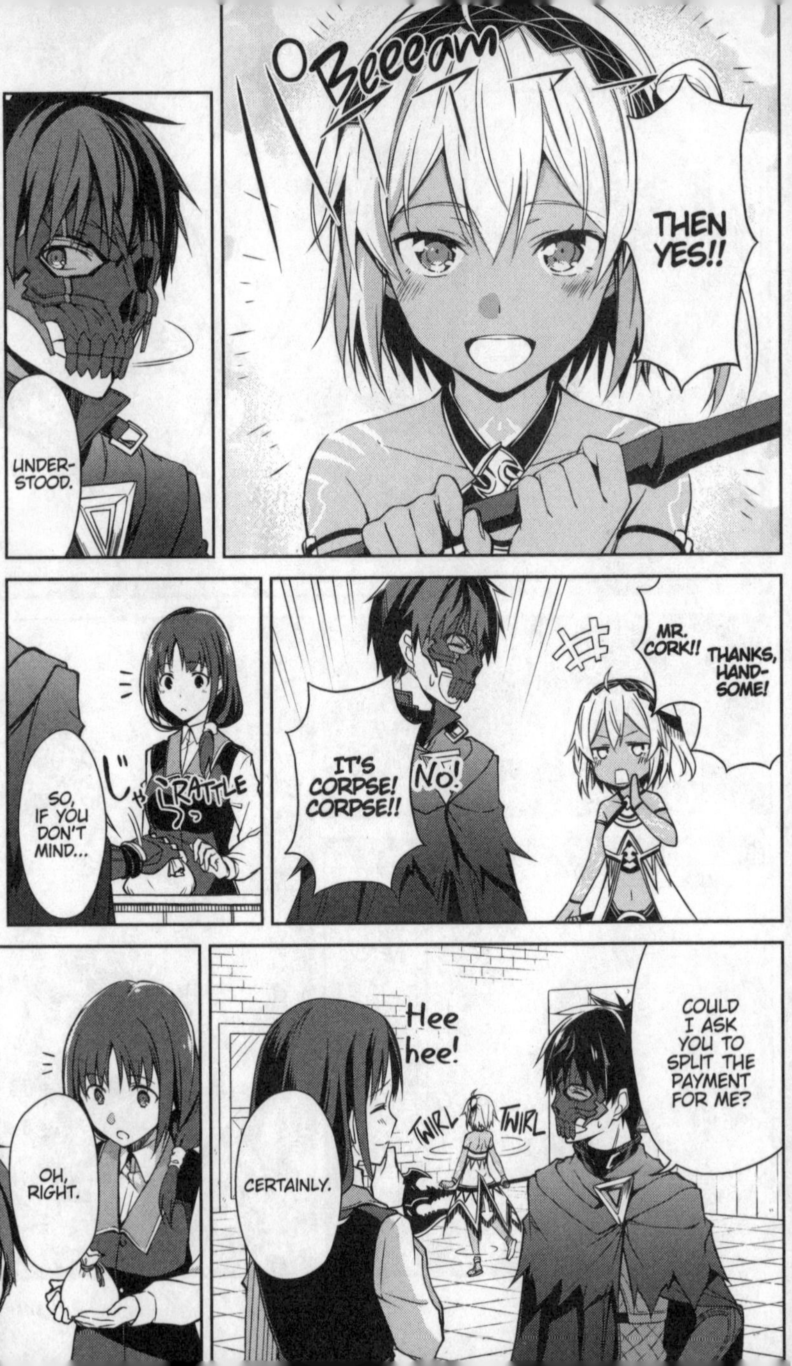
Beeeam
THEN YES!!
UNDER-STOOD.
MR. CORK!!
THANKS, HAND-SOME!
IT'S CORPSE! CORPSE!!
No!
じゃらっ
RATTLE
SO, IF YOU DON'T MIND...
COULD I ASK YOU TO SPLIT THE PAYMENT FOR ME?
Hee hee!
TWIRL TWIRL
CERTAINLY.
OH, RIGHT.

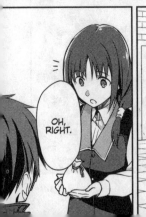

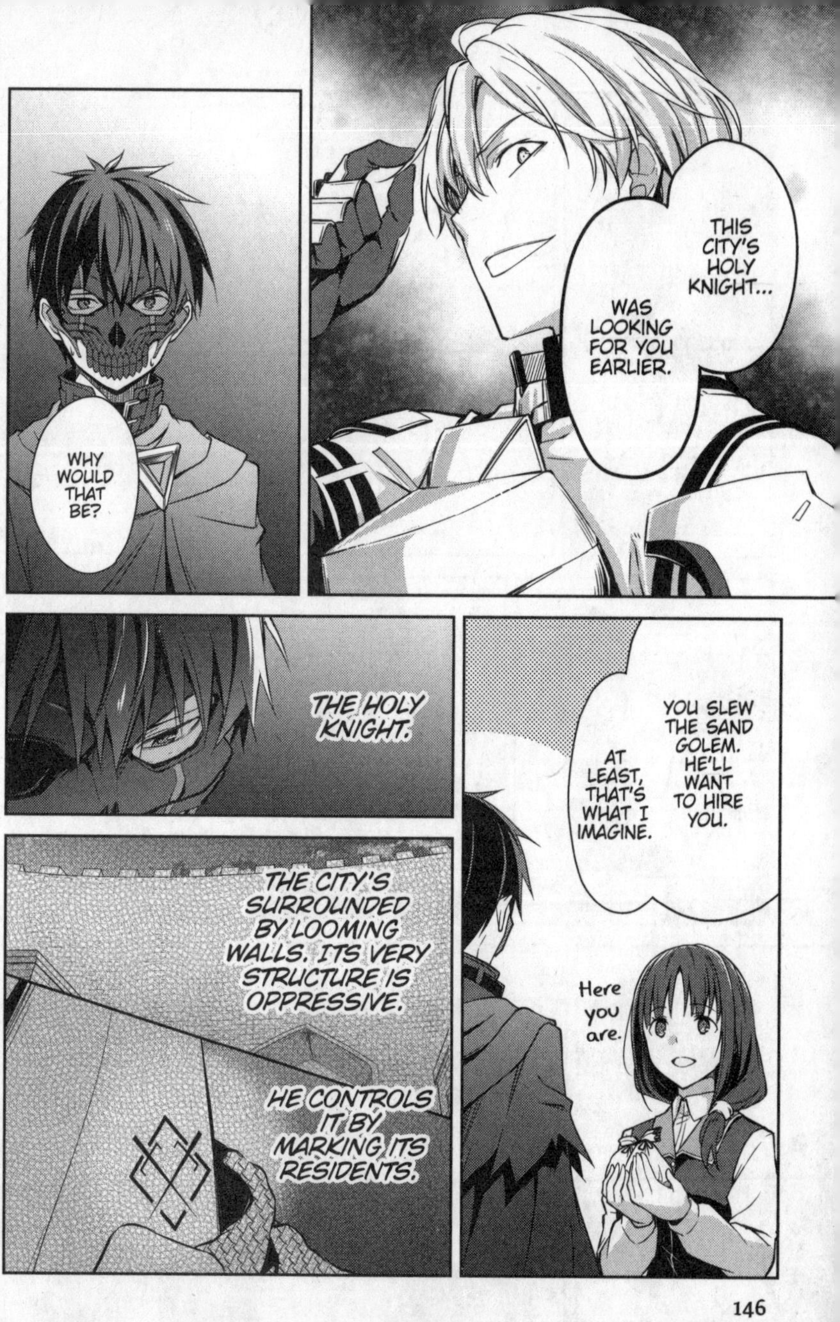
THIS CITY'S HOLY KNIGHT...
WAS LOOKING FOR YOU EARLIER.
WHY WOULD THAT BE?
YOU SLEW THE SAND GOLEM. HE'LL WANT TO HIRE YOU.
AT LEAST, THAT'S WHAT I IMAGINE.
Here you are.
THE HOLY KNIGHT.
THE CITY'S SURROUNDED BY LOOMING WALLS. ITS VERY STRUCTURE IS OPPRESSIVE.
HE CONTROLS IT BY MARKING ITS RESIDENTS.

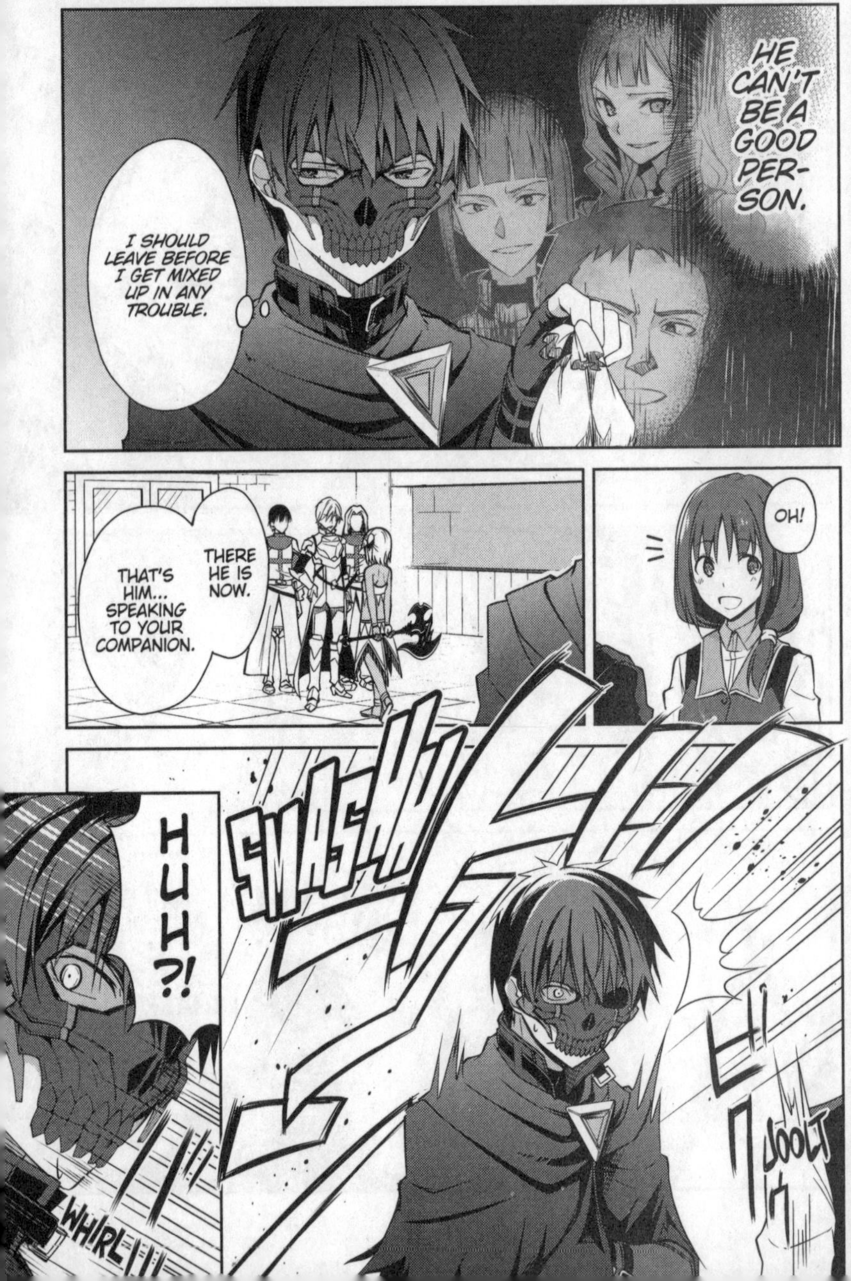
HE CAN'T BE A GOOD PER-SON.
I SHOULD LEAVE BEFORE I GET MIXED UP IN ANY TROUBLE.
OH!
THERE HE IS NOW.
THAT'S HIM... SPEAKING TO YOUR COMPANION.
SMASH
HUH?!
WHIRL

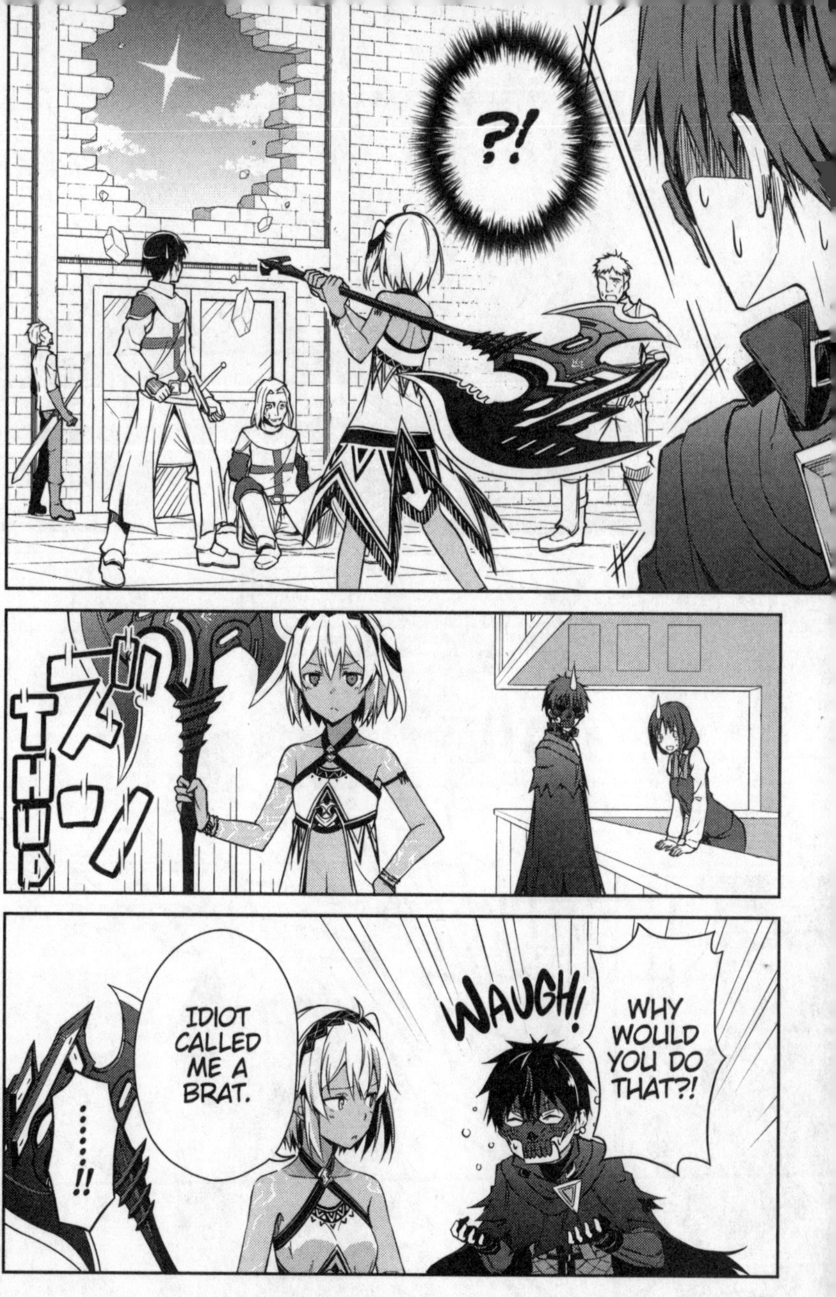
?!
THUD
WHY WOULD YOU DO THAT?!
WAUGH!
IDIOT CALLED ME A BRAT.
......!!

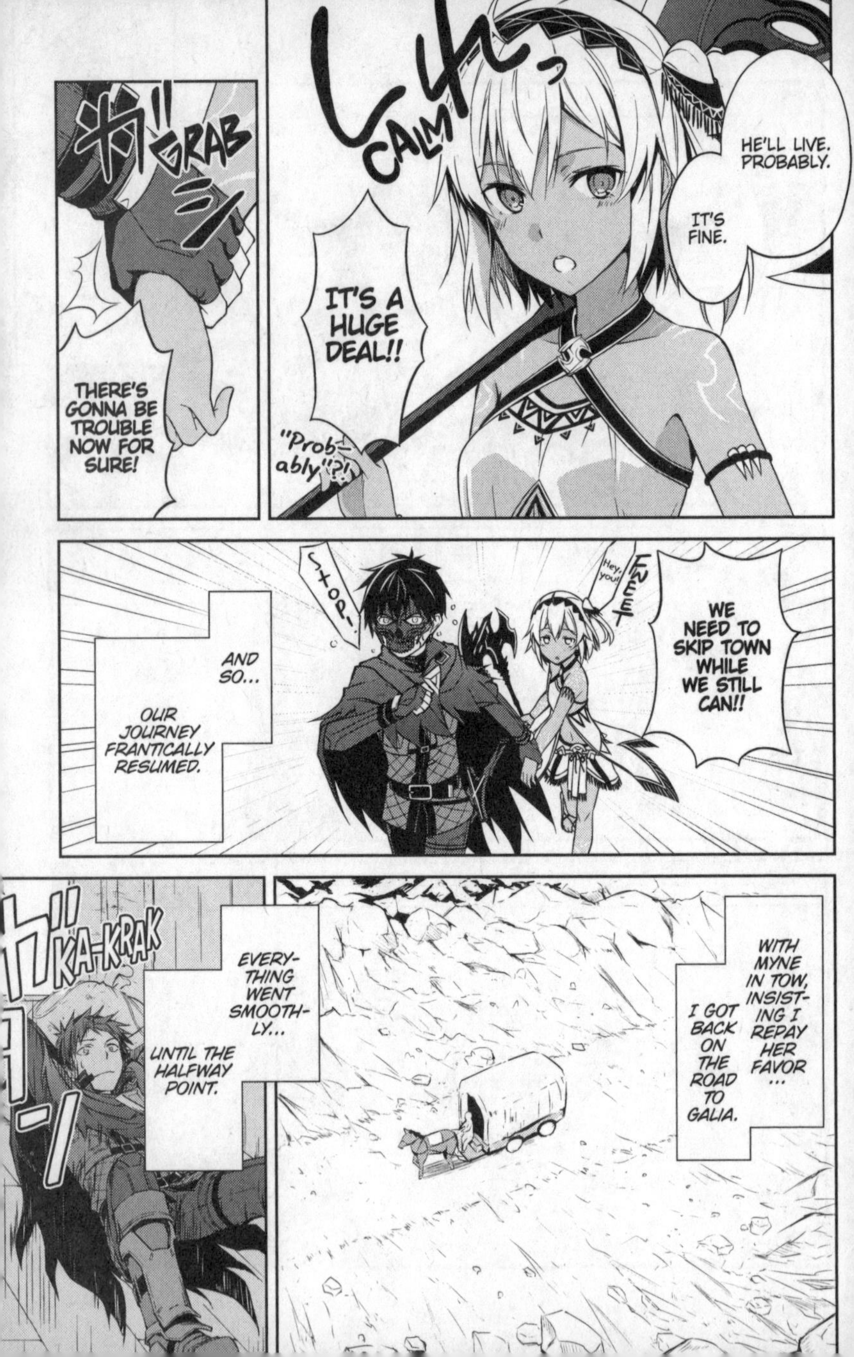
CALM
HE'LL LIVE. PROBABLY.
IT'S FINE.
IT'S A HUGE DEAL!!
"Probably"?!
GRAB
THERE'S GONNA BE TROUBLE NOW FOR SURE!
WE NEED TO SKIP TOWN WHILE WE STILL CAN!!
FWEET
Hey, you!
Stop!
AND SO...
OUR JOURNEY FRANTICALLY RESUMED.
WITH MYNE IN TOW, INSISTING I REPAY HER FAVOR ...
I GOT BACK ON THE ROAD TO GALIA.
KA-KRAK
EVERYTHING WENT SMOOTHLY...
UNTIL THE HALFWAY POINT.

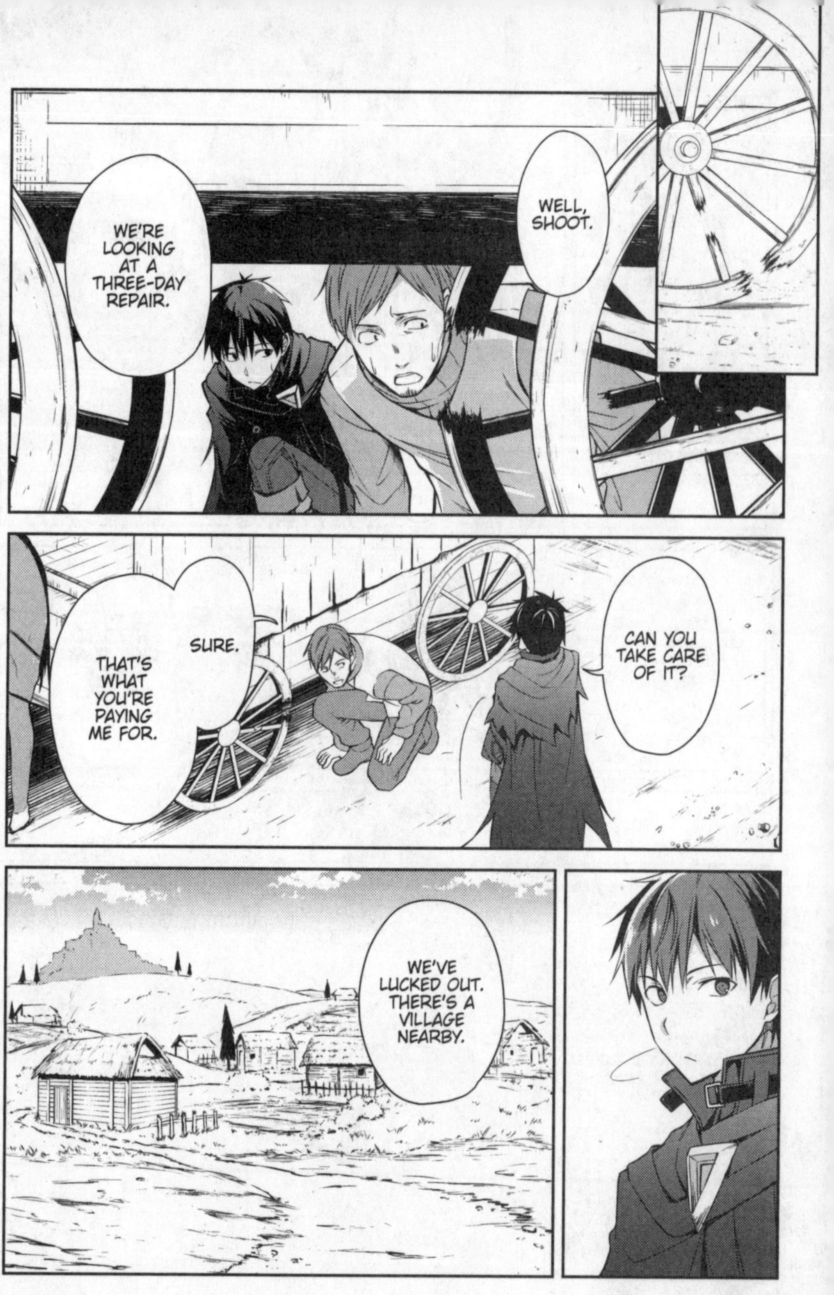
WELL, SHOOT.
WE'RE LOOKING AT A THREE-DAY REPAIR.
CAN YOU TAKE CARE OF IT?
SURE.
THAT'S WHAT YOU'RE PAYING ME FOR.
WE'VE LUCKED OUT. THERE'S A VILLAGE NEARBY.

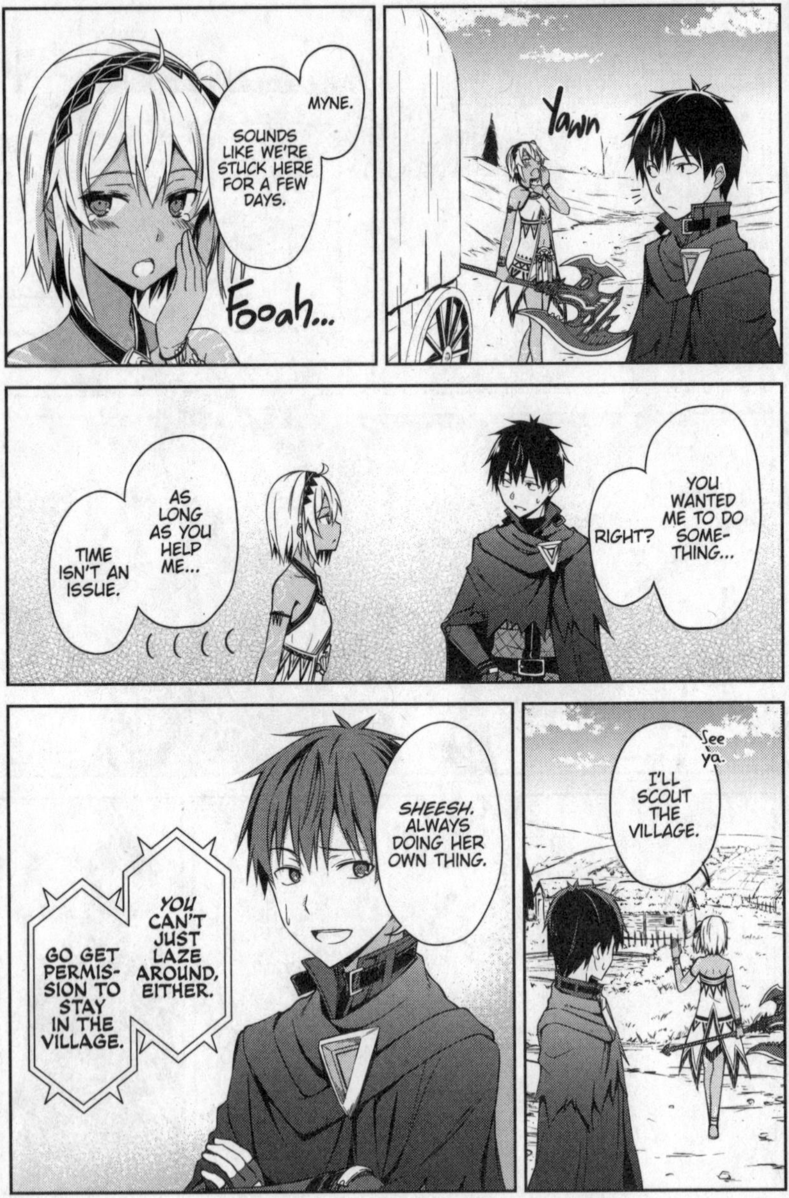
Yawn
MYNE.
SOUNDS LIKE WE'RE STUCK HERE FOR A FEW DAYS.
Fooah...
YOU WANTED ME TO DO SOMETHING... RIGHT?
AS LONG AS YOU HELP ME... TIME ISN'T AN ISSUE.
See ya.
I'LL SCOUT THE VILLAGE.
SHEESH. ALWAYS DOING HER OWN THING.
YOU CAN'T JUST LAZE AROUND, EITHER. GO GET PERMISSION TO STAY IN THE VILLAGE.

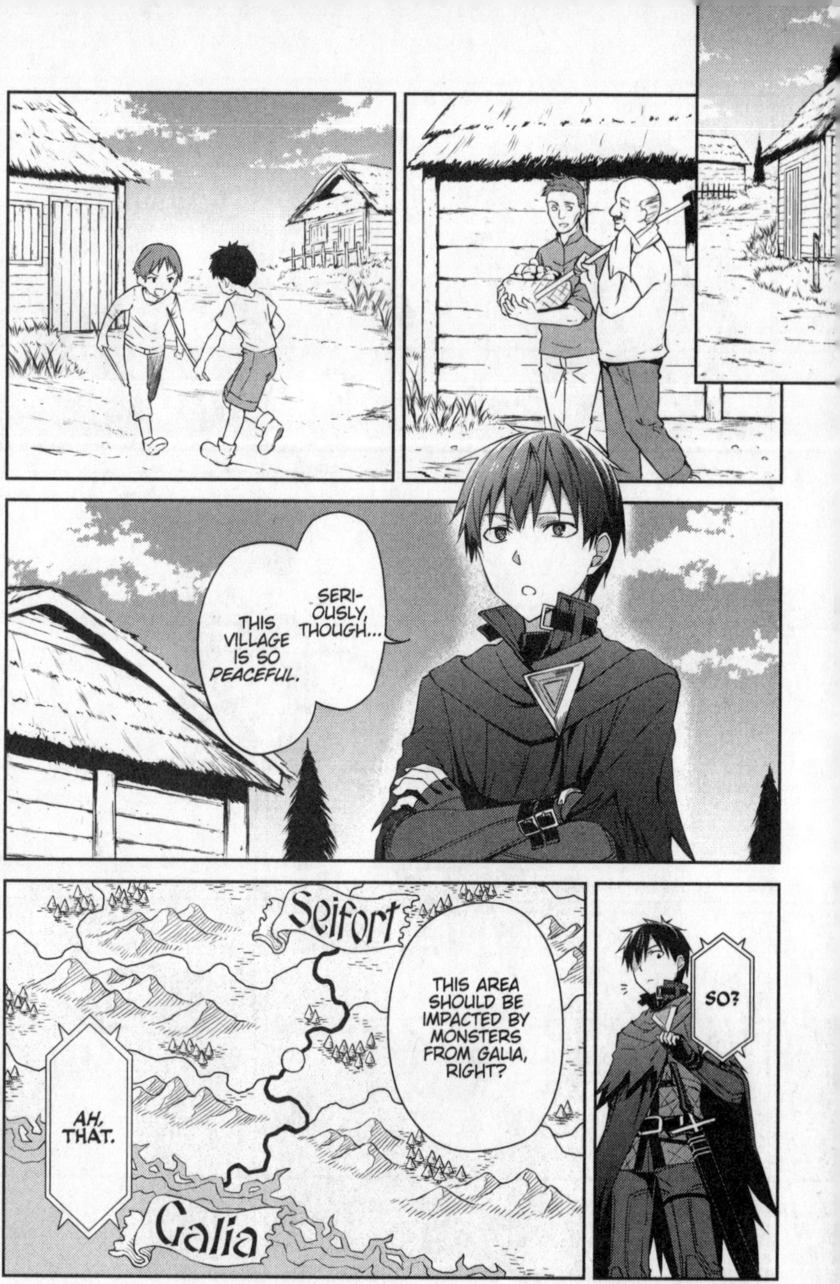
SERI-OUSLY, THOUGH...
THIS VILLAGE IS SO PEACEFUL.
SO?
Seifort
THIS AREA SHOULD BE IMPACTED BY MONSTERS FROM GALIA, RIGHT?
AH, THAT.
Galia

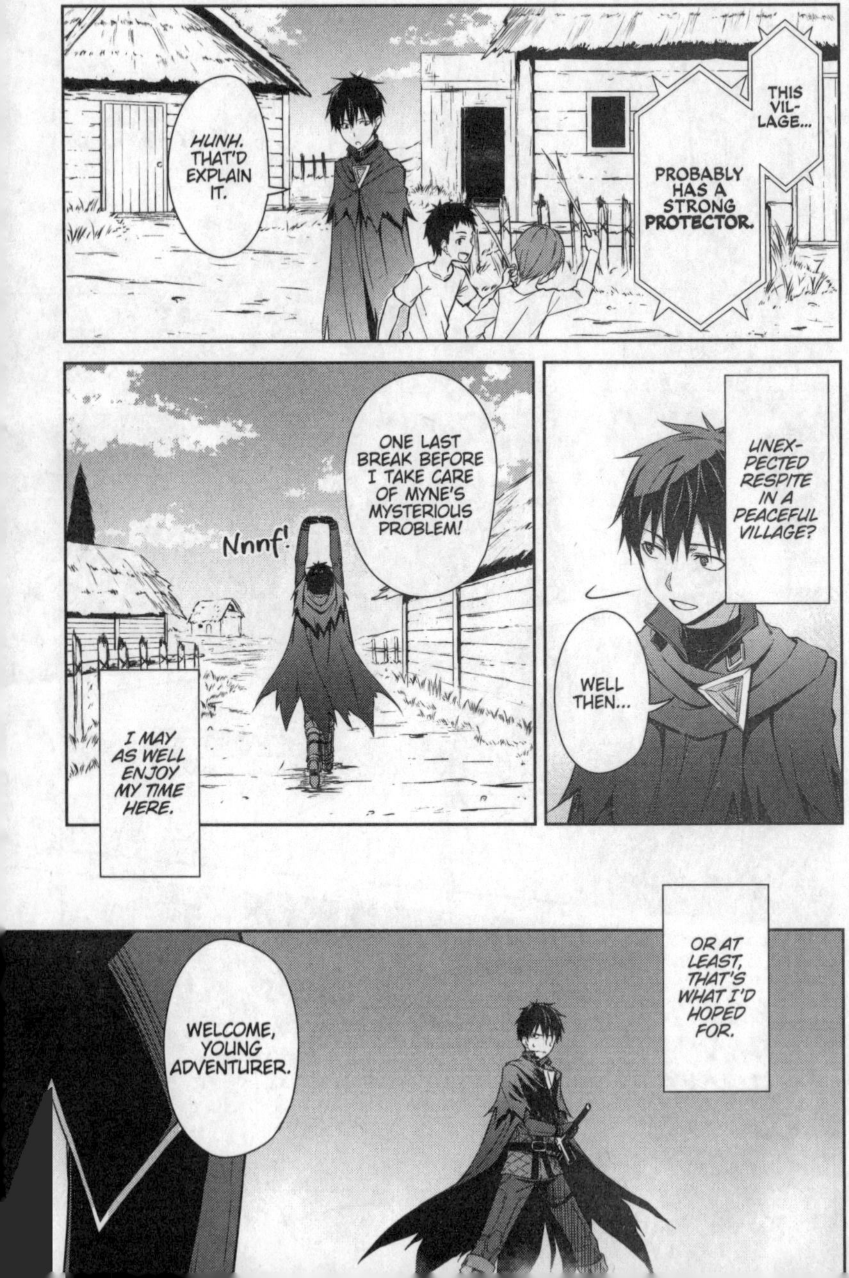
THIS VIL-LAGE...
PROBABLY HAS A STRONG PROTECTOR.
HUNH. THAT'D EXPLAIN IT.
UNEX-PECTED RESPITE IN A PEACEFUL VILLAGE?
WELL THEN...
ONE LAST BREAK BEFORE I TAKE CARE OF MYNE'S MYSTERIOUS PROBLEM!
Nnnf!
I MAY AS WELL ENJOY MY TIME HERE.
OR AT LEAST, THAT'S WHAT I'D HOPED FOR.
WELCOME, YOUNG ADVENTURER.

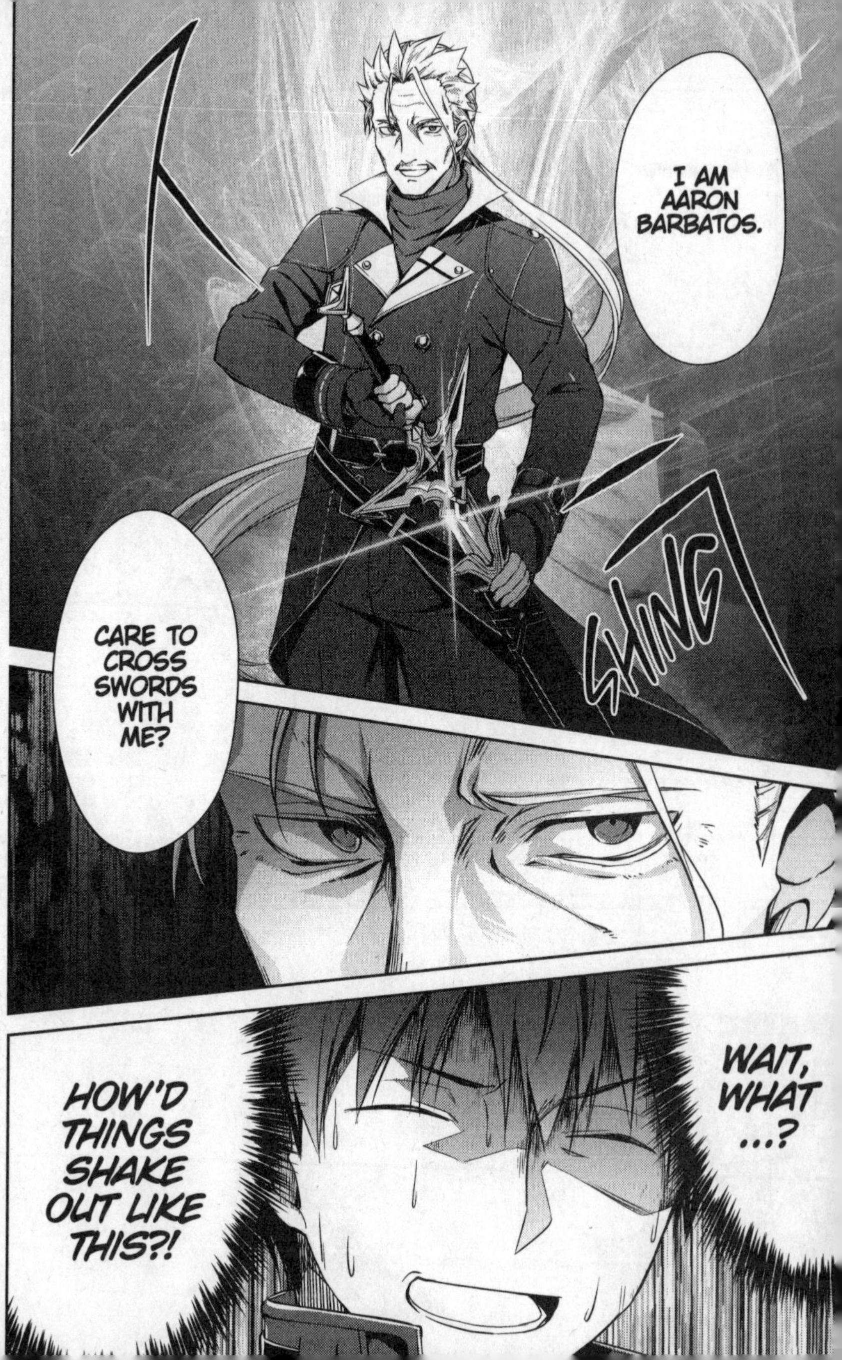
I AM AARON BARBATOS.
SHING
CARE TO CROSS SWORDS WITH ME?
WAIT, WHAT ...?
HOW'D THINGS SHAKE OUT LIKE THIS?!

BERSERK OF GLUTTONY

Afterword

Hello, and how do you do? I'm Daisuke Takino.

Berserk of Gluttony has already hit three volumes! Thank you all for picking it up.

This volume's afterword illustration is Myne in hotpants and a Wrath T-shirt. Despite the fact that she's showing more skin, I don't think she looks much sexier. That's weird! It isn't too sexy...right?

Anyway, in this volume, Myne makes her return. An abrupt reunion after she left with some cryptic words last time. That's Myne for you. She's a real free spirit!

So, maybe it's obvious at this point, but I love Myne. I've always had a thing for wildcard characters like her. Drawing her clothing patterns is a lot of work, though! A lot! I wrote "a lot" twice for emphasis because it's important! I hope you can feel all the love I put into her.

The next volume introduces another character I love, the old man Aaron Barbatos! It's like he was written for me. Stick around! I hope to see you again in the next volume!

STAFF
UTATA
Moyashi Yuki
Tsukiyo Gojuon
Ryosuke Nakagawa
Yoshihiko Yamagishi

SPECIAL THANKS
Isshiki Ichika
fame

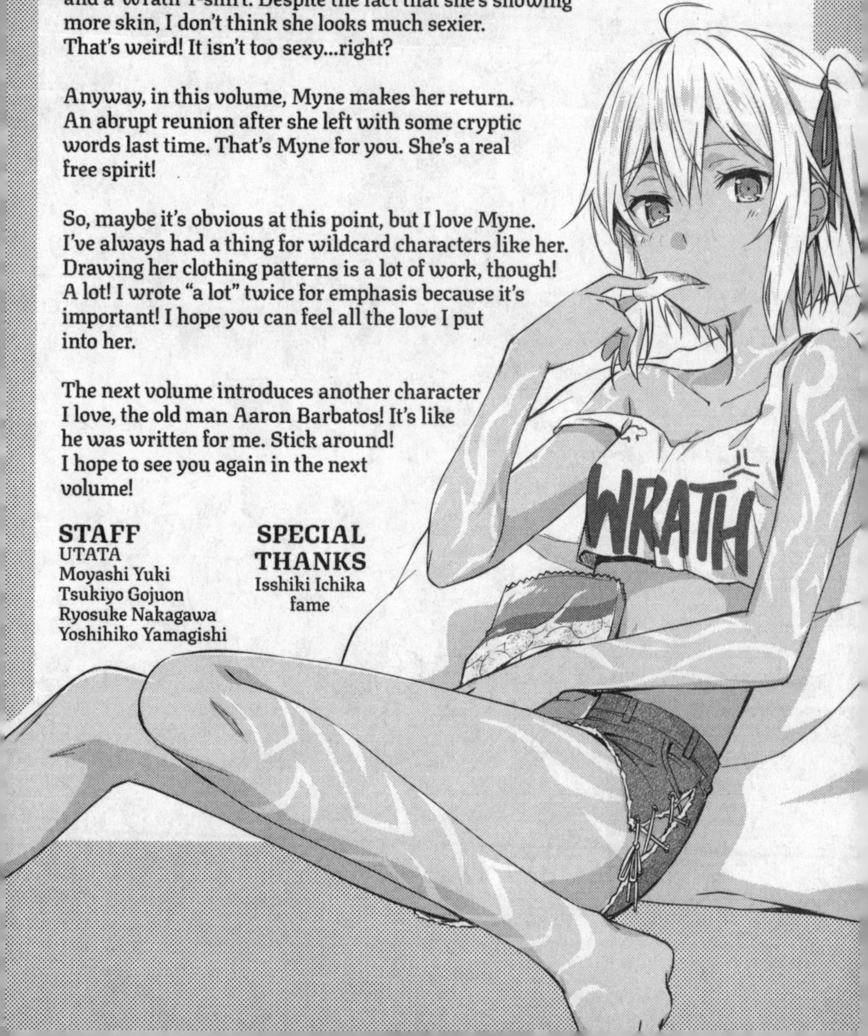
WRATH

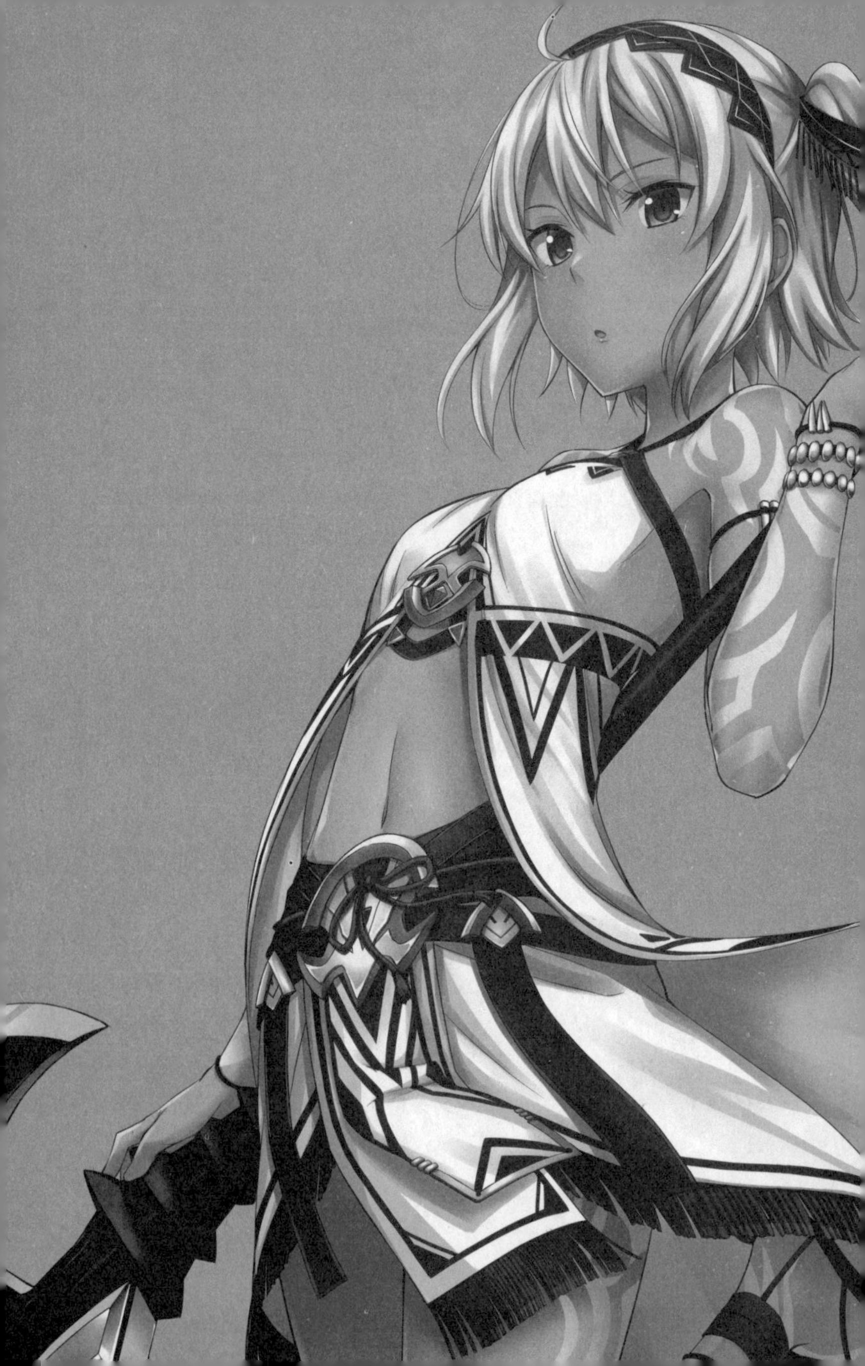

BERSERK OF GLUTTONY

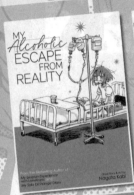
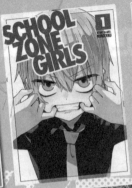
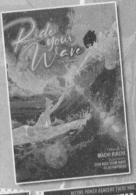
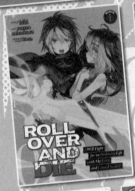
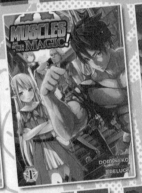
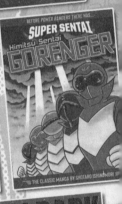
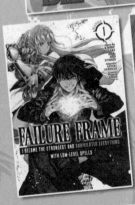
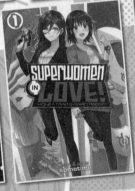
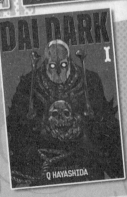

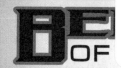

SEVEN SEA

story by **ISSHIKI ICHIKA** art by **DAISUKE TAKINO**

VOLUME 3

TRANSLATION
Amanda Haley

ADAPTATION
Sophia Tyrant

LETTERING
Arbash Mughal

LOGO DESIGN
George Panella

COVER DESIGN
Hanase Qi

EDITOR
Peter Adrian Behravesh

COPY EDITOR
Dawn Davis

PREPRESS TECHNICIAN
Rhiannon Rasmussen-Silverstein

PRODUCTION ASSOCIATE
Christa Miesner

PRODUCTION MANAGER
Lissa Pattillo

MANAGING EDITOR
Julie Davis

ASSOCIATE PUBLISHER
Adam Arnold

PUBLISHER
Jason DeAngelis

Boshoku no beruseruku -Oredake level to iu gainen wo toppa suru– THE COMIC Vol. 3
©Daisuke Takino (Art) ©Ichika Isshiki (Original Story)
This edition originally published in Japan in 2019 by
MICRO MAGAZINE, INC., Tokyo.
English translation rights arranged with MICRO MAGAZINE, INC., Tokyo.

Seven Seas press and purchase enquiries can be sent to Marketing Manager Lianne
Sentar at press@gomanga.com. Information regarding the distribution and purchase of
digital editions is available from Digital Manager CK Russell at digital@gomanga.com.

Seven Seas and the Seven Seas logo are trademarks of
Seven Seas Entertainment. All rights reserved.

ISBN: 978-1-64827-271-4
Printed in Canada
First Printing: July 2021
10 9 8 7 6 5 4 3 2 1

////// **READING DIRECTIONS** //////

This book reads from *right to left*,
Japanese style. If this is your first time
reading manga, you start reading from
the top right panel on each page and
take it from there. If you get lost, just
follow the numbered diagram here.
It may seem backwards at first,
but you'll get the hang of it! Have fun!!

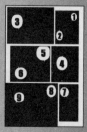

Follow us online: www.SevenSeasEntertainment.com